The third earl of Shaftesbury is often recognized as a highly influential thinker, but studies of him have hitherto been oriented narrowly around his specific contributions to ethics, religion, aesthetics and criticism. Professor Klein's study is the first to examine the extensive Shaftesbury manuscripts and offer an interpretation of his diverse writings as an attempt to comprehend contemporary society and politics and, in particular, to offer a legitimation for the new Whig political order established after 1688. It thus becomes possible to provide what has long been lacking – an account of the ideological functioning of *Characteristicks*, Shaftesbury's principal and most highly influential work.

This study of Shaftesbury offers the first extensive examination of the language of "politeness" and its uses in the eighteenth century, since the core of Shaftesbury's ideological project was his adaptation and reconstruction of ideas of politeness. Through politeness Shaftesbury reconceived the goals and procedures of philosophy in the face of the philosophical innovations of Descartes, Hobbes and Locke. Moreover, using politeness, Shaftesbury fashioned a series of politically charged cultural models. This enabled him to arrive at a new design for British discourse and cultural life, in which the traditional authority of ecclesiastical and courtly institutions was replaced with a model of a public critical culture regulated by the standards of polite and gentlemanly conversation.

Lawrence E. Klein is Associate Professor of History at the University of Nevada, Las Vegas. He is the author of several articles on aspects of eighteenth-century thought and culture: this is his first book.

Shaftesbury and the culture of politeness

Shaftesbury and the culture of politeness

Moral discourse and cultural politics in early eighteenth-century England

Lawrence E. Klein

Associate Professor
Department of History, University of Nevada, Las Vegas

CAMBRIDGE UNIVERSITY PRESS

PUBLISHED BY THE PRESS SYNDICATE OF THE UNIVERSITY OF CAMBRIDGE
The Pitt Building, Trumpington Street, Cambridge, United Kingdom

CAMBRIDGE UNIVERSITY PRESS
The Edinburgh Building, Cambridge CB2 2RU, UK
40 West 20th Street, New York NY 10011–4211, USA
477 Williamstown Road, Port Melbourne, VIC 3207, Australia
Ruiz de Alarcón 13, 28014 Madrid, Spain
Dock House, The Waterfront, Cape Town 8001, South Africa

http://www.cambridge.org

© Cambridge University Press 1994

This book is in copyright. Subject to statutory exception
and to the provisions of relevant collective licensing agreements,
no reproduction of any part may take place without
the written permission of Cambridge University Press.

First published in 1994
First paperback edition 2004

A catalogue record for this book is available from the British Library

Library of Congress cataloguing in publication data
Klein, Lawrence E.
Shaftesbury and the culture of politeness: moral discourse and cultural politics
in early eighteenth-century England / Lawrence E. Klein.
    p. cm.
ISBN 0 521 41806 2 (hardback)
1. Shaftesbury, Anthony Ashley Cooper, Earl of 1671–1713.
2. Philosophy – Social aspects – England – History – 18th century.
3. Philosophy – Political aspects – England – History – 18th century.
4. Ethics Modern – 18th century. 5. Social ethics – England –
History – 18th century. I. Title.
B1387.K57 1984
192–dc20   93–3216 CIP

ISBN 0 521 41806 2 hardback
ISBN 0 521 60752 3 paperback

Transferred to digital printing 2004

Contents

Acknowledgments	*page* ix
Bibliographical note	xi

Introduction	1
The subject	1
A language	3
A setting	8
A career	14
The argument	20

Part I Polite Philosophy	25
1 The amalgamation of philosophy and breeding	27
A philosophical vocation	27
A preface	31
Palemon in the Park	34
Classicism	41
2 Lord Ashley's *Inquiry*: The philosophy of sociability and its context	48
Seriousness	48
An Inquiry Concerning Virtue	51
Self and others	54
The "secret Anti-Epicurean view"	60
3 The notebooks: the problem of the self	70
The notebooks	70
A divided self	72
The dangers of social life	76
4 The notebooks: philosophy in the inner life	81
"Training"	81
Interiority	83
Resignation and engagement	84
Self-discourse	86
5 Philosophy in society	91
"Character"	91

viii   Contents

	Self-presentation	93
	The paradigm of conversation	96
6	Philosophical writing	102
	Philosophy as advice	102
	The "Socratick History"	107
	Characteristicks	111

Part II Polite Whiggism   121

7	From politics to cultural politics	123
	"The hinge of the whole Work"	123
	Oppositionalist and legitimist Whigs	125
	Shaftesbury's politics	131
	The civic tradition and culture	143
	The cultural politics of *Characteristicks*	150
8	The critique of the Church	154
	"Awefulness"	154
	Priestcraft and enthusiasm	160
	Shaftesbury and enthusiasm	165
	Egypt and Rome	169
9	The critique of the Court	175
	"Dazzle"	175
	The Court and the Tory interpretation of cultural history	178
	Courtliness	183
	Rome and France	185
10	The culture of liberty	195
	"Politeness"	195
	Greece	199
	Britain	202
	In sum	210

Index   213

Acknowledgments

When I began studying eighteenth-century politeness as a graduate student in Baltimore, I would have been surprised to learn that I would finish this study in Las Vegas, Nevada. I would also have been surprised at the itinerary that would lead from a city that H. L. Mencken saw as medieval to one that everyone recognizes as post-modern. In addition to the History Departments of the Johns Hopkins University and the University of Nevada, Las Vegas, I am indebted to the History Department at Stanford University, the Institute for Research in the Humanities at the University of Wisconsin, Madison, and the Center for Seventeenth- and Eighteenth-Century Studies at the University of California, Los Angeles. In writing this book, I have relied on the Library of Congress and the Folger Library in Washington, D.C., the William Andrews Clark Memorial Library in Los Angeles, and the Henry Huntington Library in Pasadena. Many of the ideas took shape under the domed roofs of the Public Record Office on Chancery Lane and the British Library on Great Russell Street in London, where I also depended on many resources of the University of London, especially the Institute for Historical Research and the files of the History of Parliament Trust. These institutions have provided me with what the eighteenth century called the necessities and decencies of the scholarly life, and, for that, I am very grateful.

After necessities and decencies, the eighteenth century situated luxuries, and the true luxury of academic life is conversation. This study is the better for the conversations I have had with Ann Bermingham, John Brewer, Michael Fried, Sun Hee Kim Gertz, Jan Golinski, Phillip Harth, David Hayton, James Jaffe, William Klein, John Michael, Nick Mirzoeff, Orest Ranum, Paul Seaver, Robert Shoemaker, Johann Sommerville, John Styles, Jay Tribby, Jane Tylus, Amanda Vickery, William Weber, and Steven Zwicker. Two friends have performed in that capacity beyond the call of duty. Dena Goodman, an indefatigable investigator and practitioner of intellectual sociability, has been a constant source of insight and encouragement in writing this book. So has David Lieberman. I am deeply and permanently in his debt for applying his intelligence so conscientiously and tactfully when called upon, more than once, to scrutinize this manuscript.

While the questions and suggestions of these scholars have shaped this project, the character of this particular study was formed at Johns Hopkins. It was Nancy Struever who introduced me to the persuasiveness of the rhetorical perspective; I am in her debt and hope my attempt here to take rhetoric seriously is some small repayment. It was John Pocock who articulated the problems that roused me to investigate politeness in the eighteenth century. Much more important, it was he who, by his example, convinced me of the power of great scholarship. While his inspiring erudition and penetration are almost too obvious to mention, I am particularly grateful for his tolerance, generosity and humanity, from which I have benefited over the years.

My ability to pursue this project has depended on others whose support has been more moral than intellectual. My London friends have made my extended stays there possible through their hospitality. Among them, I owe a unique debt to Michael Worton for his support and companionship. My extended family has been a standing source of encouragement and support, and I am particularly indebted to my mother and stepfather. Finally, my father, Sigmund Saul Klein, inspired so many of my convictions and commitments that it remains only to dedicate this book to his memory.

Bibliographical note

References to the works comprising Shaftesbury's *Characteristicks* (with the exception of "An Inquiry Concerning Virtue") are to the three-volume 1714 edition, which was published after the third earl's death but included his corrections and revisions of the first edition of 1711. The short title of the work is followed by the part and section and citation of the volume and page. References are also given in parentheses to the widely accessible modern edition, by John Robertson (London: Grant Richards, 1900; reprinted in the Library of the Liberal Arts by Bobbs-Merrill, 1964). Short titles are as follows:

"Letter"	"A Letter Concerning Enthusiasm"
"Sensus Communis"	"Sensus Communis: An Essay on the Freedom of Wit and Humour"
"Soliloquy"	"Soliloquy: Or Advice to an Author"
"The Moralists"	"The Moralists, A Philosophical Rhapsody"
"Miscellany"	"Miscellaneous Reflections on the Preceding Treatises, Etc."

The first four of these were all published separately between 1708 and 1710, prior to the appearance of *Characteristicks*.

An Inquiry Concerning Virtue was first published in 1699 and later revised for *Characteristicks*. Since the interpretation of Shaftesbury offered in part I rests on Shaftesbury's development between the original publication of the *Inquiry* and the publication of *Characteristicks*, all references to the *Inquiry* are to the original 1699 edition.

"A Letter Concerning the Art, or Science of Design ... to My Lord ***," was originally a cover letter to John Somers Concerning the treatise, "A Notion of the Historical Draught or Tablature of the Judgment of Hercules." The latter was first published in French in the *Journal des Scavans* (Amsterdam), 52 (November 1712), 483–520, and then in English in 1713. "A Letter Concerning Design" was included in some copies of the 1714 *Characteristicks*, to which all citations refer, though it

xii   Bibliographical note

only became a standard feature of the text in the fifth edition of 1732. (For the complicated history of its publication, see Kerry Downes, "The Publication of Shaftesbury's 'Letter Concerning Design,'" *Architectural History*, 27 (1984), 519–523.) References to "A Letter Concerning Design" are also given in parentheses to Benjamin Rand's edition of Shaftesbury's writings on art, *Second Characters* (Cambridge: Cambridge University Press, 1914).

The Shaftesbury Papers in the Public Record Office (P.R.O.) include a large correspondence, many notebooks, and other written records of the third earl. In cases where Shaftesbury numbered pages of notebooks, these have been provided in citations as well as folio numbers. Aside from correspondence, the most frequently cited Shaftesbury manuscripts are these:

P.R.O. 30/24/27/10   two notebooks with the head, *Askēmata*, dating primarily from 1698 to 1704, written in England and in Holland
P.R.O. 30/24/27/14   a notebook containing "Design of a Socratick History"
P.R.O. 30/24/27/15   a notebook containing material on the arts and art history and forming part of Shaftesbury's project called "Second Characters"

I cite letters by Shaftesbury to two regular correspondents who are not discussed in the text. Both Michael Ainsworth and Thomas Micklethwaite were recipients of Shaftesbury's patronage. Ainsworth was a young Dorset man whom Shaftesbury helped send to Oxford and establish in a clerical career. Thomas Micklethwaite (1678–1718) was a gentleman and friend for whom Shaftesbury long sought a government job. Micklethwaite was close to the Shaftesbury household and often acted as an agent for Shaftesbury during his absences from London.

Other abbreviations are these:

DNB   *Dictionary of National Biography*
Epictetus, *Discourses*   Epictetus, *The Discourses As Reported by*
Epictetus, *Encheiridion*   *Arrian, The Manual, and Fragments*, trans. W. A. Oldfather (The Loeb Classical Library, London: William Heinemann and New York: G. P. Putnam's Sons, 1926)

Bibliographical note

Grean, *Shaftesbury's Philosophy*	Stanley Grean, *Shaftesbury's Philosophy of Religion and Ethics* (Athens, Ohio: Ohio University Press, 1967)
Locke, *Essay*	John Locke, *An Essay Concerning Human Understanding*, ed. Peter H. Nidditch (Oxford: Clarendon Press, 1975)
Letters to Molesworth	*Letters from the Right Honourable the late Earl of Shaftesbury, to Robert Molesworth, Esq.* (1721)
Marcus Aurelius	Marcus Aurelius, *The Communings with Himself*, trans. C. R. Haines (London: William Heinemann and New York: The Macmillan Company, 1916)
Several Letters	*Several Letters Written by a Noble Lord to a Young Man at the University* (1716)
Spectator, Bond	Donald F. Bond, ed., *The Spectator*, 5 vols. (Oxford: Clarendon Press, 1965)
Swift, *Prose Works*	Herbert Davis, ed., *The Prose Works of Jonathan Swift*, 14 vols. (Oxford: Basil Blackwell, 1939–68)
Tatler, Bond	Donald F. Bond, ed., *The Tatler*, 3 vols. (Oxford: Clarendon Press, 1987)

In quoting from printed documents I reproduce the printed form exactly. I have been loyal to vagaries of manuscript spelling and punctuation, except in a few cases where silent changes have been made for clarity's sake. Dates are given as they appear in the manuscripts except that January 1 is taken as the beginning of the year. In the Public Record Office Calendar of the Shaftesbury Papers, some letters are incorrectly dated. When, on the basis of internal evidence, I have assigned a letter a different date from that in the Calendar, I have indicated that they have been "redated."

All pre-1900 imprints were published in London unless otherwise indicated.

Introduction

The subject

Anthony Ashley Cooper, the third earl of Shaftesbury, is often assigned an important role in having shaped the interests and ideas of a wide range of eighteenth-century writers, in Britain and on the Continent. This role has several facets. He is perhaps best known as a sentimental moralist whose insistence on natural sociability and a moral sense was highly influential among ethical writers. He is also well known as a deist of a strongly anti-ecclesiastical bent. Moreover, his interest in the arts has made him an object of study by those concerned with the histories of philosophical aesthetics and criticism.

This study presents Shaftesbury as a political writer. He has not been entirely ignored from this standpoint, but scholarly attention has focussed on a brief spell in the 1690s when he was closely associated with a circle of advanced Whigs in which radical religious and political ideas flourished. It is symptomatic of the lack of attention to Shaftesbury's political concerns that there has been little attention to the ideological significance of his major work, *Characteristicks of Men, Manners, Opinions, Times*, of 1711. One objective of this study is to provide a political analysis of this important text.

My intention, however, is not simply to draw attention to another side of Shaftesbury, since I follow Joseph Rykwert's suggestion that the fundamental matrix of Shaftesbury's thought was socio-political:[1] his moralism, his deism, and his aesthetic interests were all harnessed to a political project. Moreover, far from being an exercise in Whig radicalism, that project was nothing less than the legitimation of the post-1688 Whig regime. As, in his view, the Revolution had definitively established the dominance of gentlemen over English society and politics, so it ushered in an era of gentlemanly culture, the norms and content of which he was attempting to envision.

[1] Joseph Rykwert, *The First Moderns: The Architects of the Eighteenth Century* (Cambridge, Mass., and London: The MIT Press, 1980), p.156.

But a close look at Shaftesbury is more than an opportunity to reassess his particular historical place. Since, as I argue, the centerpiece of his complicated project was his notion of politeness, he becomes an important guide to his era. The language of politeness was, of course, a major idiom in the eighteenth century, entering into a wide range of discussions. Moreover, the eminence of this idiom reflected defining characteristics of eighteenth-century society and culture. Recent scholarly interest in the history of manners and the development of the public sphere as well as long-standing efforts to understand the social and institutional organization of old regime societies have combined to move such topics as civility and politeness nearer the foreground of scholarly concern in the early modern period. The study of Shaftesbury's writings opens perspectives on cultural institutions and practices of the eighteenth century, helping us to see what politeness was intended to convey and what historical circumstances it was intended to conceptualize.

Shaftesbury's *Characteristicks* was one of several works during the reign of Queen Anne in which politeness assumed a classic form: it need only be remembered that, within weeks of the publication of *Characteristicks*, the *Spectator* began its extraordinarily influential run. Whereas Joseph Addison and Richard Steele, in the *Tatler* and *Guardian* as much as in the *Spectator*, used the resources of print culture to disseminate polite moralism to a broad audience, Shaftesbury was, much more, the philosopher of politeness, aiming at an intellectual and social elite.

Nonetheless, Shaftesbury's opinions had resonance and exercised considerable persuasiveness through much of the eighteenth century. *Characteristicks* was an immediate success and went through at least ten editions in Britain between 1711 and the 1790s. It is well-known that, in the name of egoism, Bernard Mandeville attacked the Shaftesburian account of natural sociability and that, in the name of a polite Christianity, George Berkeley attacked Shaftesbury's deism. Whatever weaknesses in Shaftesbury's thought Mandeville and Berkeley exposed, the fact that Shaftesbury provoked such deft critiques suggests that he was, in fact, influential. And, of course, Shaftesbury had his followers. There were numerous Shaftesburians in England, but, more significantly, Francis Hutcheson was inspired by Shaftesburian ideas, passing them to numerous Scottish writers. In short, Shaftesbury needs to be taken seriously because the eighteenth century did so. The rest of this introduction sketches briefly the idiom of politeness and its relation to the general historical setting before returning to an account of Shaftesbury's career and the manner in which the argument of this book unfolds.

A language

Though "politeness" is a word of attenuated use in the contemporary world, the case was different in early modern Europe, where the prevalence of polite practices was matched by the importance of such words as "courtesy," "civility," and "politeness." According to Norbert Elias, it was the absolutist court, epitomized by Louis XIV's facility at Versailles, that dramatically increased the importance of comportment in European culture and did so much to effect the civilizing of manners.[2] However, as Marvin Becker makes clear, the elaboration of the discourse of comportment first occurred in Italy as early as the fourteenth century when an "archaic and communal" culture gave way to a "more problematic civil society." Part of this development was "the transformation of a vocabulary of courtesy and fidelity into the more subdued and less heroic idiom of civility."[3] The humanists added their own stamp to this "civilizing" enterprise, helping to disseminate it to literate people throughout Europe. In the early modern era, notions of civility were set into action wherever individuals attempted to redesign the communities in which they lived: at courts, to be sure, but also in towns and cities and among the learned, the literate, and the godly.

In later seventeenth- and early eighteenth-century England, the term "politeness' came into particular prominence as a key word, used in a variety of settings, with a wide range of meanings.[4] From the first, politeness was associated with and often identified with gentlemanliness since it applied to the social world of gentlemen and ladies. In the Whig periodicals of Queen Anne's reign, "the Politer Part of Great Britain" and the "polite People" were also "the elegant and knowing part of Mankind," "the Quality," and "the better sort."[5] However, if "politeness" reinforced an elitist ideology, it also served to make distinctions *within* the elite.

Not all gentlemen were polite since "politeness" was a criterion of *proper* behavior. The kernel of "politeness" could be conveyed in the simple expression, "the art of pleasing in company," or, in a contempo-

---

[2] Norbert Elias, *The Civilizing Process*, 2 vols. (New York: Pantheon Books, 1978, 1982), and *The Court Society* (Oxford: Basil Blackwell, 1983). The two volumes of *The Civilizing Process* (*The History of Manners* and *Power and Civility*) were originally published in 1939 in Germany; *The Court Society* first appeared in German in 1969. The translator of all these works is Edmund Jephcott.

[3] Marvin Becker, *Civility and Society in Western Europe, 1300–1600* (Bloomington and Indianapolis: Indiana University Press, 1988), p.xi.

[4] The rest of this section summarizes my article, "The Third Earl of Shaftesbury and the Progress of Politeness," *Eighteenth-Century Studies*, 18 (1984–85), 186–214.

[5] *Spectator*, No. 13 (March 15, 1711) and No. 218 (November 9, 1711), Bond, I, 59, and II, 349; *Tatler*, No. 39 (July 9, 1709), Bond, I, 281–287.

rary definition, "a dextrous management of our Words and Actions, whereby we make other People have better Opinions of us and themselves."[6] These formulations indicated the social, psychological and formal dimensions of the term. First, "politeness" was situated in "company," in the realm of social interaction and exchange, where it governed relations of the self with others. While allowing for differences among selves, "politeness" was concerned with coordinating, reconciling or integrating them. Second, it subjected this domain of social life to the norm of "pleasing." The gratification nurtured by "politeness" was psychological, the amelioration of people's senses of themselves and of others. Thus, "politeness" presupposed an intersubjective domain in which the cultivation and exchange of opinions and feelings were involved. Third, "politeness" involved a grasp of form. It was an art or technique, governing the "how" of social relations. "Politeness" concerned sociability but was not identical with it: while human sociability was a primal and original stuff requiring work, "politeness" was a refined sociability, bringing aesthetic concerns into close contiguity with ethical ones. Although "politeness" implied that sociability was enhanced by good form, tension might arise between these principles; for instance, when "politeness" declined into mere formality or ceremoniousness, it could be portrayed as hostile to true sociability.

Similarly, the psychological dimension of "politeness" was laced with complexity. On the surface, politeness oriented individuals towards each other's needs and wishes: it seemed to arise in a generous concern for the comfort of others. In reality, the polite concern for others might be a secondary effect of a far more basic self-concern. Thus, the altruistic or charitable appearance of politeness might conceal opportunistic egoism. Shaftesbury would spend much effort wrestling with the competing manifestations of sociability and egoism in social behavior.

Though "politeness" was by definition the dextrous management of words and actions, words had pride of place, and conversation was the paradigmatic arena for "politeness." Conversational "politeness" was the art of pleasing in conversation, the pursuit of verbal agreeableness. Polite conversation assumed the equality of participants and insisted on a reciprocity in which participants were sometimes talkers and sometimes listeners. It provided an opportunity for self-display at the same time that its norms disciplined self-expression for the sake of domestic peace. It was described as a zone of freedom, ease, and naturalness (though these terms assumed highly qualified meanings in so obviously artificial an activity). Writers on politeness differed about the particular subjects they deemed

[6] Abel Boyer, *The English Theophrastus* (1702), pp.106, 108. The second formulation was borrowed from La Rochefoucauld.

Introduction

suitable for conversation, but it is wrong to assume that politics or even religion was excluded by all conversational theorists. Similarly, the degree of seriousness and rationality to be expected in civil conversation varied in different accounts of it.

However, writers on conversation were uniformly generous with their recommendations and proscriptions. Conversants were warned against taciturnity, stiffness, self-effacement, and withdrawal, which starved conversation. They were also warned against excesses of assertiveness and sociability, which killed conversation more efficiently. It was wrong to dominate discussion or push one's opinions too relentlessly. Self-righteousness, self-solemnity, and gravity were odious. To terminate a conversation with dispatch, one needed only be pedantic or magisterial! Finally, affectation, the striving for effect, was noxious to conversation.

Such conversational criteria became, in theory at least, markers of the gentleman's behavior, but they were also found to have a wider relevance, becoming ascriptions of intellectual and literary endeavors. For one thing, "politeness" assumed a role in the classification of knowledge. Expressions such as "polite arts," "polite letters," and "polite learning" could be used to make the broad distinction between humanistic and artistic endeavors, on one side, and philosophical, mathematical and scientific inquiry, on the other. However, "polite" could be used to make more subtle distinctions, for instance, to indicate a "polite" approach to literature as opposed to mere philological criticism.

Such classificatory language was controversial in that it arose within the politics of a rapidly changing landscape of inquiry. As part of its polemical work, the term "polite" was meant to invoke the cachet of the gentlemanly. John Dennis asserted the particular appropriateness of "polite learning" for gentlemen, and the seigneur de Saint-Évremond wrote that he found "no Sciences that particularly belong to Gentlemen, but Morality, Politics, and the Knowledge of good Literature."[7] Saint-Évremond's trio of concerns came in time to define the perimeters of polite knowledge.

Polite learning was gentlemanly because it did not demand technical or specialist knowledge. Rather, it was generalist in its orientation, tending to the development of the whole person and keeping the person and his

---

[7] John Dennis, "The Advancement and Reformation of Modern Poetry," in Edward Niles Hooker, ed., *The Critical Works of John Dennis* (Baltimore: The Johns Hopkins University Press, 1939), I, 204–205; Charles de Marguetel de Saint-Denis, seigneur de Saint-Évremond, "A Judgment upon those Sciences, which a gentleman should apply himself to," in *Miscellaneous Essays* (1692), p.23. This essay was written between 1655 and 1661: see the edition by René Ternois of Saint-Évremond, *Oeuvres en prose* (Paris: Librairie Marcel Didier, 1962), II, 3. The original of this passage appears in the Ternois edition, II, 12.

social relations in view. It fixed knowledge in a firm ethical and social grid, flagged by such key words as "judgment" and "taste." Polite learning was also the stuff of gentlemanly conversation. What was inimical to politeness in learning was aspersed as "pedantry." This label was a social category since it damned its object as lacking qualities of a polite gentleman.[8]

This sort of language was easily moveable from discussion of kinds of subject matter to kinds of literary manner. Literary politeness served as an umbrella for a range of stylistic and critical campaigns. The central trait of stylistic politeness was sketched by a writer who observed that "Study makes a greater Difference between a Scholar and an ignorant Man, than there is between an Ignorant Man and a Brute: but the air of the World yet makes a greater distinction still, between a Polite and learned Person. Knowledge begins the Gentleman, and the Correspondence of the World compleats him."[9] The amalgamation of gentleman and scholar became a virtual paradigm of polite writing.

This ideal assigned conversation an exemplary role in written discourse, requiring that a polite text be not only gentlemanly but specifically conversational. As early as John Dryden, conversation was identified as perhaps the most important component of literary refinement.[10] In his writings, Dryden sketched a process of conversationalization that later writers would restyle as literary politeness. Not surprisingly, a language of gentlemanly social behavior was imported into discussion of texts. Since a true gentleman would bring to his writing all the knowledge and grace that he applied in all aspects of his life, good writing had precisely those qualities that the polite gentleman had. For John Hughes, "a free Air and genteel Motion" characterized the mental life of the gentleman. For Henry Felton, the gentleman's style had "inimitable Grace," "Delicacy and Civility."[11]

"Politeness" was applied to all sorts of expressive forms, validating comparison among literary and intellectual genres, but its applicability did not end there. Its further aggrandizement was bolstered by its classici-

---

[8] See Steven Shapin, "'A Scholar and a Gentleman': The Problematic Identity of the Scientific Practitioner in Early Modern England," *History of Science*, 29 (1991), 279–327. However, where Shapin emphasizes the irreconciliability of learning and gentlemanliness, I see learning being regulated by standards of gentlemanliness.

[9] Saint-Évremond, *Miscellaneous Essays*, p.206. This essay is not recognized as a genuine Saint-Évremond text and does not appear in the Ternois edition, cited above.

[10] John Dryden, "Defence of the EPILOGUE [to *The Conquest of Granada*, part II]. Or, *An Essay on the* Dramatique Poetry *of the Last Age*," in *The Works of John Dryden* (Berkeley: University of California Press, 1956-), XI, 216.

[11] John Hughes, "Of Style" (written 1697), in *Poems on Several Occasions. With Some Select Essays in Prose* (1735), I, 247–248; Henry Felton, *A Dissertation on Reading the Classics and Forming a Just Style* (1713), p.67.

Introduction

zation. The language of "politeness" could bear the burdens of literary classicism since ancient writings were said to be the epitome of "politeness."[12] Moreover, "politeness" was used to characterize classical culture generally. Saint-Évremond gave a lead to the conflation of the polite and the classical by locating among the ancients a precedent for his polite trivium of ethics, politics, and literature: "every one knows that *Greece* has given to the World, the greatest Philosophers, and the greatest Legislators: And one cannot deny, but that other Nations have taken from thence all the Politeness they have had."[13] The classicization of "politeness" bolstered the term's potency as a mode of cultural generalization and correlated it with the terms of classicist historicism.

The capacity of "politeness" to provide conceptual organization to various forms and levels of social and cultural life made it a mode of cultural discourse. Such a cultural discourse, generalizing about the moral features of individuals and groups as such features were embodied in practices, issued in estimations of "manners," "mores," "characters," and "characteristics." "Politeness" coordinated description and prescription, allowing a writer to perform verbal acts, of considerable complexity, in which the past and present of expressive forms were used for ideological purposes. It enabled a moralized and politicized view of culture of the sort that has been more commonly examined in the nineteenth century than in the eighteenth.[14] The writings of the third earl of Shaftesbury were an exemplary instance of this sort of discourse.[15]

Tracing the expansion of the range of "politeness" produces a map of a rich semantic world, about which two related generalizations can be made. First, "politeness" infused great tracts of discussion with a social register. As refined sociability was the sociability of gentlemen, so its spread extended the range of the gentlemanly. The spread of "politeness" from discourse to discourse reflects the appropriation of the world of social, intellectual and literary creation by gentlemen: it witnessed the remaking of the world in a gentlemanly image.

---

[12] Joseph Addison, *A Discourse on Ancient and Modern Learning* (1734), p.3; Jonathan Swift, "A Proposal for Correcting, Improving and Ascertaining the English Tongue," in *Prose Works*, IV, 9, 21 25–26; Jonathan Swift, "Hints towards an Essay on Conversation," in *Prose Works*, IV, 92; *Tatler*, No. 230 (September 28, 1710), Bond, III, 191–195.
[13] Saint-Évremond, *Miscellaneous Essays*, p.213.
[14] The classic study along these lines is Raymond Williams, *Culture and Society 1780–1950* (London: Chatto & Windus, 1958). See also David Watkin, *Morality and Architecture* (Oxford: Clarendon Press, 1977). Williams's study begins with Burke and Cobbett, Watkin's with Pugin: to the phenomena studied in both, eighteenth-century cultural discourse was an important prolegomenon.
[15] Another Whiggish cultural ideologist, contemporary with Shaftesbury, whose works would reward examination, was John Dennis (1657–1734).

Second, where "politeness" went, the model of refined sociability was likely to follow. Social agreeableness became a way of comprehending the values that informed not only social interactions and conversation but the range of cultural expressions and, indeed, manners in general. While the language of "politeness" could be used in the various ways just explored, it also brought these different objects into one interpretive scheme. The premises, criteria, and standards of this scheme can be most easily grasped as expressions of an idealized vision of human intercourse, peopled by gentlemen and ladies, sited in the drawing room or coffeehouse, engaged in intelligent and stylish conversation about urbane things, presided over by the spirit of good taste. "Politeness" evoked this scene of refined sociability, with its rules and participants, as against scenes in which sociability was distorted or neglected. The vision of decorous, gentlemanly sociability was embedded and implicit in the language of "politeness." Thus, the language of "politeness" acted as a master metaphor which brought to bear in different areas of discourse the expectations and standards of this vision.

Indeed, these scenes of sociability and the characters who inhabited them recurred throughout Shaftesbury's writings. Sociability was not just an abstract idea for him but a repeated figure, through which the self, philosophy, moral behavior, writing, and culture could be understood. Images of refined sociability and its opposites – unsociability and distorted sociability – recur in Shaftesbury's writing. As chapters 4 and 5 demonstrate, he used them to characterize the social stances available to the philosophic gentleman in company and, by extension, to taxonomize the basic discursive situations in society. In turn, as indicated in chapter 6, the figure of sociability informed the ideal of writing to which philosophy might aspire. Moreover, Shaftesbury saw an analogue between different forms of sociability and different institutional arrangements for culture. Thus, chapter 8, 9, and 10 show Shaftesbury using the figure of sociability to organize his politically motivated assessments of contemporary cultural institutions.

A setting

The argument at the heart of Shaftesbury's cultural politics was that, while the Church and the Court had traditionally dominated English culture to its detriment, post-1688 England and post-1707 Britain had the opportunity to create a new public and gentlemanly culture of criticism. Thus, he was using notions of sociability and politeness to attack the Tory loyalty to Church and Court in the name of a new Whiggish culture. There is an irony in this that Shaftesbury himself recognized. As we will see in chapter 7, his project depended on his ability to reassign the cultural associations of the two parties, shifting the guardianship of culture from the Tories to his own party, with its Country, Puritan and radical associations.

The irony is that Shaftesbury's project relied on discursive tools that had developed throughout the Restoration decades in cooperation with the very institutions, the Church and the Court, that he would come to attack. The shock of the mid-seventeenth-century civil breakdown reverberated long after 1660, defining the subsequent decades by a project of restoration. Since restoration involved reimposing the authority of traditional institutions over society and culture, the repressiveness of Charles II's regime should not be underestimated. At the same time, the period saw the search for new or renewed disciplines of society through which order would be encouraged without repressive force. Chapters 8 and 9 of this study explore the way in which the themes of sociability, civility, and politeness entered discussion of religion and monarchy during the Restoration period. The availability of these idioms was one important context for Shaftesbury's writing.

However, Shaftesbury was not simply seeking to capture some Tory ideological resources for use by the Whigs or to replace Tory control of traditional institutions with Whig control: he was not interested in a culture organized around a Whig Church and a Whig Court. Rather, he was trying to envision the shape of discourse and culture in new ways, and this endeavor was premised on specific social and institutional developments in late seventeenth- and early eighteenth-century England.

In this respect, Shaftesbury's project was like that of Joseph Addison and Richard Steele. Indeed, these renowned Whig cultural ideologists were all participants in a significant larger development: politeness was becoming a dominant paradigm, offering the scene of gentlemen in polite conversation as a model for discursive and cultural activity and authority. This model functioned in two ways. It offered a way to conceptualize complex and erratic social phenomena, giving them normative shape and direction. At the same time, it served as a blueprint for social and cultural creation, authorizing specific forms of activity and distributing authority in prescribed ways. Thus, this study of Shaftesbury is only introductory to a larger attempt to define an era of English cultural history corresponding to a "long" eighteenth century. On the one hand, this cultural era was post-courtly and post-godly (meaning neither "secular" nor "secularized" but "within a regime in which religion has been subjected to new political and intellectual disciplines").On the other, it was pre-professional, pre-meritocratic, and also, in a sense, pre-industrialist (that is, "prior to the moment at which the English developed a sense that their industrial character was highly problematic"). What defined this era was its politeness, which, as we have seen, conveyed ideas of the urbane, the amateur, the conversational, and the gentlemanly. Politeness was central to mapping not just cultural ideology in the eighteenth century but also the era's characteristic forms of cultural organization and practice.

The pressure for this new paradigm came from a number of directions, but perhaps most tangibly from shifts in gravity among England's discursive and cultural institutions. Notwithstanding the project of restoration, both the Court and the Church were declining as centers of discursive and cultural production. The rise and decline of the English Court as such a center has only been interpreted in segments, but it is clear that the decline was a phenomenon of the late seventeenth century and early eighteenth.[16] As for the Church, the overwhelming lesson of seventeenth-century history for the English mind was the need for religious sentiment and ideology to be under psychological and intellectual discipline and for religious institutions to be firmly under civil control.[17] The later seventeenth century and the early eighteenth did not see a decay of the religious spirit but rather its rigorous submission to social and civil discipline. This process weakened the Church's presumption of authority over discourse and culture. The best evidence for this is the decline in prestige of the English universities in this period and their abandonment by the English elite.[18]

However, another force was creating a demand for a new cultural paradigm: the new patterns of urban development in the later seventeenth

---

[16] Parts of the post-1660 story appear in: John M. Beattie, *The English Court in the Reign of George I* (Cambridge: Cambridge University Press, 1967); Howard Erskine-Hill, *The Augustan Idea in English Literature* (London: Edward Arnold, 1983); Malcolm Smuts, *Court Culture and the Origins of a Royalist Tradition in Early Stuart England* (Philadelphia: University of Pennsylvania Press, 1987); and R. O. Bucholz, "'Nothing but Ceremony': Queen Anne and the Limitations of Royal Ritual," *Journal of British Studies*, 30 (1991), 288–323. For the view that the Court maintained its traditional centrality deep into the eighteenth century, see J. C. D. Clark, Introduction to *The Memoirs and Speeches of James, 2nd Earl Waldegrave 1742–63* (Cambridge: Cambridge University Press, 1988), pp.1–18.

[17] H. T. Dickinson, "Whiggism in the Eighteenth Century," in John Cannon, ed., *The Whig Ascendancy* (New York: St. Martin's, 1981), pp.41, 46–47; Michael Heyd, "The Reaction to Enthusiasm in the Seventeenth Century," *Journal of Modern History*, 53 (1981), 258–280; Frank Manuel, *The Changing of the Gods* (For Brown University Press, by University Press of New England, 1983), pp.34–51; John Marshall, "The Ecclesiology of the Latitude-men 1660–1689: Stillingfleet, Tillotson and 'Hobbism,'" *Journal of Ecclesiastical History*, 36 (1985), 407–427.

[18] Lawrence Stone, "The Size and Composition of the Oxford Student Body, 1580–1910," in Lawrence Stone, ed., *The University in Society*, 2 vols. (Princeton: Princeton University Press, 1974), I, 3–110; Hugh Kearney, *Scholars and Gentlemen: Universities and Society in Pre-Industrial Britain, 1500–1700* (London: Faber and Faber, 1970), pp.23–25, 143–144, 157–158.

Introduction

and the eighteenth century.[19] The model of this new kind of urbanism was the West End of London, the Town, though the pattern was reproduced in provincial cities and towns all over Britain. The new urbanism had several facets: new urban forms called "Georgian" though the basic pattern was established before the Hanoverians arrived; new urban populations made up of aristocrats, greater and lesser gentry, pseudo-gentry, professionals, and commercial elements; and a new array of social, discursive and cultural institutions. Coffeehouses, clubs, assemblies, gardens, and theaters were nodal points in the network of the new urban culture. These new institutions arose as outlets of the new commercialized approach to leisure that early eighteenth-century towns allowed; but it would be a mistake to think of these facilities merely as outlets of consumption. They also enabled new forms of sociability and discussion or invigorated and expanded older ones.[20] These were loci for forms of social and cultural activity that politeness described.

This new urban world arose in close association with the growth and elaboration of print media.[21] Like the institutions of the Town, the development of a print culture was fuelled by the commercial opportunities it offered. But in choosing to spend money on print to fill leisure, people were also supporting forms of communication and association that, when they were not entirely new, were of a new order of magnitude and significance.

The decline of inherited discursive and cultural institutions and the rise of new ones posed problems of authority and legitimacy. For some, the continued and apparently unstoppable development of the Town induced a nightmare of unsupervised association and rampant conversability. Their terror was enhanced by the deregulation of the press after 1695 as well as the clear recognition that this multiplication of discursive opportunities was fuelled by commercial motives. It soon became unimaginable how traditional authoritative institutions could order and control this new discursive and cultural environment. As a result, a new way of comprehending discourse in society arose, the paradigm of politeness. The paradigm of politeness offered an alternative to the reliance on

[19] The best summary of this development now available is Peter Borsay, *The English Urban Renaissance: Culture and Society in the Provincial Town, 1660–1770* (Oxford: Clarendon Press, 1989).
[20] On the commercialization of leisure, see Neil McKendrick, John Brewer and J. H. Plumb, *The Birth of a Consumer Society* (Bloomington: Indiana University Press, 1982). On the relation between the new urbanity and continuing themes in English urban history, see Jonathan Barry, "The Press and the Politics of Culture in Bristol 1660–1775," in Jeremy Black and Jeremy Gregory, eds., *Culture, Politics and Society in Britain, 1660–1800* (Manchester and New York: Manchester University Press, 1991), pp.49–81.
[21] For a survey, see Jeremy Black, *The English Press in the Eighteenth Century* (Philadelphia: University of Pennsylvania Press, 1987).

traditional authoritative institutions for ordering the discursive world, because it sought processes within the babble, diversity, and liberty of the new discursive world of the Town that would produce order and direction.

The treatment of the coffeehouse, an epitome of the new urban institutions as well as an outlet for printed matter, is illustrative of the larger process. Coffeehouses first appeared during the Civil War and proliferated during the Restoration decades. They were quickly recognized as sites not just of beverage consumption but of new and dangerous forms of association. Except in broadsides put out by proprietors to advertise their businesses, it is hard to find kind words for the coffeehouse during the Restoration period.[22] After 1688, criticisms continued to appear, but they were joined by a new and more positive assessment, which characterized coffeehouses as potential sites of rational discussion and refining interaction. Addison and Steele represented them as one arena in the struggle for politeness.[23]

Indeed, the periodicals of Addison and Steele were devoted to demonstrating the pitfalls and possibilities of discourse in the modern Town. As a whole, their works represented London as a field in which opportunities for politeness were both won and lost. While Steele and Addison operated on a much more concrete level than Shaftesbury, all three were engaged in producing a model that could account for modern discursive conditions. These Whig writers foregrounded the volubility of their society as a problem. Within that polyphony, politeness as a norm and also goal of discourse promised order and direction in a way that inherited cultural institutions might have once sought to do.

It should be obvious that the popularity of politeness as an ideological vehicle does not indicate that what went on in coffeehouses or in the print culture or, more generally, in the eighteenth century actually corresponded to the canons of politeness. However, politeness should not be dismissed simply as an irrelevant ideological gloss on a reality of an entirely different nature. Since politeness was a model of cultural action, it helped shape a wide range of cultural institutions and practices in the eighteenth century. Clubs and other schemes of intellectual sociability

---

[22] Criticisms appeared in, to name a sample: *The Coffee Scuffle* (1662); *A Cup of Coffee* (1663); *The Character of a Coffee-House* (1665), pp.2–6, 10; *News from the Coffee-House* (1667); *A Broadside against Coffee* (1672); *The Character of a Coffee House* (1673), pp.1–4. On the history of the coffeehouse, see: Aytoun Ellis, *The Penny Universities* (London: Secker and Warburg, 1956); Edward F. Robinson, *The Early History of Coffee-Houses in England* (London: Kegan Paul, Trench, Trübner and Co., Ltd., 1893); and Bryant Lillywhite, *London Coffee Houses* (London: Allen and Unwin, 1963).

[23] See *Tatler*, No. 86 (October 27, 1709), No. 153 (April 1, 1710), No. 171 (May 13, 1710), Bond, II, 46–47, 361, 439–442.

Introduction 13

proliferated in the eighteenth century, bringing together gentlemen and would-be gentlemen for recreation and edification.[24] The effect of the prestige of politeness on learned activity was not limited to the diminished stature of the universities. Learning itself, both humanistic and scientific, was often submitted to models of polite conversation and edification.[25] One aspect of the print culture was the fashioning of print culture itself on lines suggested by the patterns of polite interaction.[26] Nor were the appeals of politeness limited to the traditional elite of so-called "gentlemen." As the traditional vocabulary of gentility sagged into semantic limpness, allowing all sorts of people from the middling ranks to appropriate it, so varieties of politeness were disseminated to and embraced by the "busy" elements in society.[27]

Thus, the rise of politeness was closely associated with a reorganization of culture and social life at the beginning of the eighteenth century in which the forms of public life were expanded and elaborated. Beyond new kinds of experience and subjectivity, these changes implied new shapes for political activity. The political history of early modern Europe offers many instances in which the options of princes and aristocrats were shaped by the actions and statements of others in society. However, in the eighteenth century, those without formal political power found new institutions and media through which to exert themselves; they also found a new legitimacy in their exertions. This is what Jürgen Habermas means

[24] Peter Clark, *Sociability and Urbanity: Clubs and Societies in the Eighteenth-Century City* (Leicester: Victorian Studies Center, University of Leicester, 1986).
[25] The use of "polite" to characterize the social organization of scientific activity in the eighteenth century is well-established in the historiography of science: Arnold Thackray, "Natural Knowledge in Cultural Context: The Manchester Model," *American Historical Review*, 79 (1974), 672–709; Roy Porter, "Gentlemen and Geology: The Emergence of a Scientific Career, 1660–1902," *Historical Journal*, 21 (1978), 809–836, esp. 811–825; G. S. Rousseau and Roy Porter, eds., *The Ferment of Knowledge* (Cambridge: Cambridge University Press, 1980), pp.4, 258–263, 300–305.
[26] See Kathryn Shevelow, *Women and Print Culture* (London and New York: Routledge, 1989), pp.22–57.
[27] On early modern languages of social classification, see David Cressy, "Describing the Social Order of Elizabethan and Stuart England," *Literature and History*, 3 (1976); Keith Wrightson, "The Social Order of Early Modern England: Three Approaches," in Lloyd Bonfield, Richard M. Smith, and Keith Wrightson, *The World We Have Gained* (Oxford: Basil Blackwell, 1986), pp.177–202; and Penelope Corfield, "Class by Name and Number in Eighteenth-Century Britain," *History*, 72 (1987), 38–61. On the gentle aspirations of the non-gentle, see: Nicholas Rogers, "Money, Land and Lineage: The Big Bourgeoisie of Hanoverian London," *Social History*, 4 (1979), 437–454; Susan Staves, "Pope's Refinement," *The Eighteenth Century*, 29 (1988), 145–163; Peter Earle, *The Making of the English Middle Class* (London: Methuen, 1989), pp.5–9, 31–69, 73, 76, 85, 218; Paul Langford, *A Polite and Commercial People: England 1727–1783* (Oxford: Clarendon Press, 1989), pp.59–71. The style setters in polite consumption were not necessarily the social elite as conventionally defined but rather those with easy access to metropolitan culture: see Lorna Wetherill, *Consumer Behaviour and Material Culture in Britain 1660–1760* (London and New York: Routledge, 1988), pp.194–197.

by the appearance of a public sphere in the eighteenth century.[28] One need not characterize the public sphere as polite in order to admit that ideologists such as Shaftesbury, Addison, and Steele came to understand its workings in terms of politeness. Thus, the study of politeness helps delineate both the continuity and the break between the courtly world explored by Norbert Elias and the public sphere described by Jürgen Habermas.

A career

As the subtitle of this book indicates, the third earl of Shaftesbury used ideas of politeness to frame both a moral discourse and a cultural politics. From his earliest years, philosophy and politics are themes of his biography since he was born into a family with a high political profile and with close connections to the outstanding English philosopher of the age.[29]

The political prominence of the family was entirely the responsibility of Anthony Ashley Cooper, the first earl of Shaftesbury, for whom the title was created in 1672. As the title suggested, the family had long-standing roots in Dorset, where the first earl built his seat and that of his successors, Wimborne St. Giles. Though a parliamentarian during the Civil War, this Ashley Cooper comfortably adjusted to the Restoration, serving in Parliament, gaining royal favor, and becoming the King's minister. However, in the 1670s, Shaftesbury left office and became the leader of the Whig movement that opposed royal policies and sought, in particular, to exclude Charles II's brother, James, the duke of York, from the throne. The exclusion crisis put the first earl at the pinnacle of English politics until the collapse of the movement and his exile in 1682.[30] Though his movement failed, the first earl of Shaftesbury was a very famous and a very great man in English politics. The third earl venerated and tried to vindicate his grandfather's memory. Yet, the first earl's model was a hard one to imitate, which may have contributed to the internal conflicts that afflicted the third earl.

These conflicts may also have had their origins in the contrast between the third earl's ineffectual father and his supercompetent grandfather. Though the first earl's son was a cipher, he did marry and, in 1671, had his

---

[28] Jürgen Habermas, *The Structural Transformation of the Public Sphere*, trans. Thomas Burger (originally published 1962; Cambridge, Mass.: The MIT Press, 1989).

[29] A full account of the third earl of Shaftesbury's life can be found in Robert Voitle's biography, *The Third Earl of Shaftesbury 1671–1713* (Baton Rouge and London: Louisiana State University Press, 1984).

[30] The indispensable source on the first earl is K. H. D. Haley, *The First Earl of Shaftesbury* (Oxford: Clarendon Press, 1968); for the family background, see pp.7–15, 206–215, 221–224. Wimborne St. Giles is described in Voitle, *Third Earl of Shaftesbury*, pp.164ff.

first son, whose upbringing the first earl took over. Thus, the future third earl was reared and educated in the first earl's household. That early education was the responsibility of John Locke (1632–1704), whom the first earl first encountered in the 1660s when he needed Locke's medical expertise. However, the relation took on many dimensions in subsequent years. Most famously, Locke advised Shaftesbury on political matters and developed sophisticated arguments to support the Whig cause.[31] Locke was also close to the Shaftesbury household and was charged with educating the first earl's grandchildren. (This was the context in which Locke arrived at his *Thoughts on Education*.) This personal proximity of Locke to the future third earl helps to explain the emotional intensity that later informed the latter's search for a philosophical identity: his attack on Lockean positions involved attacking a personal connection.

The Tory reaction of the 1680s, when the Whigs were in eclipse, must have been a trial for the sensitive grandson of the greatest of the Whigs. While the attack on the first earl reached its literary zenith in Dryden's *Absalom and Achitophel*, he was vilified on a daily basis in the periodical writings of Roger L'Estrange. After Locke himself went into exile, the future third earl spent some very unhappy years at Winchester school, which no doubt encouraged his antipathy to the Tory-dominated educational establishment.[32] Shaftesbury later toured the Continent, but his responses to this journey are thinly documented. He was accompanied by John Cropley (1663–1713), a wealthy Londoner from a commercial and professional background who became Shaftesbury's closest friend and, in the later part of Shaftesbury's life, a regular correspondent.

The Revolution of 1688 was obviously a turning point in Whig fortunes. The first earl was dead by then and the second earl led a secluded life, but the latter's eldest son, now Lord Ashley, might have been expected to enter on a political career. He was young, but so was Charles Spencer, the future earl of Sunderland, when he first entered Parliament in 1695 at the age of twenty-one. However, as early as 1690, we find Lord Ashley refusing to stand for a seat.[33] While he excused himself on account of his desire to study more before entering public service, this refusal is an early instance of the tension he felt in choosing between activity and retirement. Throughout his life, he alternated between phases of

---

[31] On Locke's relationship to the Shaftesbury household, see: Maurice Cranston, *John Locke* (London: Longmans, Green and Co., 1957), pp.113–121; Haley, *First Earl of Shaftesbury*, pp.202–226; *Third Earl of Shaftesbury*, pp.7–11. The third earl provided his own account of Locke's ties with the first earl in a letter to Jean LeClerc, February 8, 1705, P.R.O. 30/24/22/2, ff.157–160.

[32] See the fourth earl's account in his life of the third earl, P.R.O. 30/24/21/226.

[33] P.R.O. 30/24/22/2, f. 108. Shaftesbury to Sir J. M., February 1690; 30/24/22/3, ff.108–109, Shaftesbury to Mr. Taylor, a Weymouth worthy, February 16, 1690.

engagement in the world and phases of self-seclusion. This tension had an intellectual impact. As we will see, engagement posed him with existential conflicts that he ultimately resolved in part through notions of politeness. Moreover, his emphasis on cultural politics may have been a way for him to achieve a political personality without active engagement in the political life itself.

Though his activities in the 1690s are hard to trace, it is likely that he did spend time in study and reflection. He exchanged some letters with Locke on philosophical topics,[34] and he also produced an edition of sermons by the Anglican divine Benjamin Whichcote, which appeared in 1698. This edition's preface, with its defense of virtue against Hobbesian egoism and Christian soteriology, anticipates important themes of Shaftesbury's later writings.[35] Most important, by 1698 (and perhaps earlier), he had written a complete version of *An Inquiry Concerning Virtue*.[36] Though he would subsequently revise the *Inquiry*, the main argument remained the same when it was incorporated into *Characteristicks* thirteen years later. Thus, Shaftesbury had reached some of his basic theological and ethical positions by the time he was twenty-seven years old.

After his initial postponement, Shaftesbury did enter politics in early 1695 when he was appointed to the Dorset seat of Poole, for which he was elected later that year. Whatever reluctance he felt about political service was overcome since he assumed an active role in the Parliament that lasted from 1695 to 1698. As chapter 7 will discuss, he was swept up in the controversies which arose in these years against the background of war with France and which fractured the Whig camp. Though much of the evidence is circumstantial, he clearly was among those oppositionalist Whigs who criticized the King and his Court Whig supporters. At this point he was closely associated with a coterie of educated younger gentlemen, including Robert Molesworth (1656–1725), Walter Moyle (1672–1721), John Toland (1670–1722), John Trenchard (1662–1723), and Andrew Fletcher (1655–1716). This circle entertained advanced political and religious ideas, including varieties of republicanism, deism, and anti-ecclesiastical critique. Their Whig politics was informed by Country and civic traditions which authorized an attack on the Court and its corrupting power, though their actual degree of radicalism is arguable. Shaftesbury always maintained warm and respectful ties with the eminent Court Whig, John Somers (1651–1716), with whom he shared not only many Whig principles and policies but an interest in the arts and learning.

---

[34] See chapter 1, pp.27–28. Few of Shaftesbury's letters before 1695 survive, while the bulk of his considerable surviving correspondence dated from after 1700.
[35] Discussed in chapter 1, pp.31–34.
[36] The *Inquiry* is discussed in chapter 2.

While these political controversies reached a peak in 1697 and 1698, the latter year was also a turning point in Shaftesbury's life. By the end of the parliamentary term, he was suffering from exhaustion. Moreover, as we will see, he was troubled by the psychic stresses of this deeply engaged form of life. He therefore decided to withdraw, a move highly unexpected from one of his class and personal background.[37] However, this withdrawal, ending the first phase of his political and philosophical life, begins the development that this book is concerned to trace. He had completed his career as a Country Whig in opposition. When he next appeared in politics, his own and the nation's circumstances had changed, and he would be moving toward a quite different perception of politics than that he entertained in the later 1690s. Similarly, with *An Inquiry Concerning Virtue*, he had completed his first philosophical endeavor. His subsequent development, involving a critique of the philosophical practice of the *Inquiry*, led to *Characteristicks*, a text of a very different sort.

Shaftesbury's retirement took the form of a journey to Rotterdam where, for over a year, he led a life of seclusion and study, though he had contact with a circle of Dutch and Huguenot acquaintances and friends. The focus of this circle was the household of Benjamin Furley (1636–1714), an Englishman who had converted to Quakerism and emigrated to Holland where, in Margaret Jacob's words, he "maintained a salon in Rotterdam, kept a splendid library of heretical books, and established his home as the *entrepôt* between English republicans, Dutch Dissenters, and French refugees."[38] For years afterward, Shaftesbury maintained a lively correspondence with Furley largely devoted to contemporary international politics. Through Furley, Shaftesbury made a number of significant acquaintances, including the great Huguenot sceptic, Pierre Bayle (1647–1706), with whom Shaftesbury exchanged letters.[39] Shaftesbury also corresponded with Jean LeClerc (1657–1736), the Huguenot theologian who, through his editing of several cosmopolitan learned journals, stood at the hub of the international republic of letters.

At this point, Shaftesbury's inner life suddenly becomes visible to us, since, on arriving in Holland, he began recording ideas and reflections in notebooks that he maintained for years to come. These notebooks are striking in their detail, in their directness, and, most of all, in the personal developments they witness, for they provide evidence of a severe personal crisis that extended over several years. The dimensions of this crisis are

---

[37] See the shocked response of Thomas Stringer, a Dorset neighbor, in letters to Shaftesbury, March 27, 1699, and May 5, 1699, P.R.O. 30/24/44/77, ff.5–6, 9–10. Stringer (1639–1702) had been close to the Shaftesbury household for decades.

[38] Margaret Jacob, *The Radical Enlightenment* (London: George Allen and Unwin, 1981), p.149.

[39] On the relation of Shaftesbury and Bayle, see Voitle, *Third Earl of Shaftesbury*, pp.86–90.

examined in chapter 3 and its consequences for Shaftesbury's development are explained in subsequent chapters.

In the middle of 1699, Shaftesbury, responding to family pressure, returned to England. Before the year was out, his father died and he officially assumed the title. Though complicated estate and family matters needed to be sorted out, he was soon engaged in politics again. War with France again threatened, but circumstances on the Continent had changed so that most Whigs, including Shaftesbury, now rallied around the King. As a member of the Lords, he was an active participant in William's final parliaments. Had William lived, Shaftesbury might have followed his grandfather in ministerial responsibility.

However, William died suddenly in early 1702. The succession of Queen Anne was a setback to the Whigs, and it precipitated another period of withdrawal and retirement on Shaftesbury's part. Again, in 1703, he went to the Continent and again his notebooks record, with intensity, his personal and philosophical reflections. By this point, Shaftesbury had begun to recognize that his tenuous health was a permanent impediment to an active public life. His return to England in 1704 from the Continent involved a disastrous Channel crossing and then months of illness. As we will see, the political profile that he maintained in the middle years of Anne's reign was cautious and peripheral.

By about 1707, he appears to have attained a new level of maturity. His most severe crises, as recorded in his notebooks, were over. He married and had a son. Most important, he started writing for a public again.

In the years after the initial publication of the *Inquiry*, Shaftesbury had written abundantly, but none of it was published at the time.[40] He filled his personal notebooks as well as others devoted to specific projects. One of these was his "Socratick History," discussed in chapter 6. Another was a short satirical manuscript, dated 1702 and called "The Adept Ladys"; its critique of enthusiasm anticipated a theme on which Shaftesbury would publish later in the decade.[41] He also wrote "The Sociable Enthusiast," an early version of *The Moralists*, the philosophical dialogue at the heart of *Characteristicks*.

Shaftesbury finally returned to print in 1708 with *A Letter Concerning Enthusiasm, to My Lord * * * * **. The letter commented on the "French prophets," the Cevennais émigrés and their English adherents who, on account of their millenial outbursts and prophetic pronouncements, were

---

[40] With the exception of *Paradoxes of State*, the topical political pamphlet that he published in early 1702. This is discussed in chapter 7, pp.140–141.

[41] "The Adept Ladys" has now been published in volume I.i (pp.376–431) of the "standard edition" of Shaftesbury's works, edited by Gerd Hemmerich and Wolfram Benda and published by Frommann-Holzboog (Salzburg).

Introduction

attracting attention in London during 1706 and 1707. *A Letter Concerning Enthusiasm* was, thus, topical and a contribution to an ongoing controversy.[42] However, the "prophets," though the occasion for the piece, occupied only a peripheral place in Shaftesbury's essay, which aimed to explore the psychology of religion and to establish standards for public exchange on religious topics.

If *A Letter Concerning Enthusiasm* used a topical issue as a point of departure, it also became a topical issue itself, for, unlike Shaftesbury's original *Inquiry Concerning Virtue*, which seems to have elicited only one response, *A Letter Concerning Enthusiasm* elicited quite a few.[43] The controversy provoked by *A Letter Concerning Enthusiasm* was the point of departure for Shaftesbury's next publication, *Sensus Communis: An Essay on the Freedom of Wit and Humour*. *Sensus Communis*, published in 1709, defended *A Letter Concerning Enthusiasm* by elaborating on its positions and exploring further the discourse of ethics and the ethics of discourse. The year 1709 also saw the appearance of *The Moralists, A Philosophical Rhapsody*. While it developed moral and religious ideas already expressed in the earlier works, it was formally a break with all that preceded it. Unlike *An Inquiry Concerning Virtue*, it was not expository and, unlike *A Letter Concerning Enthusiasm* and *Sensus Communis*, it had no topical element; rather it cast Shaftesbury's substantive concerns in a complex dialogic format. Finally, in 1710, Shaftesbury published *Soliloquy: Or, Advice to an Author*. Although Shaftesbury again managed here to intertwine his concerns with moral communication and with moral wisdom, this, among his works, was most concerned with the character of discourse. It built on views already put forth in *A Letter Concerning Enthusiasm* and *Sensus Communis*, expanding them into a discussion of the nature of culture and Shaftesbury's aspirations for British culture in his own era.

At some point when he was working on *Soliloquy*, Shaftesbury must have conceived of combining his writings into a collected work. The four works from 1708–1710 and the earlier *Inquiry Concerning Virtue* – all in somewhat revised versions – comprised the first two volumes of *Characteristicks*. In addition, Shaftesbury wrote a long excursus, entitled "Miscellaneous Reflections on the Preceding Treatises, Etc.," which filled

---

[42] See Hillel Schwartz, *The French Prophets: The History of a Millenarian Group in Eighteenth-Century England* (Berkeley: University of California Press, 1980). A bibliography of works commenting on the "prophets" appears in Schwartz's *Knaves, Fools, Madmen, and That Subtile Effluvium: A Study of the Opposition to the French Prophets in England, 1706–1710* (Gainesville: The University Presses of Florida, 1978).

[43] See the annotated bibliography of eighteenth-century works referring to Shaftesbury in A. O. Aldridge, "Shaftesbury and the Deist Manifesto," *Transactions of the American Philosophical Society*, 41 N.S. (1951), 371–372.

20   Introduction

the third volume of *Characteristicks*. The "Miscellaneous Reflections" reviewed the five works in the first two volumes, rehearsing their arguments, commenting on them, bringing new material to bear on the issues, and, more generally, discussing issues of discourse, ethics, and politics.

When *Characteristicks* appeared in the spring of 1711, Shaftesbury was gratified to learn from his publisher and other correspondents that the three-volume work was received well.[44] The success of the book prompted him to revise it for a new edition and commission a set of emblematic engravings to illustrate its main points.[45] However, by then, he had already withdrawn for the last time. For the sake of his health, he had decided to move to southern Italy. He made the trip in the summer of 1711, accompanied by his wife, though his heir was left in England. Shaftesbury settled in a villa overlooking Naples Bay, where he nursed his health, associated with local notables and virtuosi, set out to tour local monuments, and examined art works brought to him. In Naples, his reflections took a more decided turn toward the fine arts. He commissioned Paolo de Mattheis to do a massive history painting, which was the basis of his discussion of painting in *A Notion of the Historical Draught or Tablature of the Judgment of Hercules*. He sent a draft of this treatise to John Lord Somers in England with a cover letter appraising the state and prospects of art in England. This was subsequently published as *A Letter Concerning the Art, or Science of Design*. He also began assembling ideas for *Second Characters*, a companion work to *Characteristicks*.[46] Unfortunately, his health grew worse in early 1713 and he died in February at the age of forty-two.

The argument

Shaftesbury's use of politeness was traditional in that it involved a reassertion of the aristocratic principle in English society and culture; but he also innovated by endorsing the concept of the public and the role of criticism in society, and it is these features that are foregrounded in this study. Shaftesbury's self-consciously modern outlook opposed quite specific alternatives. When he advocated the hegemony of gentlemen and gentlemanliness in society, he was reacting against those agencies with which gentlemen had traditionally shared the various forms of hegemony,

[44] P.R.O. 30/24/23/8, ff.7–9, Shaftesbury to Sir John Cropley, August 1/11, 1711; ff.10–11, Shaftesbury to Thomas Micklethwaite, August 11, 1711; ff.34–36, Shaftesbury to Thomas Micklethwaite, December 8, 1711.
[45] P.R.O. 30/24/23/8, ff.57–62, Shaftesbury to Thomas Micklethwaite, January 19, 1712. On the engravings, see Felix Paknadel, "Shaftesbury's Illustrations of *Characteristics*," *Journal of the Warburg and Courtauld Institutes*, 37 (1974), 290–312.
[46] These ideas appear in the notebook P.R.O. 30/24/27/15.

namely, the Church and the King. Shaftesbury was fundamentally a Whig who, in opposition to the classic commitments of the Tories, wished to see the power of both Church and Monarch reduced. Tracing a vision of eighteenth-century politics and culture that replaced godly and courtly understandings with a public gentlemanly one is the main aim of this study.

Eschewing ecclesiastical and courtly institutions, Shaftesbury directed his program of gentlemanly formation at the moral and cultural health of the ruling elite. This program rested on two main props. One of these was high culture. Shaftesbury spent much effort analyzing past and present cultures to illustrate that, while literature and the arts were invariably hobbled by ecclesiastical or courtly influences, contemporary Britain was ready for a cultural take-off that would attest to as well as strengthen the moral and civic virtue of its elite.

However, Shaftesbury's polite gentleman was to be versed not only in the arts but in philosophy, the second prop of politeness. In a society in which the Church was a dominant institution of moral formation and cultural production, philosophy offered a plausible alternative. The trouble was that philosophy as Shaftesbury confronted it in the years around 1700 was becoming unsuitable for the moral formation of anyone. For a variety of reasons, which Shaftesbury observed, philosophy was of diminishing moral force. In order for philosophy to serve the purpose of giving moral shape to gentlemen, Shaftesbury had to confront and redirect it. The absorption of philosophy to the polite project involved Shaftesbury in dialectical operations that lead away from politics *per se* and towards the politics of intellectual disciplines, the competition to define and appropriate essential but contested terms such as "philosophy." Thus, while Shaftesbury asserted the superiority of philosophy to religion, he also had to reclaim philosophy for this project of moral formation. Polite philosophy was Shaftesbury's alternative to the modern philosophical project. In turn, polite philosophy was subsumed by the project of a polite Whiggism, his vision of modernity in society, culture, and politics under Whig auspices.

Part I of this study is organized to highlight Shaftesbury's evolution towards his mature notion of philosophical politeness, the insistence that philosophy not only articulate ethical ideas but also transform gentlemen. As chapter 1 shows, this insistence involved adopting the idea of sociability not just as the basis for human moral capacity but also as the criterion of moral communication. Chapter 2 turns back to the early *Inquiry Concerning Virtue*, in which Shaftesbury first used sociability to criticize contemporary philosophy. While some of his enduring ethical convictions are evident in the *Inquiry*, the question of the rhetoric of morals did not arise for him until after he wrote it. Indeed, from the standpoint of his mature outlook, *An Inquiry Concerning Virtue* was not polite philosophy at all. Part I turns on the inadequacy of this work as a guide to Shaftesbury's mature project (though the *Inquiry* is often taken as the key work). This is evident when one examines the intellectual crisis that engulfed Shaftesbury in the years after he completed the *Inquiry*. This crisis, discussed in chapter 3, called into question the premises underlying the *Inquiry*. It also allowed Shaftesbury to generate a new understanding of philosophical practice – as a habit of the inner life (discussed in chapter 4), as a guide to social behavior (discussed in chapter 5), and as a form of writing (discussed in chapter 6). The result of this survey is to restore *Characteristicks* as a whole to our attention and to insist on its seriousness for evaluating Shaftesbury's achievement.

As Shaftesbury's mature moral concerns were highly rhetorical, so his mature political concerns were profoundly cultural. Like other Whigs, Shaftesbury was concerned with the preservation of English liberty and the special responsibilities of the elite to guard it; but he was exceptional in his serious attention to the culture of liberty and the politics of national and elite manners. The formative conditions for moral, social, political and cultural personality and the institutional framework for intellectual and cultural production were his themes, explored in part II.

Like part I, part II also has an evolutionary organization. To take politeness seriously as an idiom of political discourse, one must contrast Shaftesbury's oppositionalist stance toward the Whig regime in the 1690s with the ideology of *Characteristicks* a decade later, which legitimated that very regime. Chapter 7 surveys the ideological options open to Whigs at the end of the seventeenth century and examines the possibilities for cultural politics against this background. It also describes Shaftesbury's engagements in practical politics for evidence of his political evolution. The subsequent chapters analyze Shaftesbury's use of politeness to establish the cultural terms of the eighteenth-century order. Chapter 8 shows how Shaftesbury coordinated the contemporary idioms of "priestcraft" and "enthusiasm" with his notions of politeness to produce a critique of the Church. Chapter 9 explains how Shaftesbury reappropriated politeness from its association with courtly society in order to produce a critique of the Court. The final chapter demonstrates how Shaftesbury used politeness positively to project a design for the culture of liberty.

Shaftesbury's writing provides one highly sophisticated version of the convictions and commitments of the era of politeness, an era pre-dating the professional ethos that came into its own in the nineteenth century and penetrates so thoroughly the modern academy. Shaftesbury wrote as a gentleman but what he wrote has become the scholarly property of historical subdisciplines: histories of ideas, religion, political thought, moral philosophy, aesthetics, literature, and various arts. By foregrounding the theme of politeness in this study, I have aimed to restore Shaftesbury to the generalist context in which he operated. Nonetheless, my readers will all be in some manner specialists. Part I covers material that will be most pertinent to philosophers and literary historians while part II covers material that will be most pertinent to historians of politics and political thought. However, readers should remember that part I and part II are phases of one argument: that Shaftesbury's quest for the proper form of moral discourse, traced in part I, involved insights about communication, the self, and solidarity that shaped the cultural models, discussed in part II, which he put to such critical and constructive use.

Part I

Polite Philosophy

1 The amalgamation of philosophy and breeding

A philosophical vocation

As a young man, the third earl of Shaftesbury already recognized his antagonism to current trends in philosophy. In 1694, at the age of twenty-three, he wrote to John Locke:

> It is not with mee as with an Empirick, one that is studdying of Curiositys, raising of new Inventions that are to gain credit to the author, starting of new Notions that are to amuse the World and serve them for Diverting or for tryall of their Acuteness ... Descartes, or Mr Hobbs, or any of their Improvers have the same reason to make a-doe, and bee Jealouse about their notion's and DISCOVERY'S, as they call them; as a practizing Apothecary or a mountebank has to bee Jealouse about the Compositions that are to goe by his name ... for my part: I am so far from thinking that mankind need any new Discoverys ... the thing that I would ask of God should bee to make men live up to what they know; and that they might bee so wise as to desire to know no other things then what belong'd to em, and what lay plain before them ... What I count True Learning, and all wee can profitt by, is to know our selves ... whilst Such are Philosophers and Such Philosophy whence I can Learn ought from, of this kind; there is no Labour, no Studdy, no Learning that I would not undertake.[1]

In distinguishing two conceptions of philosophy, the letter adumbrated Shaftesbury's mature thinking. On one side, he perceived a self-consciously innovative project, associated with Descartes, Hobbes, and their successors, which informed philosophy with a scientific understanding of the natural world. On the other, he set a Socratic and stoic conception of philosophy as a perennial wisdom constituted of self-knowledge and self-possession. What Shaftesbury missed in philosophy as practised by contemporaries was not only urgency in the quest for self-knowing wisdom but sufficient interest in ethics at all.

The letter was patently a declaration of philosophic vocation, but, under the circumstances, it was also a declaration of philosophic independence. The addressee was Locke, whom Shaftesbury must have perceived

---

[1] E. S. DeBeer, ed., *The Correspondence of John Locke* (Oxford: Clarendon Press, 1976-), V, 150–154.

as an "Improver" of Descartes and Hobbes. Locke's social and intellectual ties with the Shaftesbury household were closest during the 1670s, but the third earl of Shaftesbury maintained contacts with Locke after the death of the first earl in 1683 and indeed through the end of Locke's life in 1704. However, philosophical discussion was not a staple of that relationship. Some of the letters between them in the early 1690s do broach philosophic subjects. Indeed, Locke encouraged his correspondent and former charge to convey his reflections, but Shaftesbury seems to have felt a mixture of respect and intimidation, complicated by feeling misunderstood by Locke and ultimately out of sympathy with him: after a few stabs at philosophic exchange, the younger man developed an embarrassed and self-effacing discomfort mixed with rebellious impatience.[2] Substantive discussion disappeared from this correspondence after about 1694. Meanwhile, establishing a philosophic identity distinct from Locke and from the sort of philosophizing Locke represented became a theme of Shaftesbury's career.

As we will see in the next chapter, Shaftesbury identified Descartes, Hobbes, and their "Improvers" as modern Epicureans. As an opponent of modern Epicureanism, Shaftesbury has appeared peripheral to the central narrative of modern intellectual history (at least, in its Anglo-American version), which has concerned the rising fortunes of modern science and philosophy. In that epic, the crippling domination by scholasticism over the European mind was challenged initially and uncertainly by humanism and then much more definitively by new insights into nature and method, which gave birth to the modern distinction between science and philosophy.[3] Science then could go on to conquer nature, under the inspiration of philosophy's epistemological and analytic insight. (Despite his evident dislike of the project to which he was being recruited, Shaftesbury could be assigned a secondary role in this narrative as one who helped to extend the achievements of empiricism to the realms of morals and aesthetics.[4])

Scholasticism died, of course; but humanistic inquiry, that nexus of linguistic, moral, historical and cultural concerns, survived. Thus, the triumphal story of modern science was complemented by an account (of Continental and especially German provenance) of the continuity of humanism, arising in the Renaissance and leading through Kant and German idealism to a variety of twentieth-century outcomes. For

---

[2] DeBeer, *Correspondence of John Locke*, III, 709–710; IV, 348–351, 394–395, 666–671; V, 65–66, 123–125.
[3] On the philosophical response to science and the rise of "the problem of knowledge," see John Herman Randall, Jr., *The Career of Philosophy* (New York and London: Columbia University Press, 1962), I, 363–370.
[4] This is what motivates his inclusion in the story of moral sensationalism, on which see chapter 2.

instance, Hans-Georg Gadamer's history of hermeneutics is premised on the centrality to human self-understanding of humanistic endeavor (*Geisteswissenschaften*, the "human sciences"), the distinctiveness of humanistic endeavor from the natural sciences, and the inapplicability of the scientific program for understanding human moral, social and cultural life.[5]

Gadamer assigns Shaftesbury a role in this history, and much of my account of Shaftesbury is compatible with Gadamer's narrative. In the name of a humanistic project, Shaftesbury did oppose the encroachments of science and the reorientation of philosophy around epistemology. His humanism is evident in the fact that he took the classics seriously as models for culture and cognition. More deeply, he linked ethical and rhetorical concerns in a distinctively humanistic way, so that the attempt to recuperate sociability, for which he is famous, was linked to a less familiar attempt to recuperate language, history, and culture.

However, the entire set of presuppositions on which the triumphalist story of scientific modernity (with its complement, the embattled survival of humanistic understanding) has been put in question in recent years. A new contextualism in the historiography of science emphasizes the gap between natural philosophical endeavors in the early modern period and anything recognizable as twentieth-century science.[6] Similarly, at least some historians of philosophy are no longer satisfied with long-accepted narratives about empiricism, which took for granted the modernity of the canonical figures.[7] More subversively, as the writings of Richard Rorty indicate, contemporary redefinitions of the project of philosophy entail revising its history, since the main lines of the history of philosophy were constructed to justify a project that no longer carries faith.[8] Rorty is

---

[5] Hans-Georg Gadamer, *Truth and Method* (originally published 1960; London: Sheed and Ward, 1975), pp.10–39. Similar themes are important to Wilhelm Dilthey, Edmund Husserl, Ernst Cassirer, and Jürgen Habermas.

[6] The new contextualism refuses to assume the modernity of natural philosophical investigation in the early modern period: see Steven Shapin and Simon Schaffer, *Leviathan and the Air-Pump* (Princeton: Princeton University Press, 1985), pp.3–21. Instead, a growing bibliography emphasizes the "un-modern" aspects of early modern science (alchemy, astrology, the hermetic tradition) or the affinities between natural philosophy and other cultural idioms, such as humanistic inquiry, rhetoric, and courtly culture.

[7] For instance, Louis Loeb, *From Descartes to Hume: Continental Metaphysics and the Development of Modern Philosophy* (Ithaca: Cornell University Press, 1981), and D. F. Norton, "The Myth of 'British Empiricism,'" *History of European Ideas*, 1 (1981), 331–344. In the writings of John Dunn, John Locke emerges in all his unmodernity: see especially "From Applied Theology to Social Analysis: The Break between John Locke and the Scottish Enlightenment," in Istvan Hont and Michael Ignatieff, eds., *Wealth and Virtue: The Shaping of Political Economy in the Scottish Enlightenment* (Cambridge: Cambridge University Press, 1983), pp.119–135.

[8] Richard Rorty, *Philosophy and the Mirror of Nature* (Oxford: Basil Blaskwell, 1980), pp.131–164. The canonization process in philosophy is explored helpfully in several essays

typical of the pragmatic and post-structural turn in late twentieth-century thinking, which has undermined the old narratives by eroding the distinctions (reality versus language, nature versus culture, the scientific versus the humanistic) that made them possible.

As the boundaries of the modern shift and the status of modernity is questioned, so do all historical relations: who or what should count as modern is in doubt as is the necessity of "modernity" as the organizing principle for historical narratives. It is no longer clear that Shaftesbury's opposition to his modern Epicureans locates him on a periphery. At the least, this situation provides an opportunity to re-examine Shaftesbury. Indeed, I will argue that he is a highly modern writer, but not in some transcendental sense that cements the last five centuries into the conglomerate of modernity. Rather, he was modern on his own terms, an up-to-date writer in his own time, producing a modernity for the eighteenth century that should be understood as such, not as fulfilling the modern promise of the seventeenth century and not as forecasting the more fully realized modernity of the nineteenth and twentieth.

Moreover, the writings of Shaftesbury have an interesting resonance under conditions of the pragmatic and post-structural turn in thinking. That turn has done much to batter the autonomy of truth (itself a pillar of scientific modernity) by insistently referring all cognitive claims back to the circumstances which generate them. Since all knowledge is particular, a function of the consensus or contentions within particular communities, our cognitive strivings seem increasingly capable of being grounded only in our own discursive practices, our own forms of conversation. Indeed, conversation is making a comeback in contemporary thought.[9] As part I of this study makes clear, conversation was central in Shaftesbury's writing and a crucial tool in his attempt to identify in politeness an alternative to Descartes, Hobbes, and their "Improvers".

---

in Richard Rorty, J. B. Schneewind, and Quentin Skinner, eds., *Philosophy in History: Essays on the Historiography of Philosophy* (Cambridge: Cambridge University Press, 1984). The spirit of the collection, relevant to the observations in this paragraph and, in a more general way, to this entire study, is conveyed in a statement in the editors' introduction: "By trying to interpret past figures as having done things which culminated in what analytic philosophy is now doing, philosophers occlude lots of the ways in which works of the past figures traditionally tagged as 'philosophers' lead up to a lot of other things that are going on nowadays" (p.13). Also useful on philosophers' use of the past to define the nature of philosophy: Jonathan Rée, "Philosophy and the History of Philosophy," in Jonathan Rée, Michael Ayers, and Adam Westoby, eds., *Philosophy and Its Past* (Brighton: Harvester Press, 1978), pp.2–25.

[9] See Rorty, *Philosophy and the Mirror of Nature*, pp.389–394. Conversation has moved to the center of Jürgen Habermas's ambitious project in social theory: see chapter 5, pp.96–101 below.

A preface

Early indications of the direction in which Shaftesbury's vocation would take him are evident in his first publication, a brief preface to a collection of sermons by Benjamin Whichcote, the popular London preacher of the previous generation, that appeared in 1698. The Whichcote preface put forth ideas that we associate with the mature Shaftesbury, such as the "*Kindness, Friendship, Sociableness, Love of Company and Converse, Natural Affection,*" deeply rooted in human nature. Such a view was "*in a Manner, the Scope of all his [Whichcote's] Discourses,*" and thus Whichcote, "*for his appearing thus in Defence of* Natural Goodness, *we may call* the Preacher of Good-nature."[10]

This characteriziation of Whichcote, *prima facie* evidence of Shaftesbury's intellectual roots in the latitudinarian divinity of the Restoration, had considerable validity.[11] As we will see in chapter 8, Whichcote emphasized the sweet and civil personality with which religion endowed the adherent. An edition of Whichcote would distribute his views more widely, but it also provided Shaftesbury a vehicle for critical initiatives that he pursued throughout his career. Human good nature needed to be defended against opponents, such as Hobbes, whom Shaftesbury condemned for his psychological reduction of all human inclinations to "*one Master-Passion,* Fear, *which has, in effect devour'd all the rest.*" According to Shaftesbury, Hobbes's move damaged ethical understanding, discouraged ethical practice, and comported well with atheism.[12]

However, with self-conscious irony, Shaftesbury pointed out that Christian stress on human sinfulness was tantamount to Hobbes's atheistic hostility toward human good nature. This unpromising view of human nature, Shaftesbury suggested, derived from a misguided sense that natural human virtue posed a threat to revelation. Among particular doctrines by which religious writers exacerbated this purported rivalry

---

[10] Benjamin Whichcote, *Select Sermons of Dr. Whichcot*, ed. Anthony Ashley Cooper (1698), sigs. A5r–v, A8r. According to Robert A. Greene, Shaftesbury exaggerated the strength of Whichcote's endorsement of "good nature," partly by means of creative editorial work: "Whichcote, Wilkins, 'Ingenuity,' and the Reasonableness of Christianity," *Journal of the History of Ideas*, 42 (1981), 230, 243–244. On this and other Whichcote editions, see Isabel Rivers, *Reason, Grace, and Sentiment: A Study of the Language of Religion and Ethics in England, 1660–1780* (Cambridge: Cambridge University Press, 1991), I, 42–43.

[11] For the view that Shaftesbury *was* a Cambridge Platonist, see Ernst Cassirer *The Platonic Renaissance in England*, trans. James P. Pettegrove (Austin: University of Texas Press, 1953), pp.160–165. On the other hand, Roger L. Emerson warns against assimilating deistic writings to Anglican divinity in "Latitudinarianism and the English Deists," in J. A. Leo Lemay, ed., *Deism, Masonry and the Enlightenment* (Newark, Delaware: University of Delaware Press, 1987), pp.19–48.

[12] Whichcote, *Select Sermons*, sigs. A4v–A5r, A6r–v.

between good nature and revelation was that of reward and punishment in a future life. In Shaftesbury's view, the emphasis on "Terror *and* Punishment," on the one hand, and "*Reward*," on the other, displaced the love of goodness for its own sake because it made decent behavior a matter of prudence and calculation.[13]

While perfectly explicit in referring to Hobbes, Shaftesbury's clerical target was ambiguous. By condemning "*Sects*" whose religion was founded in "*Moroseness, Selfishness, and Ill-will*," Shaftesbury suggested enthusiasts of a Calvinistic stripe. He explicitly excepted the Church of England from the imputation of such unchristian bad temper.[14] On the other hand, the doctrine of future rewards and punishments that he attacked was central to Anglicans of both Low and High Church convictions.[15] Thus, the Shaftesburian commitment to sociability was menaced not only by contemporary philosophy but also by contemporary religion.

However, the Whichcote preface sounds another Shaftesburian theme as well. The first sentence announced: "*Amongst those many Things which are made Publick; it may be thought perhaps, of* Sermons; *that they are, of any other, least wanted; and for the future, least likely to be found wanting.*"[16] Here the reader was promised a discussion of ecclesiastical discourse, though the tone of the sentence suggested that the exact purchase of the discussion might be hard to fix. Though a declarative sentence, its declarative force was considerably sapped by a conditional verb form and a qualifying adverb. Moreover, the main verb of the clause ("wanted") was equivocal, allowing the reader to contemplate either, with satisfaction, the abundance of sermons or, with discontent, the degree to which modern readers were confronted by unrelished goods. In the sentence, Shaftesbury's conditional and equivocal formulations created a semantic ambiguity in which irony was free to lurk.

In fact, Shaftesbury's discussion of sermons in the preface played on a series of ironic contrasts leading to the reflection that it must not be concluded "*that because we see not an apparent Change for the better, in the Lives of Christian Professors; that, therefore all* Preaching *is ineffectual.*"[17] The multitude of sermons was set, ironically, against the

[13] Whichcote, *Select Sermons*, sigs. A5v, A6r–v, A7r.
[14] Whichcote, *Select Sermons*, sig. A6r.
[15] Francis Atterbury, High Church and Tory, defended the doctrine against Benjamin Hoadly, Low Church and Whig: see *Fourteen Sermons Preach'd on Several Occasions. Together with a Large Vindication ...* (1708), pp.i–lxix, 365–398. Atterbury's defense included many references to Latitudinarians whom he claimed as allies on the issue. John Tillotson also returned to the theme frequently: for instance, *A Sermon Preach'd Before the Queen at White-Hall, March the 7th, 1689/90* (1690), p.1; *Of Sincerity and Constancy in the Faith and Profession of the True Religion* (1695), pp.5, 314–316, 339–360, 371.
[16] Whichcote, *Select Sermons*, sig. A2r.
[17] Whichcote, *Select Sermons*, sig. A2v.

abundance of human immorality, suggesting that, for all the preaching, auditors were entirely untouched. This contrast was a variation on ironic deist commonplaces, that Christians were morally inferior to non-Christians and that the clerical establishment was the bane of religious life.[18] However, Shaftesbury gave the commonplaces a particularly discursive cast, thereby questioning the efficacy of the sermon as a vehicle of moral persuasion. The pious goals enunciated in homiletic writings were not suitably supported by their rhetorical means, and thus the sermon failed the duty of moral discourse to exercise a transformative force on its audience.[19]

One may wonder at the incoherence of prefacing an edition of sermons with a condemnation of the genre. In the short run, Shaftesbury would remove this incoherence by terminating, with the Whichcote edition, his career as editor of clerical texts. In the longer run, he would devote much of his energy to defining and producing a moral discourse to succeed where sermons failed. As for the Whichcote edition itself, Shaftesbury had good rhetorical reasons for choosing to edit Whichcote. Though he characterized Whichcote's writing as unpolished,[20] Shaftesbury's options, among writers who advanced ideas of natural sociability, were limited. The intellectual genealogists of sociability locate Shaftesbury's immediate ancestors among certain natural law writers and among the Cambridge Platonists.[21] However, whether one thinks of Richard Cumberland's *Treatise of the Laws of Nature* or Henry More's *Enchiridion ethicum* or Ralph Cudworth's *True Intellectual System of the Universe*, such sources on sociability were very different in genre and style from Whichcote's

---

[18] The irony of religious barbarity overshadowed the entire Restoration period as the continuing debate about the relation between religion and ethics showed: Rivers, *Reason, Grace, and Sentiment*, pp.8–12. Indeed, it is a basic trope of the Enlightenment: Peter Gay, *The Enlightenment* (New York: Alfred A. Knopf, 1975), pp.31–32. According to Rivers (p.36), the latitudinarians often noted the ethical superiority of the heathen moralists to Christians. Deists deployed the irony against the established Church: Justin Champion, "The Ancient Constitution of the Christian Church," Cambridge doctoral dissertation, 1989, pp.118–126.

[19] Anxiety about the efficacy of sermons had been a continuing concern in the Anglican Church in the later seventeenth century. See, for example: Simon Patrick, *A Friendly Debate between a Conformist and a Non-Conformist*, 3rd edn (1669), pp.4–6, 15–16, 47, 147, 194–201; John Warly, *The Reasoning Apostate* (1677); Joseph Glanvill, *An Essay concerning Preaching* and *A Seasonable Defence of Preaching* (1678); Simon Patrick, *A Discourse of Profiting by Sermons* (1683).

[20] Whichcote, *Select Sermons*, sig. a1r.

[21] Cassirer, *Platonic Renaissance in England*, pp.160ff.; John Passmore, *Ralph Cudworth* (Cambridge: Cambridge University Press, 1951), pp.96–99; Grean, *Shaftesbury's Philosophy*, pp.137, 138, 155, 161, 173; Voitle, *Third Earl of Shaftesbury*, pp.114, 120, 123, 127; Norman Fiering, *Philosophy at Seventeenth-Century Harvard* (For the Institute of Early American History and Culture, Williamsburg; Chapel Hill: The University of North Carolina Press, 1981), pp.178–180, 195.

sermons, let alone the writings of the mature Shaftesbury. These works were lengthy and systematic, abstract and abstruse, laced with a vocabulary, partly neoscholastic and partly neologistic. By contrast, the Whichcote sermons were simple, direct, and easily accessible.[22] If, as the discussion of sermons indicated, Shaftesbury was already concerned with problems of moral persuasion, then Whichcote's sermons probably appeared, among Restoration defences of sociability, as texts that might best prove readable by a wider audience and so reach their mark.

Shaftesbury's Whichcote edition represented a kind of first attempt at solving the problem of moral discourse, at bridging the gap between text and audience. The epigraph Shaftesbury chose for the volume, taken from Matthew (XI.15), captured his concern: "He that has Ears to hear, let him hear." If epigraphs seek to encapsulate the identity of the work that follows, this one encapsulated not a doctrine that the work asserted but rather a process of communication that the work sought to consummate. The relation between moral assertion and moral persuasion was a concern for Shaftesbury at the outset and a theme of his maturity.

Palemon in the Park

In his 1694 letter to Locke, Shaftesbury rejected what he perceived as the modern philosophical project for the sake of moral wisdom. In the Whichcote preface of 1698, he indicated virtue was menaced not just by philosophers but by clerics as well. Since Shaftesbury situated his own enterprise against these two alternatives, these early moments in Shaftesbury's life are helpful in plotting the trajectory of his career. This is evident when we turn to *Characteristicks*, Shaftesbury's exploration of polite philosophy.

Shaftesbury expressed his philosophical ideal in a sentence of apophthegmatic concision when he wrote: "To *philosophize*, in a just Signification, is but To carry *Good-Breeding* a step higher."[23] Part I of this study is an extended gloss on this statement, which, on the most general level, describes Shaftesbury's project itself. Shaftesbury's own philosophizing, that is, involved elevating and dignifying "good-breeding," or, more generally, the language of politeness, by putting it to new and conspicuous use. For Shaftesbury, discussion of philosophy was inextricable from matters of "politeness," "manners," "good-breeding," "refinement," "taste," and "conversation."

One aim of this unlikely amalgamation was to point philosophic

---

[22] On the literary style of various Cambridge Platonists: C. A. Patrides, *The Cambridge Platonists* (London: Edward Arnold, 1969), pp.33–35.
[23] "Miscellany" III.i, III, 161 (Robertson, II, 255).

inquiry in different directions from those which it had travelled in the last century. Explaining the continuity of philosophy and good breeding, Shaftesbury wrote: "For the Accomplishment of Breeding is, To learn whatever is *decent* in Company, or *beautiful* in Arts: and the Sum of Philosophy is, To learn what is *just* in Society, and *beautiful* in Nature, and the Order of the World."[24] Breeding and philosophy treated similar domains of experience and issued in similar forms of knowing. Like good breeding, philosophy concerned human relations and formal patterns. The desire for a normative grasp of human interactions issued in ethics and the desire for a normative grasp of forms issued in aesthetics. It was these topics that Shaftesbury thought should occupy the true philosopher.

The continuity of breeding and philosophy also helped to underpin a very characteristic Shaftesburian theme, precisely the proximity of ethics and aesthetics. Moral perceptions were much like aesthetic ones, he argued, in ways that have long been of interest to scholars. Thus, Shaftesbury's well bred gentleman, who appreciated "BEAUTY in *outward Manners* and *Deportment*" and in the arts, was on the verge of an understanding of "a *Beauty* in *inward Sentiments* and *Principles*." This conflation of the ethical and the aesthetic was underpinned by the high status Shaftesbury assigned to taste.[25]

By pointing out the continuity between philosophy and politeness, Shaftesbury was prescribing contents, cognitive results, and modes of apprehension for philosophy. However, much more was at stake in the continuity, as we are invited to reflect at the opening of the philosophical dialogue, "The Moralists," where Philocles addressed Palemon:

> WHAT Mortal, if he had never chanc'd to hear your Character, PALEMON, cou'd imagine that a genius fitted for the greatest affairs, and form'd amidst Courts and Camps, shou'd have so violent a Turn towards Philosophy and the Schools? Who is there cou'd possibly believe that one of your Rank and Credit in the *fashionable* World, shou'd be so thorowly conversant in the *learned* one, and deeply interested in the Affairs of a People so disagreeable to the Generality of Mankind and Humour of the Age?
>
> I BELIEVE, truly, You are the only well-bred Man who wou'd have taken the Fancy to talk Philosophy in such a Circle of good Company as we had round us yesterday, when we were in your Coach together, in *the Park*.[26]

Philocles expressed wonder, for he raised an image of what, he said, the world least anticipated: the man familiar with society and business who was also conversant with philosophy. Thus, Philocles proposed Palemon

---
[24] "Miscellany" III.i, III, 161 (Robertson, II, 255).
[25] "Miscellany" III.i, III, 154 (Robertson, II, 251–252) and III.ii, III, 161, 162, 179–180 (Robertson, II, 255, 266–267).
[26] "Moralists" I.i, II, 181–182 (Robertson, II, 179).

as a kind of prodigy, defying conventional expectations. Palemon was a man of both deep discourse and affairs, a figure of both learning and fashion, a philosopher and a gentleman – in fact, an avatar of philosophy and politeness.

The passage immersed Palemon in a distinct scene. As Palemon represented an innovation in the demography of characters, so the scene presented a kind of geographical innovation. In the opposition of Courts and Camps, on one hand, and Schools, on the other, the antagonism between social life and learning was given a geographical, or environmental, embodiment. These locales had distinct and exclusive characters, according to Philocles. Meanwhile, the scene of Palemon's confrontation of the fashionable world with the learned one occurred in a coach in a park, suggesting that certain kinds of urbane and gentlemanly locations might offer a suitable locale for the sort of synthesis that Palemon himself embodied.

This concern with the site of philosophy was important, for it implied that philosophy had to meet specifically social criteria. Philosophy could not be hermetic, an undertaking of the cloister or the ivory tower. Rather, it had to be placed in the midst of society (at least of a certain level). Underlying Philocles' characterization of Palemon's novel social personality and the novel site in which he operated was a novel activity: talking philosophy in a circle of good company. This had to be something more than the settling of philosophical dust on the greenery of social life. We infer this because Palemon did not sacrifice his good breeding in the process. Something synthetic had happened, and a new activity – polite philosophy – was created. Indeed, the scene of Palemon in the Park was a representation of the philosophic practice in which Shaftesbury himself sought to engage in his life and writings.

Endorsing urbane spaces, gentlemen, and moral conversation, Shaftesburian politeness produced a new map of cultural space, in which cultural sites with their protocols of admission and operation were redefined and revaluated. This appraisal of discursive and cultural spaces was part of wider patterns of cultural transformation in the later seventeenth and early eighteenth century. It was hardly accidental that Addison also defined the *Spectator*'s aims as relocating philosophy and, so, remapping the cultural world. The passage is well known: "It was said of *Socrates*, that he brought Philosophy down from Heaven, to inhabit among Men; and I shall be ambitious to have it said of me, that I have brought Philosophy out of Closets and Libraries, Schools and Colleges, to dwell in Clubs and Assemblies, at Tea-Tables, and Coffee-Houses."[27] In both this

[27] *Spectator* No. 10 (March 12, 1711), Bond, I, 44. On the Ciceronian source for this passage, see below note 43.

prospectus of the *Spectator* project and Shaftesbury's introduction to "The Moralists," philosophy was being dragged from what were represented as solitary or cloistered environments to worldly and sociable ones. Of course, the differences between the passages suggest many contrasts between Shaftesbury's vision of culture and Addison's: Addison's tone was matter-of-fact while Shaftesbury's was rarefied; Addison's clientele was a wide segment of the upper and middling population while Shaftesbury's was more restrictively gentlemanly; Addison's project was more harnessed to the sites of ordinary life while Shaftesbury's, again, was more exclusive. However, it would be a mistake to ignore the important similarities: both were proposing to shift what they called philosophy from certain locales and to resituate it in new ones.

In fact, both Shaftesbury and Addison sought to extricate philosophy from the same venues. The academic institutions ("Schools and Colleges") or locales of private investigation ("Closets and Libraries"), mentioned by Addison, were objects of persistent attack in Shaftesbury. The emblematical engraving, adorning the first page of "The Moralists" in the 1714 edition of *Characteristicks*, could serve to illustrate the *Spectator* passage. The engraving is a triptych representing three venues for philosophic practice. On the left is a schoolroom with a master and scholars, engaging in a verbal exercise. On the right is a solitary alchemist in his laboratory, surrounded by experimental equipment and natural curiosities. In the middle, Philosophy herself stands, alone, on a stage, the public stage before the audience of the world – where Shaftesbury thought philosophy should be.

The alternatives to a public philosophy require examination, since the scholars in their college and the alchemist in his laboratory were meant to have a powerful resonance. They represented the same menaces to virtue that appeared in the Whichcote preface, namely, the Church and modern philosophy.

The traditional institutions of education on the left side of the engraving called to mind the fatuities of scholasticism. If scholasticism was moribund when Shaftesbury wrote, it had not yet been fully interred, and so it still menaced collegians by seducing them to mistake "the Solution of those Riddles of the Schoolmen" for "Wisdome." Shaftesbury marshalled quite standard complaints against it, depicting scholastics as obsessively inventing and manipulating terms, making systems, and perfecting formalities.[28]

---

[28] P.R.O. 30/24/20/143, Shaftesbury to Michael Ainsworth, February 25, 1707; "Soliloquy" III.i, I, 289–290 (Robertson, I, 188–189); "Moralists" I.i, II, 185 (Robertson, II, 5). On the endurance of scholasticism, see William T. Costello, *The Scholastic Curriculum at Early Seventeenth-Century Cambridge* (Cambridge: Harvard University Press, 1958), and

Moreover, Shaftesbury found it easy to trace this failure to the institutional arrangements implied in the very name of scholasticism. As "The Moralists" lamented, philosophy was "no longer *active* in the World" but rather "immur'd ... (poor Lady!) in Colleges and Cells."[29] Scholasticism was school learning, which, as we will see, was a paradigmatically impolite social configuration for learning since the philosopher was likely to be a cleric, not a worldly and secular-minded layman, and the philosophic medium was likely to be a lecture rather than conversation. The close identification of the philosophical current with academic institutions opposed directly Shaftesbury's aspiration for a reconciliation between learning and the social world.

However, the traditional institutions of education had a much more extensive valence for Shaftesbury, since they were both agents and emblems of an intellectual and political culture to which he was vehemently opposed. They were the epitome and center of all he hated, the bastions of ecclesiastical power in matters of the mind and in affairs of the state. The universities were essentially branches of the Church and acted aggressively in effecting the Restoration cultural and political project. Though the Revolution of 1688 shocked the universities, Whig regimes took decades to get a secure hold on them and, during Shaftesbury's life, this conversion was hardly complete. Oxford in particular became the center for High Church Toryism, some of it quite radical. Shaftesbury's correspondence recurs to the pernicious character of the universities.[30]

Shaftesbury wanted philosophy to serve as the alternative foundation for intellectual and political culture; but, as the engraving indicated, philosophy was confined to the cabinets, closets, and laboratories of virtuosi. However, the image was aimed not just at the indulgence by learned gentlemen in the fussy and amoral inanities of natural investigation. We should remember that, in his 1694 letter to Locke, Shaftesbury identified modern philosophy with empirics and the pursuit of curiosities. The alchemist in the engraving is a representation of the modern philosophical project.

Shaftesbury granted that modern philosophy had been instrumental in

G. V. Bennett, "The Curriculum," in L. S. Sutherland and L. G. Mitchell, eds., *The History of the University of Oxford* (Oxford: Clarendon Press, 1986), V, 469–491.

[29] "Moralists" I.i, II, 184 (Robertson, II, 4–5); also, "Sensus Communis" III.iv, I, 123 (Robertson, I, 82).

[30] On Oxford Toryism, see G. V. Bennett, "Loyalist Oxford and the Revolution," "Against the Tide: Oxford under William III," and "The Era of Party Zeal 1702–1714" in Sutherland and Mitchell, *History of the University of Oxford*, pp.9–97. On the remodelling of Cambridge under Whig auspices, see John Gascoigne, *Cambridge in the Age of the Enlightenment* (Cambridge: Cambridge University Press, 1989), pp.71–114. For Shaftesbury's hostility to university Toryism, see P.R.O. 30/24/20/143, Shaftesbury to Michael Ainsworth, May 10, 1707, and December 30, 1709.

loosening the grip of scholasticism on the European mind. For instance, Locke was "of admirable Use against the Rubbish of the Schools; in which most of us have been bred up."[31] But generally any of Shaftesbury's praise of the modern philosophers was entirely *faute de mieux*. The next chapter is devoted to Shaftesbury's critique of modern ethical ideas, but his rejection of modern philosophy had a more general aspect.

Modern philosophy failed to meet an essential criterion: "all that we call improvement of our Minds in dry & empty Speculation, all Learning or whatever else either in Theology or other Science wch has not a direct & immediate Tendency to render us honester, milder, juster, & better, is far from being justly so call'd." This statement led to a sweeping dismissal of the collected forces of philosophy:

all that Philosophy wch is built on the Comparison & Compounding of Ideas, complex, implex, reflex, & all that Dinn & Noise of Metaphysicks, all that pretended studdy & Science of Nature call'd natural Philosophy, Aristotelian, Cartesian or wtever else it be, all those high Contemplations of Starrs & Spheres & Planets & all that other inquisitive Curiouse parts of Learning are so far from being necessary Improvements of the Mind, that without the utmost Care they serve only to blow it up in Conceit & Folly, & render Men more stiff in their Ignorance & Vices.[32]

This passage denied the claims to philosophical status of two sorts of endeavor, aside from residual scholasticism.

The easier to recognize is "that pretended studdy & Science of Nature." Since "philosophy" could refer to both natural and moral studies, Shaftesbury was anxious to assert not only the distinction between the study of natural things and true moral philosophy but also the preeminence of the latter. In various places, Shaftesbury indicated that science (or natural philosophy) was illegitimately called "philosophy" and, in fact, constituted moral distraction, directing consciousness away from self-knowledge, which was the object of true philosophy.[33] It should be underscored that he objected not just to scientific studies but also to the philosophical reflection on natural concepts, such as matter, motion, time, and space.[34]

However, Shaftesbury also wished to deny philosophical status to

[31] P.R.O. 30/24/22/7, Shaftesbury to James Stanhope, November 7, 1709. A more generous appraisal appears in P.R.O. 30/24/20/143, Shaftesbury to Michael Ainsworth, February 25, 1707. See also: Shaftesbury to Michael Ainsworth, June 3, 1709, *Several Letters*, p.41; "Sensus Communis" II.ii, I, 95 (Robertson, I, 65).
[32] P.R.O. 30/24/20/143, Shaftesbury to Michael Ainsworth, January 28, 1709.
[33] "Soliloquy" III.i, I, 289–291 (Robertson, I, 188–189); "Miscellany" III.i, III, 159–160 (Robertson, II, 254–255); "Moralists" I.i, II, 189–190 (Robertson, II, 8); P.R.O. 30/24/27/10, pp.91, 360 [ff.47r, 236v].
[34] "Moralists" III.i, II, 368–369 (Robertson, II, 111–112); "Soliloquy" III.i, I, 299 (Robertson, I, 194); P.R.O. 30/24/27/10, pp.90–91, 156 [ff.46v–47r, 79v].

another form of intellectual endeavor: in the passage quoted above, "all that Philosophy wch is built on the Comparison & Compounding of Ideas, complex, implex, reflex." This was nothing other than Lockean epistemology, in which comparing and compounding simple ideas were among the basic operations of the mind and foundational for more complex ideas and, therefore, for knowledge.[35] One cannot say that Shaftesbury ever really grappled with the appeals of such inquiries. His technique was rather the frequent and superficial, not to mention petulant, dismissal in the name of a more directly moral consciousness: "What speciouse Exercise is found in those wch are call'd *Philosophicall Speculations*! the *Formation* of *Ideas*, their *Compositions, Comparisons, Agreement & Disagreemt*! What is this to the purpose?"[36] While most keen to ridicule Locke's approach, he also made slighting references to "clear ideas" and to elements in the Cartesian cogito, indicating a willingness to tar Descartes with the same brush.[37]

As Shaftesbury was not interested in the new learning of the seventeenth century, so he was not interested in one of its outcomes, the reorientation of philosophical reflection around questions of knowledge. The fact is that neither Descartes nor Hobbes nor Locke regarded epistemology as a self-subsistent subject or as a fulfillment of the entire goal of philosophy. It was the subsequent process of their canonization that created the impression that they had; indeed, they were canonized as part of the process by which modern philosophy defined its identity as epistemological. Nonetheless, Shaftesbury's ridicule of the language of "ideas" was a protest against the gravitation of philosophy towards epistemological concerns. Epistemology did not address the sorts of problems in which Shaftesbury was interested, nor was Shaftesbury interested in the sorts of problems which epistemology was generated in order to solve.

If such was the fate of modern philosophy, it could hardly serve as an alternative to the Church. Philosophy itself had to be reclaimed and remade into the ethical–aesthetic nexus suggested by the continuity of breeding and philosophy. Nor, in its ethical and aesthetic mode, could the orientation of philosophy be theoretical. Rather, it had to be practical and existential. Politeness in philosophy constituted a demand that philosophy participate in the fashioning of elite identity and legitimacy.

Like Addison, Shaftesbury wanted to bring philosophy out of "Schools

---

[35] Locke, *Essay* II.xi–xii, pp.157–158, 162–163.
[36] P.R.O. 30/24/27/10, p.90 [f.46v]. This passage, one of the earliest in the stoic notebooks (written in 1698 in Rotterdam), had a precise echo in the later "Soliloquy" III.i, I, 299 (Robertson, I, 194). See also P.R.O. 30/24/27/15, p.99r [f.107r]. For agreement and disagreement of ideas, see Locke, *Essay* IV.i, p.525.
[37] P.R.O. 30/24/27/10, p.90 [f.46v]. On the *cogito*, "Miscellany" IV.i, III, 193 (Robertson, II, 275).

and Colleges" and "Closets and Libraries." For both of them the new destination of philosophy was a zone we can call the public. Addison associated the public, quite concretely, with the venues in metropolitan London, where men and women of the middling and upper sort could engage in discussion of matters of public concern. In Shaftesbury, the destination of philosophy was less concrete and less demotic: it was the space of gentlemanly conversation, dramatized in the example of Palemon in the Park. This was the zone that was being denominated sociable and polite, as opposed to the unsociable and impolite spaces occupied by clerics and virtuosi. Polite philosophy implied a new space of public discourse and culture, occupied by a literate gentlemanly audience receptive to philosophy and a literate gentlemanly authorship purveying it.

The immersion of philosophy in society placed formal demands on it. Palemon did not just intrude intellection into conversation, but, like other philosophical models invoked by Shaftesbury, joined "what was deepest and most solid in Philosophy, with what was easiest and most refin'd in Breeding," achieving a polite philosophical manner.[38] Philosophy had to be controlled by taste, construed here not as a mode of apprehending truths but as a mode of regulating expression. Thus, the merger of breeding and philosophy produced a philosophy that was not only ethical and aesthetic in substance and practical and existential in nature, but also discursive in shape. Philosophy had to embody wisdom, enunciating in every way the character of its commitments. As against the medieval and the recent inheritance, Shaftesbury sought to reassert the identity of philosophy with moral wisdom, persuasively expressed.

Classicism

The engraving at the outset of "The Moralists" can be read as a comment on the history of philosophy. If both the medieval inheritance and the modern response were mistaken approaches to philosophy, it is not surprising that the ancients were a source of inspiration. Though classicism is sometimes identified with nostalgic longing and escapist flight from the world as it is, the classicist usually deploys the authority of instances from the classical world to mount a contemporary project, shaking the complacency of intellectual, artistic and political incumbents by bringing a classical frame of reference to bear on whatever is recent, modern or contemporary.[39] Though rendering philosophy polite was

---

[38] "Soliloquy" II.ii, I, 255 (Robertson, I, 167).
[39] See J. G. A. Pocock, "Time, Institutions and Action," in *Politics, Language and Time* (New York: Atheneum, 1973), pp.233–272.

itself a novel exercise, Shaftesbury repeatedly located antique origins for his project by linking it to a series of moments in ancient philosophical discourse going back to the very origins of moral philosophizing itself. By contrast to the unhistorical or anti-historical turn of Shaftesbury's modern Epicureans, Shaftesbury's classicism insisted that philosophy be responsible to its past. Furthermore, recognizing and embracing the historically bounded nature of philosophic inquiry implied that philosophic activity was enmeshed in culture and that philosophers were embedded in the life of their society.

Shaftesbury delineated his own project by diverse references to ancient philosophy, but the process was epitomized by his view of Socrates, whom he embraced as a pre-eminent philosophical model. Though Shaftesbury did not complete the major work on Socrates that he had planned, his admiration for Socrates left traces throughout his writing.[40] Aside from serving as the originator of philosophy, Socrates seems to have had a double appeal to Shaftesbury. First, Socrates put philosophy at the center of human activity as the pursuit of moral wisdom, constituted from self-knowledge and issuing in self-actualization and self-possession.[41] Second, Shaftesbury looked to Socrates as an exemplar of moral philosophy pursued in the midst of humanity. Socrates' philosophical activity was continuous with the discourse of the city, making philosophy accessible to the audience of citizens surrounding him. The "Solemn & Severe Character" often assigned to the archetypal philosopher was "contrary to what was his way," for Socrates' manner was "of a more open free & polite Conversation."[42]

Thus, Socrates spoke to Shaftesbury's deepest moral and discursive concerns in a way adumbrated in the source of Addison's formulation of the *Spectator* project, Cicero's well-known appraisal of Socrates' role in philosophical history, as "the first to call philosophy down from the heavens and set her in the cities of men and bring her also into their homes and compel her to ask questions about life and morality and things good and evil."[43] Socrates served here to legitimate the notion of philosophy as principally ethical in nature. (The "heavens" from which Socrates took philosophy was the cosmos, about which the reflections of Pythagoras and other pre-Socratics centered.) Socrates also legitimated a conver-

---

[40] This project is discussed in chapter 6, pp.107–111 below.
[41] This was a common perception of Socrates, going back to Cicero and, indeed, Plato: see Eugene F. Rice, Jr., *The Renaissance Idea of Wisdom* (Cambridge, Mass.: Harvard University Press, 1958), pp.8, 32, 39, 154, 163, 186ff. See also Gadamer, *Truth and Method*, p.20.
[42] P.R.O. 30/24/27/14, p.91 [f.50r].
[43] Cicero, *Tusculan Disputations*, trans. J. E. King (Loeb Classical Library, London: William Heinemann and New York: G. P. Putnam's Sons, 1927), V.iv.10, pp.434–435.

sational philosophic practice and a general philosophic audience. (Again Pythagorean contrasts are helpful since Pythagorean practice was gnomic or mystical and its audience, that of initiated sectarians.)[44]

Shaftesbury's intermingled moral and discursive concerns were evident in a genealogy in which Socrates, "containing within himself the several Genius's of Philosophy, gave rise to all those several Manners in which that Science was deliver'd." Those manners turn out to be four, the sublime, the comic, the methodical, and the simple (or, indeed, the polite), each associated with one of Socrates' disciples. Plato, "of noble Birth and lofty Genius, who aspir'd to Poetry and Rhetorick," took the sublime route. Second, Antisthenes, "of mean Birth, and poorest Circumstances, whose Constitution as well as Condition inclin'd him most to the way we call *Satirick*, took the reproving part, which in his better-humour'd and more agreeable Successor [Diogenes] turn'd into the *Comick* kind." Third, Aristotle was the progenitor of the methodical (or scholastic) manner of philosophizing.[45] (The fourth, as we will see, was Xenophon the polite.) Such epithetical characterizations implied a distinctive way of thinking about philosophy, since Shaftesbury differentiated Platonism, Cynicism, and Peripateticism by stylistic criteria. Here, the kinds of early philosophy were not schools of thought but philosophical "manners" (where "manner" conflated two distinct ideas, a mode of inquiry and a manner of expression). This sort of categorization assigned weight not to particular ideas or doctrines but to formal qualities with which philosophy presented itself and by which it could be recognized and situated.

At least in the cases of Plato and Antisthenes, Shaftesbury also noted social origins, calling attention to the link between social identity and philosophic manner. The significance of this point is evident in the status Shaftesbury assigned to the fourth of Socrates' putative philosophical successors. This successor was Xenophon, "another noble Disciple, whose Genius was towards Action, and who prov'd afterwards the greatest Hero of his time." Xenophon "took the *genteeler* Part, and *softer* Manner. He join'd what was deepest and most solid in Philosophy, with what was easiest and most refin'd in Breeding, and in the Character and

[44] In this sense, Shaftesbury's other ancient sources were Socratic: the emperor-philosopher Marcus Aurelius epitomized the active life, even if his writings were introspective memoranda; the freed slave Epictetus was known through notes taken at his public discourses by the loyal Arrian, so that the Epictetan text (except for the brief *Encheiridion*) represented a philosopher engaged in a public activity.

[45] "Soliloquy" II.ii, I, 254–256 (Robertson, I, 166–167). Shaftesbury here worked out of the doxographical tradition. According to Diogenes Laertius, Socrates' successors were Plato, Xenophon, and Antisthenes (II.47), the latter of whom was succeeded by Diogenes the Cynic (I.15; VI.2, 15, 21). Antisthenes in fact had no direct relation to the Cynics: see Donald R. Dudley, *A History of Cynicism* (London: Methuen & Co., Ltd., 1937), pp.1–16.

Manner of a Gentleman." Distancing himself from the styles struck by the other post-Socratics, Xenophon represented "that natural and *simple* Genius of Antiquity," consisting (as Shaftesbury remarked elsewhere) of "Chastity, Simplicity, Politeness, Justness."[46]

Thus, Xenophon represented an exemplary version of the Socratic enterprise. That a Xenophon, so conceived, could serve as a model illustrates the turn that Shaftesbury wished to give philosophy. Socially Xenophon was the noble gentleman whose activity in the world comported with serious intellectual pursuits. Intellectually he combined the refinement of the gentleman with the solidity of the scholar. From the modern standpoint, it is indeed remarkable that Xenophon should have assumed philosophical significance at all, since, when not viewed as a historian, he is usually portrayed as a memoirist and popularizer – a source about ancient philosophy but nothing more. He was dropped from the philosophical canon by the end of the eighteenth century.[47]

Shaftesbury's characterization of Xenophon points in two significant directions: first, toward Cicero, and second, toward politeness itself.

For one thing, this Xenophon can be understood in Ciceronian terms. As a synthetic figure, combining, first, knowledge and action and, second, philosophy and breeding, Xenophon suggested the Ciceronian goal of merging wisdom and eloquence. In antiquity and later, the goal of reconciling philosophy and rhetoric grew out of their hostility as disciplines. Their claims about human nature, the possibilities of human knowledge, the relation of knowledge and action, and the right forms of education clashed. Cicero was neither the first nor the last to attempt a negotiated settlement; yet, his was a particularly ample and distinguished effort and a highly influential one.[48]

In *De oratore*, Cicero advocated the synthesis of eloquence and wisdom as a reintegration of entities that had been sundered. While *sapientia* had originally encompassed knowledge and rhetorical power in the context of the active and civic life, he said, contemplative principles had arisen to

---

[46] "Soliloquy" II.ii, I, 254–255 (Robertson, I, 167); P.R.O. 30/24/27/10, p.243 [f.178r].

[47] Xenophon was treated extensively in Thomas Stanley's *History of Philosophy* (1655) and modestly in Johann Jakob Brucker's *Historia critica philosophiae*, 2nd edn (Lipsiae, 1767), but, by the nineteenth century, he had been eliminated from works such as Johann Gottlieb Buhle's *Geschichte der neuern Philosophie* (Göttingen, 1800–1804) and Heinrich Ritter's *Geschichte der Philosophie* (Hamburg, 1829–1853).

[48] Jerrold E. Siegel, *Rhetoric and Philosophy in Renaissance Humanism* (Princeton: Princeton University Press, 1968), pp.3–30; M. L. Clarke, *Rhetoric at Rome* (London: Cohen & West, Ltd., 1953), pp.9, 52–58; Alain Michel, *Rhétorique et philosophie chez Cicéron* (Paris: Presses Universitaries de France, 1960). On the cognitive importance of rhetoric, see Nancy Struever, *The Language of History in the Renaissance* (Princeton: Princeton University Press, 1970). On the humanists' view of Cicero, see Quentin Skinner, *The Foundations of Modern Political Thought* (Cambridge: Cambridge University Press, 1978), I, 84–101.

situate *sapientia* in the context of "tranquillity and leisure." Conceived as an occupation unto itself and cultivated in limitless leisure, learning became increasingly specialized and, more important, divorced from public needs and civic action. Moreover, the learned now spent their whole lives "in the sciences that were invented for the purpose of moulding the minds of the young on the lines of culture and of virtue [*ad humanitatem atque virtutem*]."[49] That Cicero was deeply concerned with cultivating the mores of a ruling elite makes his project a precedent for Shaftesbury's.

He mounted the case for the reconciliation of philosophy and rhetoric on the basis of the inadequacies of each discipline in the absence of the other: the uselessness of wisdom in the absence of persuasive power was symmetrical with the perniciousness of eloquence in the absence of knowledge. However, Cicero did opt to call his ideal "the orator" since the civic framework imposed a simultaneous responsibility to truth and to eloquence. While admitting that philosophy legitimated claims to knowledge, he insisted that rhetoric secured knowledge to the social world by relating truth to practical issues, by making truth accessible to the ordinary intellect, and by disciplining knowledge according to common sense. Cicero's synthetic design was distinguished by its subsumption of rhetoric and philosophy to the service of public life and the standards of good Roman citizenship.[50]

Shaftesbury's Xenophon accorded with the aspirations of Cicero's program. This Xenophon, like Cicero himself, was a man of action and politics as well as a man of learning and writing. Moreover, in his writing, he managed to combine learning with refined expression. Insofar as Xenophon embodied Shaftesbury's philosophical ideal, he illustrated a Ciceronian aspect of the entire project.[51]

However, while resorting to the ancients for models and inspirations, Shaftesbury also refracted classical references through eighteenth-century idioms. Shaftesbury's Xenophon had the air of an idealized English gentleman. Shaftesbury's persuasiveness to his audience owed much to the way in which he conflated so advantageously the classical and the contemporary. When James Stanhope became intoxicated with the Shaftesburian ideal, Shaftesbury told him: "For your comfort you know well enough that though you have few companions in this way among the

---

[49] Cicero, *De oratore*, trans. E. W. Sutton and Horace Rackham (Loeb Classical Library, London: William Heinemann and Cambridge, Mass.: Harvard University Press, 1942), III.xiv.54–xv.58, II, 42–47.
[50] *De inventione* I.i.1; also, *De oratore* III.xxxv.142; Michel, *Rhétorique et philosophie chez Cicéron*, pp.5–16, 78.
[51] Other Ciceronian resonances in Shaftesbury are discussed in chapter 7, pp.148–150 below.

moderns, you have the best of ancient heroes to keep you in countenance, and that these latter were not only used to carry with them the books of philosophers, but their persons too, if they could tempt them abroad." Likening Stanhope's interest in philosophy to that of ancient heroes made of Stanhope a modern Xenophon, or at least a modern Scipio Africanus.[52] In a sense, Shaftesbury's *Characteristicks* wrote this compliment large and extended it, generally, to the men and women of Stanhope's class.

A signal instance of the "modernization" of antiquity was Shaftesbury's transformation of the Ciceronian reconciliation of philosophy and rhetoric into a Shaftesburian reconciliation of philosophy and breeding. This change obviously bespoke the differences in cultural idiom between the Greco-Roman world and that of early eighteenth-century Britain. In the first, rhetoric was not just a discipline but a cultural form profoundly related to the conditions of ancient existence. In the second, rhetoric was a diminished entity, maintaining a place in educational curricula but hardly a capacious enough mold in which to cast a philosophical and cultural program. However, the modern discipline of politeness had important affinities with classical rhetoric. Like classical rhetoric, modern politeness aimed at persuasion through the skillful use of formal means. Also like rhetoric, politeness assumed that all knowledge, insight, and expression arose in specific social and discursive situations. Thus, the fully realized polite gentleman combined learning and other virtues with the ability to deploy them skillfully as occasion demanded. More important, politeness could inspire an account of human life in which ethical and political possibilities were grounded in a recognition of their linguistic, historical and cultural character.[53]

Shaftesbury's promotion of politeness sets a limit on the interpretive relevance of his classicism. Though he did not pronounce on the set-piece quarrel of the Ancients and the Moderns, it is fair to say that Shaftesbury did value ancient achievement in morals and literature more than he valued the modern achievement in natural philosophy and epistemology. At the same time, he thought appropriate forms of modern greatness were

---

[52] P.R.O. 30/24/22/7, ff. 490–492 (pp.9–13), Shaftesbury to James Stanhope, November 7, 1709. See also P.R.O. 30/24/21/197, James Stanhope to John Cropley, February 13, 1712; P.R.O. 30/24/21/204, James Stanhope to John Cropley, April 26, 1712. According to Cicero, Africanus, when on campaign, carried Xenophon's writings with him: *Tusculan Disputations*, II.xxvi.62. Stanhope (1672–1721) was a high-minded Whig who fought in the Spanish campaigns of Queen Anne's reign, served in Parliament, and, under George I, became Secretary of State.

[53] On contrasts between classical rhetoric and modern politeness, see Daniel Javitch, *Poetry and Courtliness in Renaissance England* (Princeton: Princeton University Press, 1976), pp.18–49.

The amalgamation of philosophy and breeding

to be expected now that its political and cultural foundations were being laid.[54] Thus, his affinities with the ancients were subordinate to a modernist project. In Shaftesbury's case, the relation of "ancient" and "modern" is more complicated and more interesting than one of antagonism, as that relation is usually characterized.[55] Therefore, though understanding the intellectual traditions from which Shaftesbury wove his texts is important, sources do not provide an adequate account of the nature of his engagements. Indeed, despite the renunciation of novelty in his letter to Locke, with which this chapter began, Shaftesbury came to see himself as an innovator, whose "Design" was "to advance something *new*, or at least something *different* from what is commonly current in PHILOSOPHY and MORALS."[56] Respecting that claim helps to locate Shaftesbury in his discursive context. Hence, the centrality assigned in this study to "politeness" and "taste" and "conversation" and "good humor" and "breeding" and so on – a glossary easily recognizable as eighteenth-century idiom but hardly the stuff of which histories of philosophy and political thought have been made.

[54] For his great cultural expectations, see chapter 10.
[55] Joseph Levine's *The Battle of the Books: History and Literature in the Augustan Age* (Ithaca and London: Cornell University Press, 1991) tends to ignore the modernist uses of classicism.
[56] "Miscellany" III.i, III, 154 (Robertson, II, 251–252).

2 Lord Ashley's *Inquiry*: the philosophy of sociability and its context

Seriousness

Shaftesbury's first serious attempt to actuate his philosophical vocation was *An Inquiry Concerning Virtue*. He wrote it in the later 1690s and, though he seems not to have intended immediate publication, it appeared when John Toland, a member of his circle, had it published in 1699. Much later, the fourth earl of Shaftesbury said that the third earl had objected to the publication and bought up all the copies. But, as A. B. Worden has pointed out, Shaftesbury seems to have cooperated in the translation of the treatise into French by Pierre Desmaizeaux (1673–1745), Huguenot émigré and free-lance man of letters in the international intellectual scene.

Moreover, Shaftesbury included a revised version of the *Inquiry* in *Characteristicks* and assigned it a strategic importance.[1] Here one must remember that the early editions of *Characteristicks* had three volumes: the first containing "A Letter Concerning Enthusiasm," "Sensus Communis," and "Soliloquy"; the second, the *Inquiry* and "The Moralists"; and the third, "Miscellaneous Reflections." According to Shaftesbury, the heart of the endeavor was the second volume. He called the first volume "preparatory" to the second and distinguished the critical task of the first volume from the constructive task of the second. Whereas in the first volume he deployed "his *sapping* Method and *unravelling* Humour" and assumed a *"sceptical* Mein," in the second volume, particularly in the

---

[1] A. B. Worden has suggested that Toland significantly reshaped the text of the early edition: A. B. Worden, introduction to Edmund Ludlow, *A Voyce from the Watch Tower, Part Five: 1660–1662* (Camden Fourth Series, vol. 21, London: Royal Historical Society, 1978), pp.24, 28–29. However, the differences between the earlier and later versions of the *Inquiry* were largely matters of polish. The substantial differences (such as the emphasis on the aesthetics of moral insight in the later version) are traceable to developments in Shaftesbury's thinking rather than Shaftesbury's correction of views Toland foisted on the earlier version. See: A. O. Aldridge, "Two Versions of Shaftesbury's *Inquiry Concerning Virtue*," *Huntington Library Quarterly*, 13 (1949–1950), 207–214; Robert Voitle, "Shaftesbury's Moral Sense," *Studies in Philology*, 52 (1955), 17–38. Since one of my themes is the distance between the thinking of the mature Shaftesbury and his first effort in philosophy, I have cited the *Inquiry* in the 1699 edition.

Inquiry, he "discovers himself openly, as a plain *Dogmatist*, a *Formalist*, and *Man of Method*." In the *Inquiry*, not only did he plainly assert his philosophical positions, but he also adopted the method and style of formal philosophy, "*dry* Reasonings."[2]

While mounting the *Inquiry* as the central text of *Characteristicks*, Shaftesbury framed it ironically and ambivalently. The very qualities that promoted the *Inquiry* deprived it of any claim to politeness: not only did it lack the ease and playfulness of the polite world, but its gravity, formality, and "dogmatism" stood in stark contrast to polite attributes. Though the *Inquiry* defended human sociability, the text itself was somehow unsociable. The extent of the ambivalence is evident in the identification of the *Inquiry* with writing fit for "the *patient* and *grave* READER ... who in order to *moralize* can afford to retire into his Closet, as to some religious or devout Exercise."[3] This ironic assessment indicates the change in Shaftesbury's views about the standards for moralist writing between the later 1690s, when he wrote the *Inquiry*, and the later 1700s, when he depicted Palemon in the Park as the model philosopher.

The purchase of these remarks will become clearer as my argument unfolds, but neither irony nor ambivalence effaced one key assertion – that the *Inquiry* was more methodical and more formal than anything else that Shaftesbury published later. The *Inquiry* was a work of exposition, to rely on Berel Lang's reflections on philosophic genre. In the expository mode, according to Lang, the implied author positions himself outside of or independently of what he is writing about, conceiving of philosophy's role as directed to analyzing the features of reality already formed and given.[4] The expository text offers an orderly analysis with a logical progression toward a coherent representation of reality: it should be, as John Locke said of *An Essay Concerning Human Understanding*, "an Edifice uniform, and consistent with it self," "all of a piece."[5] Such a text is an attempt to realize a vision of philosophical discourse as nothing but logically ordered propositions. Meanwhile, the voice of the philosophic expositor aims for inconspicuousness or even transparency, refusing to call attention to itself or situate itself. Since the language seems not to emanate from a particular voice, it seems to avoid idiosyncrasy, partiality,

---

[2] "Miscellany" III.i, III, 134–135, 142–143 (Robertson, II, 239–240, 244); IV.i, III, 189–190 (Robertson, II, 273–274). See also "Miscellany" I.i, III, 7–8 (Robertson, II, 161); IV.ii, III, 225–226 (Robertson, II, 295); V.ii, III, 284–285 (Robertson, II, 333); and P.R.O. 30/24/23/8, ff.45–52, Shaftesbury to Thomas Micklethwaite, December 29, 1711.
[3] "Miscellany" IV.i, III, 191–192 (Robertson, II, 274).
[4] Berel Lang, *The Anatomy of Philosophical Style* (Oxford: Basil Blackwell, 1990), p.35.
[5] Locke, *Essay* I.iv.25, pp.102–103. Much is made of the essayistic qualities of this "essay" by Rosalie Colie in "The Essayist in His *Essay*," in John Yolton, ed., *John Locke: Problems and Perspectives* (Cambridge: Cambridge University Press, 1969), pp.234–261, but that is to underplay the compelling logical form of the work.

distortion, and subjectivity. This depersonalized quality is underpinned by seriousness and absence of humor. To this extent, the language appears to be a sufficient mirror of an autonomous reality. This is the basis of its authority.[6]

The expository aspirations of the *Inquiry* were patent since it was a systematic and logical exploration of the questions it posed about religion and virtue. As we will see, the *Inquiry* proceeded in an orderly way, combining definitions and their further specifications with logical deductions and natural observations. Its outline was abstract, and it offered a proof. Moreover, the voice in which the piece was written was precisely that inconspicuous one characteristic of the expository mode. These traits all stood in contrast to the polite style that Shaftesbury would use in his mature writings.

This, no doubt, explains the appeal the *Inquiry* has had, among all of Shaftesbury's writings, to historians of philosophy. As Berel Lang points out, professional philosophy in the nineteenth and twentieth century has staked its identity and authority on the expository mode.[7] It is not surprising then that historians of philosophy find it easiest to recognize philosophy in the past when it is in the mode of exposition. Aside from the interest that has attached to any substantive matters addressed by it, the *Inquiry* has been formally attractive: it is the Shaftesburian work in which digressiveness, ornamentation, and belletristic self-indulgence have least harried philosophical and intellectual-historical detectives in their search for the moral theory of the third earl. It is in the *Inquiry* that Shaftesbury is to be found looking most as a philosopher ought: seriously.[8] Since one of Shaftesbury's aims in the works that framed the *Inquiry* in *Characteristicks* was to complicate the question of seriousness through a defense of polite raillery, this search for his serious side is unhistorical, at the least.

---

[6] Lang, *Anatomy of Philosophical Style*, pp.11–44; John Richetti, *Philosophical Writing: Locke, Berkeley, Hume* (Cambridge, Mass., and London: Harvard University Press, 1983), pp.4–47 (on transparency, p.8). Mikhail Bakhtin called such expository writing monologic, a species of "direct and unmediated object-oriented discourse," which "recognizes only itself and its object, to which it strives to be maximally adequate": "Discourse in Dostoevsky," in Caryl Emerson, ed., *Problems of Dostoevsky's Poetics* (Minneapolis: University of Minnesota Press, 1984), pp.186–187.

[7] Lang, *Anatomy of Philosophical Style*, pp.12–13, 20–22, 38f.

[8] The seriousness of the *Inquiry* is the basis for interpreting Shaftesbury in: James Martineau, *Types of Ethical Theory* (Oxford: Clarendon Press, 1885), II, 451; James Bonar, *Moral Sense* (London: George Allen & Unwin, 1930), p.26; Robert Voitle, "Shaftesbury's Moral Sense," *Studies in Philology*, 52 (1955), 18. The philosophical anthologists also rely almost entirely on the *Inquiry* (in the *Characteristicks* version): see L. A. Selby-Bigge, ed., *British Moralists* (Oxford: Clarendon Press, 1897); D. D. Raphael, ed., *British Moralists 1650–1800* (Oxford: Clarendon Press, 1969); D. H. Monro, *A Guide to British Moralists* (London: Wm. Collins Sons & Co., 1972); J. B. Schneewind, *Moral Philosophy from Montaigne to Kant* (Cambridge: Cambridge University Press, 1990).

Indeed, the very search for serious moral theory has led to a neglect of everything in *Characteristicks* except for the *Inquiry*. Carried further, it has led D. D. Raphael to dismiss Shaftesbury's endeavors entirely. In Raphael's view, *everything* Shaftesbury wrote on morals was vague or loose: "In the course of his essays, written for the gentleman of culture and taste, are to be found simply certain suggestions which were taken over, adapted and elaborated into an explicit theory by Hutcheson."[9] Even at his most serious then, Shaftesbury did not make the grade. Raphael cannot be faulted for pointing out Shaftesbury's failure to meet requirements set by the modern philosophical profession. He is only wrong in using this failure as a ground for denying Shaftesbury any relevance to the history of moral discourse. As Raphael himself makes clear, gentlemanliness and taste were measures of the Shaftesburian project, not systematicity and deductive coherence. Since the goal here is to define what Shaftesbury actually had in mind as the correct shape of a philosophical enterprise, the purchase of gentlemanliness and taste as criteria for a philosophical project are matters for examination, not dismissal. In this investigation, the *Inquiry* can only be a point of *departure*. For, in the end, the *Inquiry* did not meet Shaftesbury's own developing criteria for philosophical endeavor.

It will take part I of this study to demonstrate the manner in which the original *Inquiry* did not satisfy Shaftesbury's mature philosophical ambitions. However, Shaftesbury did remain loyal to the key ideas he first articulated in the *Inquiry*. Not only did a revised version of the *Inquiry* occupy a central place in *Characteristicks*, but the *Inquiry*'s central ideas were summarized and rehearsed (and also revised) at several points in the other essays.[10] It is therefore important to set these ideas in the context of Shaftesbury's more general response to contemporary philosophy. From the beginning, this critique centered on the way that modern philosophy evaded, misconstrued or bungled questions of human social and ethical relations. In the *Inquiry*, Shaftesbury articulated the main principles of an ethical theory intended to supply what contemporary philosophy did not offer.

An Inquiry Concerning Virtue

In substance and in polemical force, the *Inquiry* was directly continuous with the Whichcote preface, which Shaftesbury wrote about the same

---

[9] D. D. Raphael, *The Moral Sense* (London: Oxford University Press, 1947), pp.16–17.
[10] The clearest instance is provided by *Sensus Communis*, in which a rehearsal of the *Inquiry*'s positions (parts II and III) is sandwiched between reflections on the nature of public discourse (parts I and IV). The *Inquiry*'s themes of cosmic order, natural soci-

time. The *Inquiry* was a moral treatise defending the possibility of individual ethical action in accordance with real ethical standards on the basis of natural human propensities to exist companionably with others. Thus, Shaftesbury was revealed in his first major work as a philosopher of sociability. Moreover, the polemical vectors of the *Inquiry* pointed in the same directions as did those of the Whichcote preface: the *Inquiry* pursued explicitly and implicitly the argument of the preface to Whichcote, that virtue had to be saved from clerics and philosophers.

As befits a piece of philosophy in the expository mode, the *Inquiry* had an analytic organization, each of its two parts posing a discrete question. Part I concerned the relation between religion and ethics, asking: "HOW FAR VIRTUE ALONE COULD GO: AND HOW FAR RELIGION WAS EITHER NECESSARY TO SUPPORT IT? OR ABLE TO RAISE AND ADVANCE IT." In other words, what was the connection between having certain beliefs and acting virtuously.[11] To answer it, Shaftesbury needed a typology of religious beliefs (from atheism to perfect theism), to which the first section (I.i) was devoted. He also needed a definition of moral action, which he accomplished in the second section (I.ii) by laying out the principles of cosmic design and the nature of human being. He therefore could, in the third section (I.iii), estimate the moral impact of the various forms of religious belief: atheism, he concluded, neither threatened nor enhanced the possibilities for moral action, while religious beliefs, when proper, encouraged morality but, when defective, were responsible for much harm in the world.

The principal question of the second part of the *Inquiry* concerned the reasons to be virtuous. It was subtitled "Of the Obligations to Virtue," by which Shaftesbury meant the inducements to virtuous action. The argument here was what one might call empirical, since it was based on

ability, and the autonomy of virtue are the principal subjects of *The Moralists*, part II, in which the *Inquiry* itself becomes a subject for discussion among the participants of the dialogue (II.iii). In addition, "Miscellaneous Reflections" reflects on the *Inquiry* at several points, chiefly throughout Miscellany IV.

[11] *Inquiry* I.i, pp.3–4. If, as Shaftesbury said, exploring this question had been suggested "by the example of others" (p.4), Bayle's *Pensées diverses sur la comète* (which first appeared in 1682) was a likely inspiration. Bayle argued on the basis of a Calvinist anthropology that religious belief of any sort exercised little force in leading people to moral action. Shaftesbury shared Bayle's desire to ease ethics out of the grasp of religion without the extremity of Bayle's approach to the question, which made rather remote the possibility of any genuine ethical action. Shaftesbury's anthropology, consistent with English Latitudinarian rather than Calvinist divinity, allowed greater power to human rationality and altruism. See A. O. Aldridge, "Shaftesbury and the Deist Manifesto," *Transactions of the American Philosophical Society*, 41 N.S. (1951), 307–308; Grean, *Shaftesbury's Philosophy*, pp.184–188; and Voitle, *Third Earl of Shaftesbury*, pp.87–90, 123.

observations of "*the Oeconomy of the Passions.*"[12] Shaftesbury demonstrate that happiness and goodness went together, sir oneself and serving others were one and the same, and virtue w... reward.

Though the *Inquiry* was not fully explicit, it developed the polemic, suggested in Shaftesbury's preface to Benjamin Whichcote's sermons, against both modern Christianity and modern philosophy.

Recurring to the tension between virtue and religion that was a leitmotif of English thinking since the middle of the seventeenth century, the first part of the *Inquiry* concluded that religion could influence morals for worse. In part I of the *Inquiry*, there is little to suggest that Christianity in particular was at fault, but part II contained a long section developing the position already put forth in the Whichcote preface, that the doctrine of future rewards and punishments was not an aid to true virtue. Regardless of its truth as a dogma, it reduced virtue to an object of calculation rather than an object of value in itself. His hostility to this doctrine became one of Shaftesbury's signature positions.

The insistence on the autonomy of virtue in the *Inquiry* also led to a critique of current trends in philosophy, which the mature Shaftesbury regarded as manifestations of Epicureanism. In the final section of this chapter, we will examine the way in which the issues Shaftesbury initially raised in the *Inquiry* were subsumed into a larger critique of modern Epicureanism. By doing that, we will be able to indicate the specific targets of Shaftesbury's critique. Though the *Inquiry* is not explicit, its arguments do carry through Shaftesbury's intention, announced early in his 1694 letter to Locke, to distinguish himself from "Descartes or Mr Hobbs, or any of their Improvers."

The *Inquiry* addressed two particular tendencies in moral thinking. First, it sought to refute ethical nominalism and scepticism by ascribing to morals an ontological foundation, assured by the design of the cosmos. Though this ontological foundation did not fit into the pattern of an emerging naturalist ethics based on affection and leading to Hutcheson and Hume, Shaftesbury relied on it to secure his moral theory.

Second, the *Inquiry* argued against egoism in moral thinking by founding human moral capabilities in the affections. He insisted that at least some human affections were sociable ones so that selflessness was a natural human capacity and human behavior could not be reduced to a display, albeit complex, of egoism. By contrast to the former point, this emphasis on "the emotional impulses that prompt to social duty" has long been regarded as a highly significant move by historians of ethical

---

[12] *Inquiry* II.i, p.94.

theory.[13] This may be true, but Shaftesbury was less a sentimentalist than he is usually made out to be.

This is important for two reasons. First, the critique of contemporary religion in the *Inquiry* revolved around an understanding of the way in which sociable affections were distorted by culture. To understand this, we have to look at what Shaftesbury said not just about the affections but also about their objects and the ideas that disposed their orientation.

Second, the emphasis on affections creates the impression that Shaftesbury was principally interested in exploring human moral equipment. He did so, but his observations about moral cognition did not occupy much of the *Inquiry* and were subsumed by other questions. In fact, the purpose for which Shaftesbury considered the affections has been ignored. He was principally interested not in the capacities through which humans acquired moral knowledge but rather in the criteria which established virtuous action. Fundamentally concerned with fathoming the relations of the self to others, the *Inquiry* can be seen as an attempt to produce an ethical outlook that would balance the claims of self and others, autonomy and relation. It was this theme which haunted Shaftesbury in the years after he wrote the *Inquiry*, and, as later chapters will show, it was his attempts to wrestle with it that generated the idea of polite philosophy.

Self and others

According to the *Inquiry*, morality consisted in pursuing one's relatedness to others and the world, but it depended on one's capacity to act independently. The claims of both relatedness and autonomy were registered in the fact that Shaftesbury defined moral goodness by reference to both. Another way of putting this is that Shaftesbury defined goodness, understood as a quality of agents, with respect both to its objects and to its origins.[14]

On the one hand, goodness was a direct function of relation: the goodness of parts could not be estimated except by reference to the wholes to which they belonged. This principle was inscribed into the universe, a unified system under unified guidance, designed for good purposes by the creator. This system was composed of sub-systems, themselves composed of sub-systems, in a regressing pattern leading down to the individual. In other words, the universe was a hierarchy of

---

[13] Henry Sidgwick, *Outlines of the History of Ethics for English Readers* (London: Macmillan and Co., 1886), p.181.

[14] Shaftesbury's account seems to imply a distinction between the "goodness" of acts and the "virtue" of actors, but his use of these words does not systematically follow the implicit distinction: see Grean, *Shaftesbury's Philosophy*, pp.226–227.

individuals and mediating systems all subsumed by the general system. These essentially metaphysical presuppositions were the foundation of real ethical principles.[15] Though his later reading in the Roman stoics confirmed these ideas, their more immediate sources were Richard Cumberland and Ralph Cudworth.[16]

For human individuals, the relevant wholes were families, tribes, polities, and ultimately the species. Goodness required that one be oriented toward "the good of his Kind, or of that System ... where he is included, and of which he is a PART."[17] Thus, cosmic design established relatedness, which was the basis for ethics; relatedness, moralized, gave rise to an ethic of cooperation. This ethics on a real foundation was meant to counter notions that, as we will see, Shaftesbury found rampant in contemporary philosophy: that ethical principles might be arbitrary conventions or products of divine fiat.

While participating in a larger circle of human engagement was a necessary moral criterion, it was not sufficient since goodness had to arise in the depths of the self. Virtue required an interior motion or affection and, ultimately, a rational recognition of the good. In the Western ethical tradition, an insistence on moral autonomy had been deepened with the rise of Protestantism. Moral autonomy among the ancient moral philosophers was largely an autonomy of self-knowledge and self-governance. However, Reformation Protestantism, developing strands already present in Christian thinking, made "the purity and intention of the heart or will ..., the sine qua non of true virtue."[18]

Shaftesbury endorsed this concern with absolute sincerity and the concomitant deepening of the interior world. While good and evil had reference to a cosmic system, discussion of virtue was incomplete without reference to matters of motivation and intention: "in a sensible Creature, that which is not done through any affection (and consequently with no knowledg, consciousness or perception at all) makes neither good nor ill in the nature of that Creature." The statement made clear that goodness was defined by real moral agency. Shaftesbury elicited the example of the creature who basically hated others but who, out of fear for himself, performed a good act. Such a creature, Shaftesbury said, was not good on

---

[15] *Inquiry* I.ii, pp.13–16.
[16] On Shaftesbury and Cumberland, see Grean, *Shaftesbury's Philosophy*, pp.174, 211–212. On Shaftesbury and Cudworth, see John Passmore, *Ralph Cudworth* (Cambridge: Cambridge University Press, 1951), pp.96–99.
[17] *Inquiry* II.i, p.84.
[18] Norman Fiering, *Moral Philosophy at Seventeenth-Century Harvard: A Discipline in Transition* (For the Institute of Early American History and Culture, Williamsburg; Chapel Hill: University of North Carolina Press, 1981), pp.94–95; Jonas Barish, *The Antitheatrical Prejudice* (Berkeley: University of California Press, 1981), pp.80–96.

account of the good act performed: nothing here mitigated the creature's "ill Nature or ill Disposition," though a good may have occurred "without good Nature, good Disposition, or good Intention."[19]

What was required for virtue was a pure and autonomous motion. The manner in which Shaftesbury established this autonomy is the best known, if not always best understood, feature of the *Inquiry*. Shaftesbury wrote that humans were by nature sociable and that this sociability arose, in the first instance, in their very affections. If his reflections on parts and wholes led to a criterion for goodness, his reflections on natural affective sociability guaranteed the "performability" of that criterion among humans: there was a natural fit between the human make-up and the moral imperatives structured into the cosmos.[20] In asserting natural affective sociability, Shaftesbury was moving forward a reassessment of the affections, in which emotionality was assigned the determining role in human personality, that had been proceeding for fifty years.[21] Though such philosophical egoists as Thomas Hobbes and the French Augustinians had offered such a reassessment by insisting on the radically passionate character of all human action, Shaftesbury (not without predecessors) was using the affections to combat egoism.

However, for Shaftesbury, the affections were only the foundations of human morality. Human morality, though it arose in the feelings, was a phenomenon of consciousness and rationality as well. While humans were naturally sociable and naturally capable of virtue, they were not, to speak precisely, naturally good or virtuous. Virtue required training and work, for virtue was not merely an affective disposition, but affection raised to a conscious principle in the rational agent by reflection on affection and the sorts of actions endorsed by affection. He wrote that if a creature was sociable but could not reflect on what he did or approve of what others did, making "that idea or conception of Goodness, or a good Action done through good Affection, to be an object of his Affection, he has not the name of being virtuous: for thus, and no otherwise, he is capable of having *a sense, in any kind, of what is right or wrong.*"[22] Here, Shaftesbury offered the notion which has been his entire claim on the attention of some commentators. The "moral sense" (an expression he did not use)

---

[19] *Inquiry* I.ii, pp.17–19.
[20] J. B. Schneewind's expression in "The Divine Corporation and the History of Ethics," in Richard Rorty, J. B. Schneewind, and Quentin Skinner, eds., *Philosophy in History* (Cambridge: Cambridge University Press, 1984), p.179.
[21] This development is a major theme in Fiering, *Moral Philosophy at Seventeenth-Century Harvard*, pp.5, 157–165, 176–181, 195–198, and also in Albert O. Hirschman, *The Passions and the Interests: Political Arguments for Capitalism before Its Triumph* (Princeton: Princeton University Press, 1977), esp. pp.12–48.
[22] *Inquiry* I.ii, p.27–29.

was nothing more than the consciousness of affections and their significance. Moreover, the expression was introduced not to elucidate the innovation (if it deserves that name) of founding human morals on sociable affections but rather to underscore a demand for self-consciousness, and therefore moral autonomy, on the part of the moral actor.

Thus, in the *Inquiry*, sociability and moral autonomy were complementary notions. While moral insight required hiving oneself off from external authority and deploying the resources of the interior (affection and reason), the fundamental insight of moral feeling and reflection was one's connectedness to others and the fundamental demand that one act in ways that benefited them. The difficulties of these requirements were immense and, as we will see in chapters 3 and 4, Shaftesbury would discover many of them. Here it is important to note the unproblematic presentation of the relations between self and others in the *Inquiry*.

According to Shaftesbury, human sociability was a reliable criterion of morality. By "sociability" here, I refer to those affections that Shaftesbury said drew people out of solitude into fruitful connection with others. This understanding of sociability depended on an analysis that distinguished affections according to their object: first, "the natural ones towards the Kind," which carried the self towards goods other than its own; second, "the self-ones," which carried the self only towards its own private good; and, third, those perverse or unnatural affections which served the good of neither self nor others, whose object was destruction for its own sake.[23]

This scheme created a place for selflessness, securing the self against radical egoism. The existence of natural affections meant that the human had impulses towards others which had no ground in self-referring affections or calculations. At the same time, the self affections themselves had a legitimate albeit cramped place. As Shaftesbury said himself, he had no intention of setting up a "perfect opposition" between these two sorts of affection, despite the observed fact that acting on the natural affections often frustrated the propensities of the self-referring affections.

Indeed, the *Inquiry* identified various forms of accommodation between self-referring and other-referring affections. On the one hand, self affections were necessary for the preservation and prosperity of the self and might even contribute to the general good.[24] On the other, acting on the sociable affections redounded to the greater satisfaction of the self. This was the major thrust of part II of the *Inquiry*, where Shaftesbury asserted that sociability was the only basis for human happiness: "for every

---

[23] This analytic of the affective life, implicit in many assertions in part I, such as I.ii, p.26, or I.iii, p.52, was presented explicitly at the outset of part II.i, pp.88–89.

[24] *Inquiry* II.i, pp.85, 90–92; also, I.ii, pp.19–22.

particular in its System, to work *to the good of that System or Public*, and *to its own good*, is all one, and not to be divided."[25] On this basis, part II of the *Inquiry* has been read as a proto-utilitarian account of morals.[26] Such a reading certainly conflicts with the point of part I, which was to create an ethic free of prudential, self-interested calculation. Shaftesbury recognized the danger sufficiently to put up some impediments to this reading. To detach pleasure from egoism, he insisted that true pleasures were either the natural affections themselves in their operations or the immediate effects of natural affections.[27] Here, as elsewhere, Shaftesbury insisted on clarifying human motivation. Whatever rewards redounded in the direction of the self from its own sociability, the definition of and motivation for goodness did not refer to the self. Ethical sociability was constituted by a large measure of selflessness.

While denying that sociability and egoism might be indistinguishably linked, Shaftesbury was quite aware of the impediments to virtuous sociability. First, the affections might be disordered in a number of ways: not only might natural affections and the self affections be too strong or too weak, but affections of the perverse or destructive sort might be present. The solution to this impediment was a proper balance (or "Oeconomy") among the natural and self affections and, of course, the exclusion of unnatural affections.[28]

Second, the affections might be well ordered but mistaken in their objects: "where this good Aim is ever so much; and where the Affection towards Right is ever so strong; yet if through Superstition or strange Custom and Vogue, or through any wildness or extravagancy of Opinion, there come to be very gross mistakes in the assignment or application of the Affection," then vice is present. The impediment here was a matter not of affection but of "opinion," "custom," "fashion," "belief," "education," and so forth. Indeed, "ill Religion", in the forms of superstition and enthusiasm, was most likely to misguide the affections.[29] The solution to these common anomalies was a more accurate application of the sense of right and wrong.

The impediments to virtue that Shaftesbury admitted are important, first, because they make it less easy to imagine him as a Panglossian cartoon not only of naïveté and sentimental optimism but of a danger-

---

[25] *Inquiry* II.i, p.87.
[26] Ernest Albee, "The Relation of Shaftesbury and Hutcheson to Utilitarianism," *Philosophical Review*, 5 (1896), 24–35; Grean, *Shaftesbury's Philosophy*, pp.242–243; Voitle, *Third Earl of Shaftesbury*, p.130.
[27] *Inquiry* II.ii, p.108.
[28] *Inquiry* I.ii, pp.29, 34; I.iii, p.52; II.i, pp.94–100; II.ii, p.149.
[29] *Inquiry* I.ii, pp.30–33; I.iii, pp.45–51; II.i, p.100.

ously feeble critical intellect.[30] More significant, the impediments to virtue were in important respects sociological or cultural. Though the *Inquiry* was principally concerned with the distortions that religious beliefs imposed on consciousness, the point could be generalized. Shaftesbury's analysis of the ways in which natural affections could be transformed and transmogrified by external "opinions" invited a cultural discourse since it offered categories by which individuals could be located with respect to social or cultural formations. Such categories ultimately served the purposes of cultural analysis that will be discussed in part II of this book. Given these categories, moral autonomy was very important, promising a point of refuge at which the "opinions" of society could be evaluated and discriminated amongst. However, the demand for moral autonomy put a heavy burden on the self. Shaftesbury's experience, subsequent to writing the *Inquiry*, called into question the extent to which the sort of autonomy depicted in the *Inquiry* was possible.

While the *Inquiry* was, among other things, a case for moral improvement on the basis of the education of the emotions, it did not address closely the processes by which humans might move towards virtuous sociability. The text contained little indication of the difficulties that might attend enacting in reality the assent given by the mind to the *Inquiry*'s propositions. Nor did the text make any suggestion about how such difficulties might be tackled. The text, in short, did not reckon with moral inertia. Tellingly, the *Inquiry* did not mention the will.

Moreover, the text's genre and style implied that intellectual clarity was a sufficient instrument for moral edification. As an effort at demonstration, the text urged the reader to embrace its analyses and conclusions. The convinced reader of the *Inquiry* might be expected to recognize the moral pattern of the universe and, if he were a convinced egoist, integrate a limited self-concern into a general altruistic stance. Even were he not an egoist, he might be expected to moderate his self-concern by cultivating his natural affections. He also might be expected to embrace virtue for its own sake rather than on the basis of superstition or prescription (which might involve some rearranging of religious opinions previously taken for granted). However, as the substance of the *Inquiry* avoided questions of moral struggle, so its form was not conducive to addressing those questions. In the years that followed the writing of the *Inquiry*, moral struggle became the theme of Shaftesbury's inner life. He would seek forms of philosophic practice and discourse that could address such struggle.

---

[30] See *Inquiry* II.i, p.99. For an account of Shaftesbury as continuing Locke's Pauline pessimism but without soteriological hope, see W. M. Spellman, *John Locke and the Problem of Depravity* (Oxford: Clarendon Press, 1988), pp.184–202.

The "secret Anti-Epicurean view"[31]

We have already seen how the classics played a part in Shaftesbury's definition of polite philosophy. However, ancient philosophy also provided Shaftesbury with specific categories with which to clarify the state of modern morals. The *Inquiry* advanced ideas that, in the course of time, Shaftesbury came to understand as stoic and anti-Epicurean.

Shaftesbury applied a simple scheme of ancient philosophical history to modern philosophical dispute. In all of antiquity, there were never "any more than Two real distinct Philosophys":

> the one derived from Socrates, and passing into ye old Academic, ye Peripatetic, & Stoic; ye other derived in reality from Democritus, & passing into ye Cyrenaic and Epicurean. ... The First therefore of these two Philosophys recommended Action, Concernment in Civil Affairs, Religion &c: The Second derided All, and advised In-action & Retreat; & good Reason. – For the First maintained yt Society, Right and Wrong was founded in Nature, & that Nature had a Meaning, & was Her self, that is to say, in her Wits, well Governed & administer'd by one Simple & Perfect Intelligence. The Second again derided This, & made Providence & Dame Nature not so sensible, as a doating old Woman. The First therefore of these Philosophys is to be called ye Civil, Social, Theistic: the Second, ye Contrary.[32]

For Shaftesbury, this grand opposition between stoic and Epicurean absorbed the entire variety of ancient opinion.[33]

In this dyadic confrontation, Shaftesbury was an unambivalent partisan of the stoics. Positions articulated in the *Inquiry* – the depiction of a designed, orderly and harmonious cosmos, the notion of natural human sociability, optimism in the face of evil – were congenial to the stoic tradition. Later, as we will be observing, his writings, especially the manuscripts, became saturated with the specific influence of Epictetus and Marcus Aurelius.[34] As Shaftesbury more and more immersed himself in ancient writings, he came to identify himself as an opponent of Epicureanism, ancient and modern. "Epicureanism" assigned a common genealogy to a variety of contemporary intellectual positions and rooted

---

[31] An expression Shaftesbury used to characterize the philosophical polemic underlying his investigations in art: P.R.O. 30/24/27/15, p.43r [f.51r].

[32] P.R.O. 30/24/22/7, Shaftesbury to Pierre Coste, October 1, 1706.

[33] This account, though simplistic, had some validity inasmuch as Zeno's attack on Epicurean privatism in the name of public duty linked the stoics to the classical philosophers and translated the spirit of the *polis* into a more cosmopolitan framework. Like Plato and Aristotle, also, Zeno sought to correlate reason, knowledge and virtue with *eudaimonia* while Epicurus grounded *eudaimonia* in pleasure: Marcia Colish, *The Stoic Tradition from Antiquity to the Early Middle Ages*, 2 vols. (Leiden: E. J. Brill, 1985), I, 9; J. M. Rist, *Stoic Philosophy* (Cambridge: Cambridge University Press, 1969), pp.19–20.

[34] A comprehensive account of the intellectual components of the ancient stoic tradition can be found in Colish, *Stoic Tradition*, I, 7–60. Shaftesbury's relation to stoic thinking is pursued further in chapters 3 and 4.

their defects in a highly individualistic and nominalistic attitude that, Shaftesbury alleged, descended from Epicurus himself.[35]

Epicurus had rebelled against the notion that philosophy was a theoretical exercise, dismissing Platonic ideas and Aristotelian categories in favor of a sensationalist epistemology and a nominalist view of language. Philosophy was to be a practical activity helping individuals achieve happiness. Epicurus therefore set himself the goal of removing the myths, superstitions, and false hopes that disturbed serenity. Though he did not renounce the gods entirely, he depicted the world as a domain without supernatural interference, running on materialist principles. For Epicurus, Democritean atomism explained nature and thereby banished such stoic emphases as teleology, order, design, and providence.[36] This dismayed Shaftesbury, who called atomism "the Faith of Epicurus" and "*Atomes & Void*, a plain negative to Deity."[37] Shaftesbury challenged the Epicureans to account for cosmic order in an atomist's universe.[38]

Who among the moderns was propagating an Epicurean view of the cosmos? Shaftesbury was not quite explicit, though the broad brush of his "Epicureanism" probably took in the variety of seventeenth-century materialism, atomism, and mechanism. Unlike the Cambridge Platonists, Shaftesbury preferred allusion to specificity and so refrained from elaborating arguments against current metaphysical opinions.[39]

It is easier to identify the ethical trends in contemporary philosophy that Shaftesbury opposed as expressions of Epicureanism. Epicurus's metaphysical commitment to individualism had important implications

---

[35] On nominalism and early modern thought, see: Meyrick Carré, *Realists and Nominalists* (London: Oxford University Press, 1946), pp.123–124; Michael Oakeshott, introduction to Thomas Hobbes, *Leviathan* (Oxford: Basil Blackwell, 1947), pp.xii, lii–liv. On Epicurus in early modern Europe, see: Lynn Joy, *Gassendi the Atomist* (Cambridge: Cambridge University Press, 1987); T. F. Mayo, *Epicurus in England* (College Station, Texas, 1934).

[36] A. A. Long, *Hellenistic Philosophy* (New York: Charles Scribner's Sons, 1974), pp.20–42; Eduard Zeller, *The Stoics, Epicureans and Sceptics*, trans. O. J. Reichel (London: Longmans, Green, and Co., 1892), pp.410–425.

[37] P.R.O. 30/24/27/10, pp.92, 248 [ff.47v, 180v]. On several occasions, he invoked a tag, inspired by Marcus Aurelius: "Either Atomes or Deity." See Marcus Aurelius IV.3, VI.10, VIII.17, IX.39. Shaftesbury attacked the Epicurean view of divinity in P.R.O. 30/24/27/10, p.249 [f.181r] and in "Moralists" II.iii, II, 268 (Robertson, II, 53).

[38] P.R.O. 30/24/27/10, p.287 [f.199r]. A revised version of this passage appeared in "Moralists" III.i, II, 358 (Robertson, II, 105).

[39] Nonetheless, a passage written for the revised version of *The Moralists* reveals some of the metaphysical projects he abhorred, namely, those of Benedict de Spinoza, René Descartes, and John Locke: P.R.O. 30/24/26/6, f.32r–v. This manuscript is a bound volume of handwritten supplements to the original version of *The Moralists*, called "The Sociable Enthusiast." This passage was not included in the revised version. On the versions of this text, see: S. F. Whitaker, "The First Edition of Shaftesbury's *Moralists*," *The Library*, 5th series, 7 (1952), 235–42; Horst Meyer, *Limae Labor: Untersuchungen zur Textgenese und Druckgeschichte von Shaftesburys "The Moralists"* (Peter Lange: Frankfurt am Main, 1978); Voitle, *Third Earl of Shaftesbury*, pp.313–319.

for moral and social theory. As natural events were caused by the interactions of atoms, so social life was explained by the interactions of self-oriented individuals. Individuals pursued pleasure, which was the aim of life and the equivalent of human happiness. The Epicurean dismissed the pursuit of virtue for its own sake as a stoic delusion. Indeed, moral principles were themselves simply the result of convention.[40] A corollary of the assertion that the human was a self-oriented, pleasure-seeking, pain-avoiding animal was the contention that humans had no natural leanings toward society, which the Epicureans saw as an expediency, confected by individualistic men better to assure their own peace. (Lucretius later historicized Epicurean views producing a naturalistic and materialistic account of the genesis of human society, which confirmed its expediential character.[41]) Unlike the stoic, the Epicurean was likely to retreat from the public sphere and to cultivate an aloofness from both domestic and civil affairs. While love and marriage were to be avoided, friendship was the social form promising the least disturbance and the most pleasure.[42]

Shaftesbury saw Epicurean ethics as a challenge to his own positions. Metaphysical atomism led to "Weakness and irresolution in the Opinion concerning *Man's being Sociable by Nature.*"[43] Epicurean hedonism had to be countered by a vigorous assertion of the antagonism between virtue and pleasure.[44] In Shaftesbury's view, the Epicurean aloofness from family and politics implied suppressing the social and extirpating instinct since "*Relations, Friends, Countrymen, Laws, Politick Constitutions, the Beauty of Order and Government,* and *the Interest of Society and Mankind,* were Objects which, [Epicurus] well saw, wou'd *naturally* raise a stronger

---

[40] The remains of Epicurus available to Shaftesbury were in Diogenes Laertius, *Lives of Eminent Philosophers,* X.150. See Long, *Hellenistic Philosophy,* pp.69–71; Zeller, *Stoics, Epicureans and Sceptics,* pp.445, 462–464.

[41] Lucretius, *De Rerum Natura,* V.958–961, 1019–27.

[42] Diogenes Laertius, *Lives of Eminent Philosophers,* X.118, 143, 148. See Long, *Hellenistic Philosophy,* p.62; Zeller, *Stoics, Epicureans and Sceptics,* pp.445–465. On Epicurean practice, see M. L. Clarke, *The Roman Mind* (Cambridge, Mass.: Harvard University Press, 1956), pp.27, 30; Bernard Frischer, *The Sculpted Word: Epicureanism and Philosophical Recruitment in Ancient Greece* (Berkeley: University of California Press, 1982), p.xiv; A. J. Festugière, *Epicurus and His Gods,* trans. C. W. Chilton (Oxford: Basil Blackwell, 1955), pp.41–42.

[43] P.R.O. 30/24/27/10, pp.100–101 [ff.51v–52r]; see also p.210 [f.161v].

[44] The autonomy of virtue is an important idea in *An Inquiry Concerning Virtue.* Shaftesbury turned the opposition of pleasure and virtue into a personal signature through his use of the story of the choice of Hercules in "Moralists" II.ii, II, 253–254 (Robertson, II, 45) and in *A Notion of the Historical Draught or Tablature of the Judgement of Hercules.* On Hercules and the stoics, see Colish, *Stoic Tradition,* I, 30–31, 41, 95, 147. For further references, see James McLachlan, "The Choice of Hercules: American Student Societies in the Early Nineteenth Century," in Lawrence Stone, ed., *The University in Society,* 2 vols. (Princeton: Princeton University Press, 1975), II, 449–494.

Affection than any which was grounded upon the narrow bottom of mere SELF."[45] Here was Epicurus as a social atomist, seeking to reduce humans to solitary individuals. It was this trait of the Epicureans that earned them Cicero's disdain.[46] Likewise, for Shaftesbury, Epicurus began to look like a philosopher of selfishness.

Thus, Shaftesbury's reading of Epicurean social atomism prepared for a critique of aspects of seventeenth-century philosophy, which seemed to him a rejuvenation of ancient Epicureanism. One instance was the rise of theorists of self-love who rejected the "*natural* Materials" of social affection in order to build "after a more uniform way": "They wou'd new-frame the Human Heart; and have a mighty fancy to reduce all its Motions, Ballances and Weights, to that one Principle and Foundation of a cool and deliberate *Selfishness*." However, while Epicurus recognized that social affection had to be suppressed, his "Revivers" sought "to alter *the Thing*, by shifting a Name": "They wou'd so explain all the social Passions, and natural Affections, as to denominate 'em *of the selfish kind*." While pretending to give an account of human psychology, the philosophers of egoism only proffered "a piece of conceptual legislation" (in Steven Lukes's expression): they committed themselves to an interpretive norm according to which all human behavior would be understood as maneuvering on the part of a calculating ego.

Shaftesbury cited Thomas Hobbes and John Wilmot, the earl of Rochester, as proponents of philosophical egoism and, elsewhere, referring to "Distributers and petty Retailers ... who have run Changes, and Divisions, without end, upon this Article of *Self-Love*," he cited the duc de La Rochefoucauld.[47] By linking Hobbes, Rochester, and La Rochefoucauld, Shaftesbury indicated that he was rebelling not just against Hobbes but against a general climate of philosophical egoism. Contemporaries frequently connected Hobbes with the sort of libertinism represented by Rochester. The particular tie between the two issued from Gilbert Burnet's account of Rochester's death-bed 'conversion' when Rochester confessed that reading Hobbes turned him into the paths of voluptuousness. Even if this story was a fabrication, certain passages of Rochester's "Satyr against Reason and Mankind" had a definite Hobbesian ring.[48]

---

[45] "Sensus Communis" III.iii, I, 117 (Robertson, I, 78).
[46] Alain Michel, *Rhétorique et philosophie chez Cicéron* (Paris: Presses Universitaires de France, 1960), p.112.
[47] "Sensus Communis" III.iii, I, 116, 118, 120 (Robertson, I, 78, 79, 80); Steven Lukes, *Individualism* (Oxford: Basil Blackwell, 1973), p.99. On early modern egoism, see Nannerl Keohane, *Philosophy and the State in France* (Princeton: Princeton University Press, 1980), pp.183–197, 273–277, 289–303.
[48] See David M. Vieth, ed., *The Complete Poems of John Wilmot, Earl of Rochester* (New Haven and London: Yale University Press, 1968), p.99.

Moreover, if (as has been asserted) Rochester's perspective was shaped by Lucretius, one can see further justification for Shaftesbury's associating Rochester with Hobbes.[49] Just what Epicurean or Lucretian stamp Hobbes himself may have borne is not at issue. However, he was at least on occasion called an Epicurean by contemporaries.[50] For Shaftesbury, Hobbes was perhaps the arch-Epicurean in recent philosophy, advocating materialism, atomism, and egoism. Finally, in mentioning La Rochefoucauld, Shaftesbury was specifying another seventeenth-century version of egoism, namely, the Augustinian tradition that informed Jansenism. La Rochefoucauld was not a Jansenist but he had personal associations with Jansenists and his writing bore the Augustinian imprint.[51]

However, philosophical egoism was not the only Epicurean feature that Shaftesbury located in contemporary currents of thought, for egoism was related to the denial of the ontological reality of morality. As the Epicureans depicted a universe without informing moral characteristics, so, according to Shaftesbury, modern moralists denied the ontological foundations of ethical principles. "But so far are our modern Moralists from condemning any unnatural Vices, or corrupt Manners, whether in our own or foreign Climates, that they wou'd have VICE it-self appear as *natural* as VIRTUE; and from the worst Examples, wou'd represent to us, 'That all Actions are *naturally indifferent*; that they have no Note or Character of Good, or Ill, *in themselves*; but are distinguish'd by mere FASHION, LAW, or *arbitrary* DECREE.'"[52] Virtue and vice, according to the moderns, were not naturally distinct; without a real or natural foundation, ethical principles became purely conventional, either the artificial device of whomever had power in the social order or the arbitrary decrees of God.

Both Thomas Hobbes and John Locke typified modern moralism, according to Shaftesbury. Having explicitly labelled Hobbes an Epicurean revivalist, Shaftesbury devoted several pages of "Sensus Communis" to Hobbes's ethical insights. According to Shaftesbury, these amounted to the proposition that ethical principles had no basis in reality

---

[49] S. I. Mintz, *The Hunting of Leviathan* (Cambridge: Cambridge University Press, 1962), p.142.

[50] By Pufendorf and Barbeyrac: Richard Tuck, *Natural Rights Theories* (Cambridge: Cambridge University Press, 1979), p.175; Istvan Hont, "The Language of Sociability and Commerce: Samuel Pufendorf and the Theoretical Foundations of the 'Four-Stages Theory,'" in Anthony Pagden, ed., *The Languages of Political Theory in Early-Modern Europe* (Cambridge: Cambridge University Press, 1987), p.259. See also Mintz, *Hunting of Leviathan*, p.32.

[51] Keohane, *Philosophy and the State of France*, p.289.

[52] "Soliloquy" III.iii, I, 352 (Robertson, I, 227); also, III.i, I, 298 (Robertson, I, 193) and "Sensus Communis" III.i, I, 107 (Robertson, I, 72).

but were established in society by one artificial means or another (force, custom, and so forth).[53]

Though he never called Locke an Epicurean,[54] it should be clear that Locke was a signal instance for Shaftesbury of the infestation of the best thought of the era by Epicurean motives. In fact, Shaftesbury's Epicurean interpretation of Locke allowed him to see both the epistemology and key elements of the political theory as components of a unified and pernicious program.

Shaftesbury read Locke as continuing the nominalist project of Hobbes. He assigned a Hobbesian paternity to "all those they call *Free-Writers* nowadays." Then, conceding his personal respect for Locke and his admiration for Locke's views on other matters, he noted that Locke "did, however, go in the self-same track," spawning Matthew Tindal and others. In the end, Shaftesbury said, Locke's influence in moral thinking was more devastating than that of Hobbes, whose "Character and base slavish Principles in Government took off the Poyson of his Philosophy." Meanwhile, "'Twas Mr. LOCKE that struck at all Fundamentals, threw all Order and Virtue out of the World."[55]

He did this, in Shaftesbury's view, much in the manner of Hobbes:

> Virtue, according to Mr. LOCKE, has no other Measure, Law, or Rule, than *Fashion* and *Custom*: Morality, Justice, Equity, depend only on *Law* and *Will*: And GOD indeed is a perfect *Free Agent* in his Sense; that is, *free to any Thing, that is however Ill*: For if he wills it, it will be made Good; Virtue may be Vice, and Vice Virtue in its Turn, if he pleases. And thus neither *Right* nor *Wrong*, *Virtue* nor *Vice* are any thing in themselves; nor is there any Trace or Idea of them *naturally imprinted* on Human Minds. Experience and our Catechism teach us all![56]

Like Hobbes, Locke propagated the conventional character of morality and a nominalist view of God.

While Shaftesbury's version of Lockean ethics was partly caricature, it did respond to the uneasy assortment of elements among Locke's ethical reflections. The passage just cited was a response to Book II, chapter 28, of *An Essay Concerning Human Understanding*, in which Locke distinguished among three sorts of "Moral Rules, or Laws, to which Men generally refer," namely, divine law, civil law, and the "Law of *Opinion* or *Reputation*." Though Locke was engaged here in description, he also made clear that divine law was "the only true touchstone of *moral*

---

[53] "Sensus Communis" II.i, I, 91–93 (Robertson, I, 62–63).
[54] Shaftesbury did once apply the Epicurean label to Locke on account of his ideas about vacuums (in *Essay* II.xiii.23): "Soliloquy" III.i, I, 301 (Robertson, I, 195).
[55] Shaftesbury to Michael Ainsworth, June 3, 1709, in *Several Letters*, pp.38–39.
[56] Shaftesbury to Michael Ainsworth, June 3, 1709, in *Several Letters*, pp.40–41; also, P.R.O. 30/24/22/7, ff.490–492, Shaftesbury to James Stanhope, November 7, 1709.

Rectitude."[57] He had already asserted in the *Essay* that, despite the access that human reason gave to God and divine expectations, "the true ground of Morality" was strictly "the Will and Law of a God, who sees Men in the dark, has in his Hand Rewards and Punishments, and Power enough to call to account the Proudest Offender."[58] Moral prescriptions were thus the commands of God, enforced by divine sanctions: they were not part of any natural order.[59] Shaftesbury took exception to this antinaturalism. Nor did Shaftesbury trust other strains (hedonistic, rationalistic, jusnaturalistic) that appeared in Locke's moral thinking. Though Locke asserted that knowledge of conduct should be man's chief regard and that moral knowledge was as capable of certain demonstration as mathematics, the *Essay* was very slim in its coverage of the ethical third of Locke's "Division of the Sciences."[60] Nor did other writings of Locke perform the promised demonstration, which seems to have receded from his interests over time to be replaced by a more nominalist view of moral instructions as God's commands and moral excellence as an individual's "calculation of extra-terrestrial self-interest."[61]

Nor was this the end of Locke's treachery to virtue. In Shaftesbury's view, the assault on virtue among neo-Epicurean moralists had a double thrust: while it denied the reality of real ethical principles, it also denied humans the natural capacity to act virtuously. Hobbesian egoism was, for Shaftesbury, a pure expression of the tradition. As for Locke, Shaftesbury assimilated the Lockean critique of innate ideas to considerations about the inherent capacity of humans for virtue.

Locke had given the critique of innate ideas, directed not so much at Descartes as at the Cambridge Platonists, a powerful statement in Book I of the *Essay*. Shaftesbury dismissed the discussion of innate ideas as a red herring, one of the "childishest Disputes" in which philosophers had engaged. This dismissal came easily since Shaftesbury did not see the debate in an epistemological context. Locke's question in the *Essay* was how do humans know and part of his answer was not by innate ideas. However, Shaftesbury interpreted the question of innate endowments as a question not about the origins of human knowledge but about the origins

---

[57] Locke, *Essay* II.xxviii.6–8, pp.351–352.
[58] Locke, *Essay* I.iii.6, p.69.
[59] John Colman, *John Locke's Moral Philosophy* (Edinburgh: Edinburgh University Press, 1983), p.5.
[60] Locke, *Essay* I.i.6, IV.iv.7, IV.xxi, pp.46, 565, 720.
[61] John Dunn, "The Politics of Locke in England and America in the Eighteenth Century," in *Political Obligation in Its Historical Context* (Cambridge: Cambridge University Press, 1980), pp.57–58. Two versions of Locke's moral ideas are: Richard I. Aaron, *John Locke*, 3rd edn (Oxford: Clarendon Press, 1971), pp.256–266, and W. van Leyden, introduction to John Locke, *Essays on the Law of Nature* (Oxford: Clarendon Press, 1954), pp.69–76.

of human virtue. Once the question had been transferred from the realm of epistemology to that of ethics, Shaftesbury was committed to innate sociability, though he was willing to dispense with the innateness of "ideas." The innateness of philosophical propositions was irrelevant because what mattered was "whether the Passion or Affection towards Society was such," that is, natural and coming of itself, or taught by art, the "Product of a Lucky Hit of some first Man who inspir'd and deliver'd down the Prejudice."[62] Thus, Shaftesbury found Locke's refutation of innate ideas irrelevant.[63]

The central point in Shaftesbury's objection to the Lockean critique of innate ideas was the implication that humans were entirely formed by their experience. This Lockean view excluded the possibility of natural sociability. At this point, it was possible for Shaftesbury to link the author *An Essay Concerning Human Understanding* with the author of the *Second Treatise of Government*. It was also possible to address the natural law tradition that shaped the thinking of both Hobbes and Locke.

From the Shaftesburian perspective, natural law took on an interestingly Epicurean rather than the more usual stoic cast.[64] Natural law thinking began with an act of abstraction since the theory was grounded on attempts to imagine the condition of humans in the absence of society. The abstract individual was an irreducible human entity, a human essence, with basic capabilities and drives, from which everything social and cultural had been hived. Denominated "natural," this non-social human being could be discussed as inhabiting a state of nature (either fictive or historical). Since man in nature was an individual, he necessarily was concerned with his own condition and preservation. This self-referentiality did not necessarily exclude sociability: Hugo Grotius, for example, had supplemented the individual's self-preserving mechanisms with natural or innate sociability. However, following Grotius, the natural individualism that had always been part of the tradition turned decisively toward natural egoism, first in John Selden and then more famously in Hobbes, for whom the abstract individual was decidedly anti-social.

Given these premises, natural law theory went on to suppose a history in which society or the state emerged from the natural situation of atomic individualism. By the nature of the case, society or the state was not natural, but rather an artificial contrivance to compensate for the defects of nature. It was also instrumental since it came into existence to meet the

---

[62] Elsewhere, however, Shaftesbury appears to have had a somewhat deeper investment in the innateness of ideas: P.R.O. 30/24/22/7, ff.490–492, Shaftesbury to James Stanhope, November 7, 1709.
[63] Shaftesbury to Michael Ainsworth, June 3, 1709, in *Several Letters*, p.39.
[64] This summary derives from Tuck, *Natural Rights Theories*, and Hont, "The Language of Sociability and Commerce", pp.253–276.

needs and further the aims of the atomic individuals. Such an account depended on a creative or constitutive moment in which individuals turned themselves from natural into social or political beings. The idea of a contract might be introduced to represent the transition from nature to society, though the conceptual difficulties of imagining the transition produced much discussion of obligation and promises – just what was it that differentiated the moral terrain of nature from that of society.[65]

Shaftesbury's commitment to natural human sociability invalidated not only the egoism of natural law theories but the entire process of abstraction underpinning them. If one accepted natural sociability, then atomistic individuality was a simple fiction, no starting point for philosophical discussion of humans in society. While Shaftesbury did mention self-preservation, he gave it a social turn: "if anything be *natural*, in any Creature, or any Kind; 'tis that which is *Preservative* of the Kind it-self, and conducing to its Welfare and Support." The preservation of selves could not be conceived except in a social context. The "natural" state of humans was already one of sociability. Shaftesbury wrote:

If *Eating* and *Drinking* be natural, *Herding* is so too. If any *Appetite* or *Sense* be natural, the *Sense of Fellowship* is the same. If there by any thing of Nature in that Affection which is between the Sexes, the Affection is certainly as natural towards the consequent Offspring; and so again between the Offspring themselves, as Kindred and Companions, bred under the same Discipline and Oeconomy. And thus *a Clan* or *Tribe* is gradually form'd; *a Publick* is recogniz'd.

Because of the ineluctable continuum of social feeling and action from the most immediate to more remote human relations, there was no frontier marking a passage from the presocial to the social. The *"Tribe"* came into being by a process of accumulation. Likewise, that *"a Publick* is recogniz'd" implied that the public already existed before it was acknowledged. Shaftesbury refused to conceive of a natural condition of disaggregated individuals since the most elemental human condition was already too mediated by sociability. He exclaimed, with clear reference to the natural law idiom: "How the Wit of Man shou'd so puzzle this Cause, as to make Civil Government and Society appear a kind of Invention, and Creature of Art, I know not."[66]

Shaftesbury dismissed contemporary social and political theory as only "Cavils of a Philosophy, which speaks so much of *Nature* with so little Meaning."[67] Part of what made natural law theories seem Epicurean to

---

[65] Tuck, *Natural Rights Theories*, pp.90 (Selden), 105–106 (post-Selden), 126 (Hobbes), 168–169 (Locke).
[66] "Sensus Communis" III.ii, I, 110–111 (Robertson, I, 74–75). Shaftesbury also argued here that natural law could not provide any satisfactory account of moral obligation.
[67] "Sensus Communis" III.ii, I, 109–110 (Robertson, I, 73–74).

Shaftesbury was their depiction of natural human atomism. This atomism was the product of an abstraction and bespoke the larger abstract and deductive character of natural law theory. Had Shaftesbury depicted natural law as another species of neo-scholasticism, he would not have been entirely wrong. In his mature writings, Shaftesbury rejected abstract and deductive approaches to human social life in favor of approaches that, in his view, were truly persuasive morally. This meant rethinking the character of philosophy as an activity and as a form of writing. In the process, he developed an ironic stance toward the *Inquiry*, his effort at an expository philosophy of sociability. We turn now to those experiences that led him to develop a polite philosophy.

It is worth mentioning that Shaftesbury once called Epicureanism an "un-polite Philosophy." He meant that the Epicurean denial of design, order, and real beauty in the universe obviated the possibility of aesthetic experience as well. Shaftesbury was well aware that the Epicureans had no use for arts and letters.[68] It is not surprising then that Shaftesbury categorized both Hobbes and Locke as "Anti-Virtuosi," who denying the ontological reality of virtue also denied the significance of form.[69]

[68] "Miscellany" II.i, III, 32 (Robertson, II, 175).
[69] P.R.O. 30/24/27/15, p.73r [f.81r].

3   The notebooks: the problem of the self

The notebooks

An Inquiry Concerning Virtue had certainly been completed by 1698, a year marking a rupture in Shaftesbury's life. Elected to the Commons in 1695, he was in the process of making a public name for himself. However, he refused to stand in the elections of 1698 in order to adopt a life of an entirely new character. Instead of actively participating in public matters, assiduously managing the affairs of his family, and otherwise enjoying the social and intellectual life in Town and Country which accompanied his status, he went to Holland where he pursued a studious retirement. The reversal was abrupt, entire and striking. If it suggests the operations of a complicated personality, the suggestion is confirmed in the personal notebooks that he began keeping when he arrived on the Continent in 1698.

"Natural Affection" was the heading under which Shaftesbury commenced his reflections at Rotterdam in August 1698. From the start, he reiterated commitments familiar from the *Inquiry*: the affective basis for human action; an ideal of human moral autarky; a conception of beneficent cosmic order. He defined natural affection as "not that wch is only towards Relations; but towards all Mankind," a universal, caring but disinterested love, informed by a wise acceptance of the overall design of nature. However, having written this, he went on to ask: "When shall this happy Disposition be fix'd, that I may feel it perpetually, as now but seldome? When shall I be intirely thus affected, & feel this as my Part grown naturall to me?"[1] Not only did he experience natural affection only occasionally and partially, but he found reason to doubt the very naturalness of the natural affections. From their opening pages, the notebooks depict Shaftesbury in difficulty.

A parallel pattern is evident under "Deity," the second heading in the notebooks. Here Shaftesbury reiterated his loyalty, first declared in the

[1] P.R.O. 30/24/27/10, p.10 [f.6v].

Inquiry, to an orderly cosmos supervised by a sentient, conscious and intelligent being. However, as under the former heading, the clarity of his assertions was occluded by the questions that followed: "Wch is most shamefull? to think of Providence as those do who count themselves Naturalists; or thinking of Providence as thou dost, to be no otherwise affected than as thou art? Wch of the two is most absurd? to have the Faith of Epicurus & beleive in Atomes; or, being Conscious of Deity to be no otherwise mov'd by his presence, than if He were not, or had no Inspection of our Thought or Action?"[2] Here Shaftesbury was not asserting the reality of an orderly providential reality against an atomistic and mechanical one but rather urgently seeking to match insight into the orderly, providential pattern with an internal condition that registered it.

The opening passages are typical of the notebooks as a whole, which witnessed the psychological landscape in which Shaftesbury's hopes for moral experience were confounded. His life was not proving as tractable as the argumentation in the *Inquiry*, and the prose showed it. The notebooks did not make simple assertions but, rather, continually juxtaposed statement and question. Since the significance of the notebooks emerges in this dynamic interplay of assertion and doubt, they will be examined here not as an elaboration of Shaftesburian views but as a dramatic encounter between those views and the existential reality of an individual.

The notebooks were, in the first place, journals of self-examination. Organized topically, they offer an irregular record of Shaftesbury's inner life, mostly between 1698 and 1704.[3] Shaftesbury is revealed in the notebooks as a gifted offspring of a gilded background, whose hypertrophied sensibility preyed on his inner conflicts to produce a late adolescent crisis, of which the notebooks provided detailed and intellectualized reportage. However, the notebooks were more than inert mirrors of his inner life, since they recorded programs for reform of the self and evaluations of its progress. The notebooks were tools of self-investigation and also of self-command, amounting to a kind of moral workbook. Finally, Shaftesbury wrote much of the material in the notebooks while immersed in deep intellectual engagement with the Roman stoics, Epictetus and Marcus Aurelius. In places, the notebooks were a commonplace book of Greek citations and Shaftesburian commentary.[4]

[2] P.R.O. 30/24/27/10, pp.16, 20, 92 [ff.9v, 11v, 47v].
[3] Many entries were dated (or are dateable by internal evidence), thus providing biographical insight. A major shortcoming of the Benjamin Rand edition of the notebooks, published in 1900 in *The Life, Unpublished Letters, and Philosophical Regimen of Anthony, Earl of Shaftesbury* (London: Swan Sonnenschein & Co., New York: The Macmillan Co.) is the deletion of the dates; it is also selective.
[4] On the character of these works, see chapter 1, note 44.

72 Polite philosophy

Shaftesbury's notebooks are obviously a very different sort of text from the *Inquiry*. While the moral discourse of the *Inquiry* had been inspired by a public quest for cognitive lucidity, that of the notebooks was deeply engaged in personal moral struggle.[5] Since Shaftesbury has been suspect as someone who made virtue too easy, this struggle and its origin in the phenomenon of sociability itself bear examination.

A divided self

The notebooks convince us of the existential impetus behind them. At a moment of crisis, Shaftesbury recalled: "Thus frequently in other Losses of Mind not knowing wch way to turn, when beset, when urg'd, when divided in opinion on Family & Publick – Emergencyes: & in reality Distracted thus. Restless Nights. Throws. Labours. Groans."[6] Such statements attest to Shaftesbury's vibrant sensitivity to the motions of his own mind and, in turn, the responsiveness of those motions to phenomena about him. The tone was not the cheerful and good-natured, indeed, polite, tone that Shaftesbury would praise and project in *Characteristicks*. The notebooks have many dark moments. "All is Corruption, & Rottenness," exclaimed the philosopher of politeness.[7]

The desperation of such passages, which were frequent in the notebooks, was a symptom of what Shaftesbury himself identified as internal conflict:

I have a Part, 'tis true, yt is fitt to come into Company, knows Company, & is known; but another Part yt is not so. I have a laughing, talking Entertaining Part yt dos all with Others, yt admires & is ravishd, wonders, praises, censures,

---

[5] There have been a number of suggestions about the relationship between the notebooks and the *Inquiry*. F. H. Heinemann ("The Philosopher of Enthusiasm," *Revue internationale de philosophie*, 6 (1952), 294–322) argues, as I do, that existential pressure led Shaftesbury to reconsider the position of the *Inquiry*. However, he says that Shaftesbury's emotional crisis forced him to "acknowledge the controlling power of reason" (p.303), a position based on ignoring the role of reason in the *Inquiry*, explored in the last chapter. Robert Voitle emphasizes the complementarity, rather than the tensions, between the notebooks and the *Inquiry*: while the *Inquiry* emphasized the stoic theme of solidarity with others, the notebooks dramatized the stoic pursuit of self-sufficient tranquillity. See *Third Earl of Shaftesbury*, pp.157–163. Esther Tiffany offered a stronger but less tenable stoic interpretation in "Shaftesbury as Stoic," *PMLA*, 38 (1923), 642–684. She recruited Shaftesbury to a tidy version of ancient stoicism, thereby privileging the notebooks over other of Shaftesbury's writings, reducing Shaftesbury's aestheticism to a cool rhetorical ploy for the sake of an ascetically ethical message, and evacuating Shaftesbury's entire discussion of natural affections of any reference to their instinctive and emotional character.

[6] P.R.O. 30/24/27/10, p.291 [f.202r]. The public context of his distress is discussed on pp.137–138 below. Domestically, he had to negotiate testy relations among his mother, his father, and the Dowager Countess, for which see K. H. D. Haley, *The First Earl of Shaftesbury* (Oxford: Clarendon Press, 1968), pp.726–727.

[7] P.R.O. 30/24/27/10, pp.76–77 [ff.39v–40r]; also p.219 [f.166r].

rejoyces, greives, and takes on (as they say) with others: and I have a still Quiet tho' not less active Part yt dos none of all this; neither admires nor lives nor pursues with others; is never pleasd as others are pleas'd; is never angry but with Itself & for what Itself can remedy; bemoans nothing; condoles with nobody; nor has with whom to congratulate.

Shaftesbury portrayed himself as populated by two personalities, one gregarious and extroverted, the other reclusive and introverted, whose diverging propensities were the source of his personal anguish in the years after 1698.

This polarity illuminated the challenge of philosophical pursuit, since the introverted part of the self was nothing other than a philosophic self, with all the marks of a stoic sage: aloof from and impassive before the vicissitudes of human emotion and opinion, it confined its actions to what was within its power. By contrast, the extroverted part of the self, the social self, instigated fears of radical heteronomy and plasticity which were absolutely pernicious to the sagacious ideal. Of the social and philosophical parts of his self, Shaftesbury wrote: "The first of these Parts is a faithless, corrupt, perfidiouse, mutinouse, sacrilegious Part. The Second is an Honest, Friendly, Just, Piouse Part; in Charity with Men, and never at odds with Deity."[8] Shaftesbury's longing for sagacity was set amidst psychological experiences, recorded throughout the notebooks, of vicissitude, passivity, and friability, which put personal identity in question. His inner incompatibilities provoked him to incessant ruminations on the theme, "Who am *I*?", often concluding that "I [may] indeed be said to be lost, or have lost My Self."[9]

It is clear that, in Shaftesbury's notebooks, sociability was a concept under pressure. It confounded the philosophical life but was also inseparable from it, since the philosophical self in its friendliness and charitableness was itself sociable. In fact, Shaftesbury later relabelled the two parts of the self "the familiar conversible, *Sociable* Part" and "ye truly sociable." Thus, in the notebooks, sociability was an ambiguous and labile entity, around which the philosophical struggle for wisdom pivoted. While the philosophical self sought to reconcile both sociability and autonomy, the social self sacrificed its autonomy for the sake of sociability.

Since Shaftesbury is, with good reason, well known as a defender of human sociability, it is important to emphasize his doubts about it. We have already seen, in chapter 2, how the *Inquiry* mounted human sociabi-

---

[8] P.R.O. 30/24/27/10, p.301 [f.207r].
[9] P.R.O. 30/24/27/10, pp.134, 285 [ff.68v, 199r]; also, pp.59–62, 79, 232 [ff.31r–32v, 40r, 172v].

lity against human egoism, but, in the notebooks, sociability was measured against the standard of autonomy and found wanting. This discrepancy stems from two different interpretive axes on which sociability could be located. One of these concerned the orientation of the self and was organized around the polarity of selfishness and altruism. This interpretive axis was the background for Shaftesbury's critique of egoism discussed in chapter 2.

However, the other interpretive axis concerned the control of the self and was organized around the polarity of autonomy and plasticity. To conceive of the self as autonomous implied that the self had a firm and irreducible identity: regardless of its tendencies to selfishness or altruism, it was a stable entity, capable of sovereignly and consistently organizing its own operations and capable of reliably portraying itself to the world. By contrast, admitting the plasticity of the self implied that the identity of the self was always in question: its operations were not underwritten by a central core; it was liable to unreliability, inconsistency, instability, and dependence. It was not autonomous in that, lacking a central core, it was radically conditioned by time, place, and situation. Thus, while the sociable self was the antagonist of the egoistic self, it might also be the enemy of the autonomous self.

Anxieties about the impact of sociability on the stability of the self found expression in the Roman stoics, for whom philosophic capacity depended on a firm distinction between what was within and what was outside one's control.[10] Ordinary humans, instead of following nature and reason, followed the mistaken standards raised by their bodily appetites and drives for wealth, power, and the esteem of others. In contrast, the stoic interrogated all appetites, emotions, and ideas, negotiating human social life with care. Indeed, the later stoics devoted far more energy to mastering the various manifestations of consciousness (*prolēpsis*, "mental picture," *phantasia*, impression, *dogma*, belief, *doxa*, opinion) than to curtailing or redirecting the forms of passion (*orexis*, appetite, *hormē*, impulse). As Marcus Aurelius wrote, "Remember that everything is but what we think it." Or, as Epictetus said, "It is not the things themselves that disturb men, but their judgements about these things."[11] Among the challenges of social life addressed by the stoics was the temptation to sacrifice autonomy for the sake of others' esteem. One had to avoid converting one's achievements into an object of others' admira-

---

[10] Epictetus, *Encheiridion*, 1; also Epictetus, *Discourses* I.ix.31–32.
[11] Marcus Aurelius II.15, p.39; Epictetus, *Encheiridion*, 5, II, 487. For Marcus Aurelius's intellectualism, see III.11, IV.7, V.16, VII.2; for self-exhortations to resist others' opinions, see III.4, IV.3, V.9, VIII.1, XII.4. Similar themes appear in Epictetus, *Discourses* I.xxi.1–4, III.i, III.xvi, III.xxiii, IV.ii.

tion. Epictetus referred critically to this propensity to make a show of oneself, to turn oneself into a display (*epideixis*).[12]

Of course, such anxieties are widely dispersed in the Western tradition. Jonas Barish analyzes them as part of a long debate about theatricality. According to Barish, the anti-theatrical prejudice belongs "to a conservative ethical emphasis in which the key terms are those of order, stability, constancy, and integrity, as against a more existentialist emphasis that prizes growth, process, exploration, flexibility, variety and versatility of response."[13] Barish's polar emphases echo those used by Richard Lanham when he juxtaposes the "central" self and the "social" self. While the former is the model in most philosophical and moralist discussions, the latter is the model of "the rhetorical ideal of life." Since Lanham proposes his polarity in connection with verbal style, he adds to the terms enumerated by Barish the polarity between the central self's seriousness, clarity, and sincerity of expression and the social self's playfulness, opaqueness, and ambiguity. Lanham makes explicit that the poles should be understood not as offering alternatives but rather as defining a standing tension:

The Western self has from the beginning been composed of a shifting and perpetually uneasy combination of *homo rhetoricus* and *homo seriosus*, of a social self and a central self. It is their business to contend for supremacy. To *settle* the struggle would be to end the Greek experiment in a complex self.[14]

In early modern Europe, the destabilizing impact of sociability was linked to new directions in thinking about the self. Whether as passionate self-assertion or prudent calculation, the ego assumed new importance in theories of social life.[15] However, the self-concern of the ego could be assigned opposing valences, positively as a form of power, negatively as a form of need. Conceived as a form of power, the ego was a propulsive and imperialistic self aiming for greater and greater spheres of security and

---

[12] See Epictetus, *Discourses* III.xii.16, used by Shaftesbury in P.R.O. 30/24/27/10, p.1 [f.2r].

[13] Jonas Barish, *The Antitheatrical Prejudice* (Berkeley: University of California Press, 1981), pp.116–117. See the illuminating use of the model of theatricality in Michael Fried, *Absorption and Theatricality: Painting and Beholder in the Age of Diderot* (Berkeley: University of California Press, 1980). David Marshall's treatment of Shaftesbury in *The Figure of Theater* (New York; Columbia University Press, 1986) emphasizes Shaftesbury's failure to fend off the threats to character posed by theatrical sociability.

[14] Richard Lanham, *The Motives of Eloquence: Literary Rhetoric in the Renaissance* (New Haven and London: Yale University Press, 1976), p.6 and more generally pp.1–9.

[15] Albert O. Hirschman, *The Passions and the Interests: Political Arguments for Capitalism before Its Triumph* (Princeton: Princeton University Press, 1977), pp.14–48. An essential resource on early modern psychological language is Norman Fiering. *Moral Philosophy at Seventeenth-Century Harvard* (For the Institute of Early American History and Culture, Williamsburg, Virginia, Chapel Hill: The University of North Carolina Press, 1981).

domination. It was against this conception of the egoistic self that Shaftesbury insisted on the self's sociability. Conceived as a need, however, the ego was radically inadequate, seeking to compensate for absences rather than to conquer and aggrandize. In this model, the appetites of the human spirit parallelled those of the body. Self-love, the self's insatiable psychological hunger for the esteem and love of others, submitted the ego to a regime of ineluctable sociability.[16]

The dangers of social life

Though Shaftesbury did not in the notebooks discuss self-love *per se*, much that he wrote there brings to mind contemporary descriptions of self-love's compulsive search for esteem because he gave a particularly psychological cast to the self's vulnerability. The real menace to the self did not lie in libidinous appetites or material ambitions, but rather in "the Plays, Diversions, Talk, Story-telling, Secrets, Confidence, & whatever else makes up that sort of Convers wch thou art so fond of, with a certain Sett of Friends."[17] This localization of the disorienting power of the world in the seductions of his own sociability was the most striking aspect of Shaftesbury's entire treatment of the self in the notebooks. Association out of "Need" brought a pathological sociability. Thus, the philosopher of sociability, writing of himself, asserted that "the Affection yt draws Thee to Sociable Acts & Commerce with Mankind" was "Sickness, & of a dangerouse kind." Sociability diverted attention from the orderly succession of true ideas to the randomness of common thought and discourse: "a Croud of other Ideas! impertinent, idle, monstrouse, Imaginations & Wild Fancyes rushing in, making havock." This displacement from the real self involved a mistaken fixation on "Name, & Character in the World," the self as it existed in others' opinion.[18]

Sometimes, Shaftesbury formulated the problem of the social self in visual terms: the social self gave itself over to the eye of a beholder, rendering itself an object of spectatorship. He asked:

is it not a thing monstrously preposterouse to be fully & absolutely convincd yt there is a Deity & of the highest Perfection; that He superintends all things, sees & knows all things & is present every where; and yet at the same time to be so little

---

[16] If Thomas Hobbes's writings portrayed the propulsive self, Pierre Nicole's showed how egoistic need laid the basis of society.

[17] P.R.O. 30/24/27/10, p.94 [f.48v]; also, p.106 [f.54v]. Shaftesbury's stoic favorites repeatedly addressed the need to corral sexual appetite and Shaftesbury was pleased by passages in Xenophon's *Memorabilia* in which Socrates lauded sexual self-control; but Shaftesbury's sexuality was sufficiently attenuated or displaced that "the hankering after Flesh" merited only the occasional reprimand. P.R.O. 30/24/27/10, p.230 [f.171v]. On Shaftesbury's own sexuality, see Voitle, *Third Earl of Shaftesbury*, pp.242–244.

[18] P.R.O. 30/24/27/10, pp.85, 122–123, 176 [ff.44r, 62v–63r, 89v].

affected by such a presence as to have more regard even for the commonest human Eye?[19]

However, in Shaftesbury's notebooks, the problem of the self was more consistently conveyed in discursive rather than visual terms: the social self gave itself over to the terms of the other, becoming the victim or prisoner of the other's language. In this connection, Shaftesbury cited one of the Epictetan admonitions: "Avoid entertainments given by outsiders and by persons ignorant of philosophy ... For you may rest assured, that, if a man's companion be dirty, the person who keeps close company with him must of necessity get a share of his dirt, even though he himself happens to be clean."[20] Conversation brought humans into contact on the basis of a common language. The desire to suppress disagreement and create impressions of consensus was a powerful force for conformity. However, if the self simply accepted the given terms, then it became oriented to the other, playing along, pleasing the other through pliability. In this way of casting the situation, the self was caught between the *voice* of the world and the *voice* of wisdom.

Because common language was a force hard to resist, Shaftesbury felt a need to fix or objectify it, so as to call it into question and undermine its power. He constantly quoted the commonplaces of the day, subjecting them to ruminative examination. Take this passage:

See thy Self. Be thy Self. First then, as Who? – A Man: not (as they say) a meer Earthling. not a worldling, but of the true World? – a Man of Quality – What Quality? the Herald-Quality? Patent-Quality? Court-Quality? or Progenitors Courtiers? (worthy Men!) Progenitrices of the Court? (worthy Women!) .... Noble Pedigree! unquestionable Pedigree! Noble Thoughts, Life, Manners, Employment of Time! Happy Great Ones! Noble and highly privilegd Great ones! See to wt privilegd, to wt entitled! ...... This is *Quality* .... and is there no better? is this the Derivation; and is there no better? is this the Breeding, Education, Instruction; and is there no better, no higher?[21]

The obvious point was that society's idea of "Quality" was highly conditioned and different from a truly philosophical understanding of the term. However, perhaps more noteworthy was Shaftesbury's effort to textualize the discourse of society and subvert it in the course of rearticulating it. It was as if Shaftesbury had to speak louder than "the world" and so, in these passages, the discourse of "the world" was being captured and stabilized, debated and defeated. Writing to and for himself, he could take grammatical shortcuts, excluding indicative syntax, distributing ellipses generously, implying points by a juggle of exclamation and

[19] P.R.O. 30/24/27/10, p.103 [f.53r]; also pp.42–43, 81, 188, 193 [ff.22v–23r, 43r, 150v, 153r].
[20] Epictetus, *Encheiridion* 33, II, 516–519.
[21] P.R.O. 30/24/27/10, pp.201–202 [ff.157r–v].

interrogation. Such writing abounds in the notebooks, and some of it even found its way into *Characteristicks*.[22]

In another instance, he castigated his admiration of outward things: "*a celebrated Beauty! a Palace! Seat! Gardens! Pictures! Italy! a Feast! a Carnivall.*" In such apostrophes, the writing echoed the talk of the Town, presented here in order to be invalidated, dessicated, and shrunk. Indeed, we find Shaftesbury trying, in the notebooks, to blunt the force of the language of "politeness" itself. Tucked in one of his notebooks appeared the minatory note: "Remember the Modern Theophraste, who calles Politeness, a more refin'd sort of Flattery. examine therefore what Politeness is consistent with Simplicity, & what not." The passage suggested not the rejection of politeness as much as the contention between different versions of it. One of these was a cosmetic or theatrical politeness. As Shaftesbury wrote: "What are all those Forms & Manners wch come under the notion of good-breeding? the affected smiles, the fashionable Bows, the Tone of Voice, & all those supple, carressing & ingratiating ways? what is this but Embroidery, Guilding, Colouring, Daubing?" The purveyors of this language "speak knowingly" of "Behaviour & Carriage," "talk of nothing but Ease, Freedome, Liberty, Unconcerndness," but the techniques that make one "agreeable in company" are "utterly wrong, harsh, dissonant; out of Measure & Tone."[23] Politeness as the art of pleasing others was fundamentally misdirected since it fixed the self's course by reference to others. As his own conflicts reveal, such politeness was highly seductive, but Shaftesbury sought to resist it, as we will see, in the name of a higher politeness.

Ordinary conversation posed other dangers too. The person who did not conform was liable to become its object: "But what will my Carriage be in company? how shall I appear in Conversation? – Dangerouse consequences! but of what kind? – least I be calld *Ill-bred*; least I be thought *Dull*, & deserve not to be calld *a Good Companion*."[24] The moral pressure on the individual came not only from the false ideas and values of the "world"'s discourse but also from the "world"'s criticism of those who rebelled against it. Many passages in the notebooks attested to Shaftesbury's vulnerability before others' judgment and his struggle to defend himself against them.

[22] There are instances in "Soliloquy" III.ii and "Moralists" III.i (in Theocles' apostrophe to Nature).
[23] P.R.O. 30/24/27/10, pp.67, 69, 79–80 [ff.35r, 36r–37v, 41r–v]. There were numerous candidates in England for a modern Theophrastus, not to mention Jean de La Bruyère, author of *Caractères* (1688), its imitators, and its translators. See Chester Noyes Greenough, *A Bibliography of the Theophrastan Character in English* (Cambridge, Mass.: Harvard University Press, 1947).
[24] P.R.O. 30/24/27/10, pp.59–62 [ff.31r–v].

In light of the hostility between a "real character" and a nugatory social self, Shaftesbury was inclined to flee the human eye and evade the human voice. Since "the world" displaced one from the self, one might only be able to constitute oneself as a substantial character in retirement and privacy. Shaftesbury's notebooks contained exhortations to withdraw from the dizzying society of others: "the Safety is in Retirement from all this sort of Convers:."[25] Such sentiments explain Shaftesbury's periods of withdrawal, notably his two stays in Holland.

However, retirement was an untenable solution. Not even in withdrawal did one elude the "eye" or the "voice" of others. Reflective contemplation could itself degenerate into "the wretched Pomp and Fucus of Meditations" engaged in "for others or with a Thought towards Others."[26] One was always in danger of parading one's virtues because the morally distracting consciousness of the other could follow one even into retreat and contemplative retirement. Therefore, Shaftesbury did not urge a radical fleeing from all civilization. As Shaftesbury knew, Marcus Aurelius had written to himself: "Men seek out retreats for themselves in the country, by the seaside, on the mountains, and thou too art wont to long intensely for such things. But all this is unphilosophical to the last degree, when thou canst at a moment's notice retire into thyself."[27] Physical retirement in itself was a sterile exercise, but the figurative retirement of an expanded interiority was deeply philosophical and a route that we will observe Shaftesbury exploring.

Besides, retirement provided no basis for a rational sociability, which was the destiny of humans. As much as the *Inquiry*, the notebooks proclaimed that humans were designed for company.[28] Like Cicero before him and for similar reasons, Shaftesbury ultimately rejected the austerest claims of stoic sagacity.[29] Shaftesbury's own social position and that of his explicit audience shaped his enterprise. He had to produce a notion of virtue which the gentleman could embrace. To be a gentleman in England was to have a public standing, to exist in the eyes of others: it required a substantial social dimension, which any ethic devised for the gentleman would have to take into account.

Thus, Shaftesbury's ultimate stance was not to evade the membrane between self and society, despite the tension he felt there. He seems to have experienced in a particularly intense way (and, luckily for us, recorded in a remarkably extensive way) the stress that social life placed

---

[25] P.R.O. 30/24/27/10, p.122 [f.62v]; also, pp.81, 125 [ff.42v, 64r].
[26] P.R.O. 30/24/27/10, p.188 [f.150v]; also, pp.104–105 [ff.53v–54r].
[27] Marcus Aurelius IV.3, p.67.
[28] For instance, P.R.O. 30/24/27/10, pp.31, 268 [ff.17r, 190v].
[29] Alain Michel, *Rhétorique et philosophie chez Cicéron* (Paris: Presses Universitaires de France, 1960), pp.113–114.

on the integrity of the self. Nonetheless, Shaftesbury aimed to negotiate this treacherous terrain, establishing, in the face of the difficulties outlined so far, a stable character that began in the inner life and ended in a reliable outward stamp. Shaftesbury's program for philosophy emerged from the need to resolve the claims of both moral autarky and sociability. Similarly, Shaftesbury did not ultimately reject politeness but rather reconstructed it. That reconstruction proceeded in the notebooks alongside Shaftesbury's condemnations of the pernicious form of politeness. While this chapter has sketched the anxieties about the social self recorded in Shaftesbury's notebooks, the next two discuss the reconstruction of politeness. The instrument of that reconstruction was a regimen, a set of patterns that began as strenuous exercise and became second nature. Politeness was initiated in the inner man by a moral training of a sort we must now investigate.

The problematic representation of human sociability in the notebooks suggests an interesting development in relation to *An Inquiry Concerning Virtue*. While Shaftesbury's earliest philosophical endeavor was substantially an attack on egoism in the name of philosophical sociability, the notebooks pointed up the challenges posed by sociability itself to human ethics and to moral autarky. The *Inquiry* had criticized the impoverishment of the isolated life, but the notebooks portrayed isolation as a refuge from the dangers of sociability. Moreover, as opposed to the confident intellectual examination of the grounds of the moral life in the *Inquiry*, the manuscript notebooks cast doubt on Shaftesbury's personal ability to achieve wisdom. Though the notebooks continued many themes of the *Inquiry*, they did so in another key entirely and with a much grimmer sense of the difficulties of moral realization. This shift in tone, this deepening of the moral picture, was reflected in the quality of the discourse itself. The logical and expository discourse of the *Inquiry* gave way in the notebooks to a highly personal discussion whose self-apostrophic form expressed the tensions revealed. Mixing the declarative, the interrogative, and the imperative, the notebooks constituted a massive project in self-discourse, an extended interaction between inner voice and inner addressee. As such, the notebooks reflected negatively on the adequacy of the ethical discourse practiced in the *Inquiry*: the expository philosophical exercise was shown to be insufficient as a transformative moral discourse.

4 The notebooks: philosophy in the inner life

"Training"

On the binding of the first volume of one set of his notebooks, Shaftesbury inscribed the Greek word, *Askēmata*, "exercises," which can be taken as a title for the notebooks. The later Roman stoic inspiration for the title is clear enough, since, on the first page of this volume, Shaftesbury copied passages from the chapter in Arrian's Epictetus, *Peri askēseōs*, "Of training" or "Of exercise."[1] However, the title indicates more than intellectual genealogy, for it describes the function of the notebooks.

The chapter *Peri askēseōs* revealed a central preoccupation of Epictetus, namely, the training that conduced to wisdom. Wisdom arose in the willingness to limit strivings to what was within the power of the moral athlete or, in Epictetus's characteristic vocabulary, "within the sphere of his moral purpose [*proairesis*]." The sphere of moral purpose was that of will and choice.[2] Since wisdom was identified with a rigorous ideal of moral autonomy, training aimed to enhance acting "without hindrance in choice [*orexis*] and in aversion [*ekklisis*]." Training was necessitated by the fact that habit, *ethos*, was "a powerful influence," and men were usually habituated to direct their choice and aversion only over external things. As Epictetus wrote, "if you allow training to turn outwards, towards the things that are not in the realm of moral purpose, you will have neither your desire successful in attaining what it would, nor your aversion successful in avoiding what it would." The response of the therapeutic stoic was to "set a contrary habit to counteract this habit."[3]

---
[1] Epictetus, *Discourses* III.xii, II, 81–87. *Askēsis* means "exercise," "practice," or "training." It is the etymological source of the English "ascetic." Benjamin Rand aptly called the notebooks a "regimen" in his edition (*The Life, Unpublished Letters, and Philosophical Regimen of Anthony, Earl of Shaftesbury*, London: Swan Sonnenschein & Co., New York: The Macmillan Co., 1900).
[2] The instrument that, in stoic writings, enabled humans to achieve wisdom was their own rational ordering and controlling part, the *hēgemonikon*, which ordered the soul so that it shared in the rational and orderly traits of the cosmos. See J. M. Rist, *Stoic Philosophy* (Cambridge: Cambridge University Press, 1969), pp.24–25, 30–31, 215–216, 220, 229–230.
[3] Epictetus, *Discourses* III.xii.3–6, II, 81–83. See also II.xviii.4–5 and III.xxii.13.

Thus, stoic exercise was a matter of rehabituation by contraries, a dialectical process.

Shaftesbury read the Roman stoics as guides to the practice of self-formation – technicians of the moral and cognitive personality – and his notebooks project a similarly therapeutic role for philosophy.[4] For Shaftesbury, philosophy provided fundamental perspectives on humanity, nature, and the cosmos, but it also had to provide the mechanisms by which the questing self might near its goals. Shaftesbury once wrote that the pursuit of wisdom was "not ye Work of Speculation meerly. 'Tis not a Newton, or Archimedes, yt excell in this. or can give help to others. There is stubborn Will to work on. Appetites & Humours, Passions & Desires are to be dealt with. and this is a Province those Philosophers are as much strangers to, as much at a Loss in, as ye Vulgar." This perception of the poverty of theory led Shaftesbury to reiterate frequently in the notebooks the practical orientation of philosophy. His aim was "inward Economy," "right Discipline, Conduct & Economy," and he elucidated the practical thrust in a range of figures – dietary, calisthenic, artisanal.[5] This emphasis in the notebooks pointed to the definitions of philosophy in the later printed works. In "Soliloquy," philosophy aimed "to teach us *our-selves*, keep us the *self-same* Persons, and so regulate our governing Fancys, Passions, and Humours, as to make us comprehensible to our-selves, and knowable by other Features than those of a bare Countenance." In "Miscellaneous Reflections," philosophy was "*Mastership in* LIFE and MANNERS."[6]

Moreover, the notebooks were a part of the therapeutic process because writing could stabilize the activity of self-reflection and perhaps thereby advance the process of moral transformation. According to Shaftesbury, the notebooks bore the same relation to the ethical life as the jottings of other practitioners (carpenters, architects, sculptors, mathematicians) did to their own work: "Why this flourishing, drawing, figuring over & over, ye same skill? what for? – What but for the Art? Not for shew: but for Exercize, Practice, Improvement... Go on then. Exercize & Write."[7] The notebooks discussed ethical processes but also actuated them. On Shaftesbury's own terms, the notebooks and the interior pro-

---

[4] On the antique sources of self-formative practice, see Michel Foucault, *The Technologies of the Self*, ed. Luther H. Martin, Huck Gutman, and Patrick Hutton (Amherst: The University of Massachusetts Press, 1988), pp.21–46. For the meditative tradition in early modern Europe, see Louis L. Martz, *The Poetry of Meditation*, rev. edn (New Haven and London: Yale University Press, 1962), pp.118–127, 150–174.

[5] P.R.O. 30/24/22/4, Shaftesbury to "Tiresias," February 5, 1704; P.R.O. 30/24/27/10, pp.64, 71, 82, 102 [ff.33v, 37r, 42v, 52v].

[6] "Soliloquy" III.i, I, 283 (Robertson, I, 184); "Miscellany" III.i, III, 159 (Robertson, II, 254).

[7] P.R.O. 30/24/27/10, pp.191–192 [f.152r–v].

cesses they recorded constituted philosophical activity at its most basic degree, what we might call the fundamental form of the philosophical life.[8]

Interiority

Since the attempt to construct a reliable moral self was undertaken in the midst of a social undertow threatening constantly to undermine the project, the central moral problem in the notebooks was that of mastering sociability. The solution given in the notebooks to this central moral problem was the enhancement of the individual's moral autonomy through the expansion and elaboration of human interiority. On lines suggested by the Roman stoics, Shaftesbury's interior space was potentially a sphere of control, in which the shaping influences of the outside world could be stilled, examined, and appraised.

In the notebooks, Shaftesbury exhorted himself to adopt an active inner life. "Resolve therefore Never to forget *Thy Self*," he wrote and, recalling the inner conflicts described in the last chapter, he proceeded: "How long is it that thou wilt continue thus to act two different parts, & be two different Persons? Call to mind what thou art . . . recollect thy Self wholly within thy Self. be One intire & self same Man: and wander not abroad, so as to loose sight of *the End*, but keep that constantly in view."[9] His experience of personal fragmentation brought forth a breathtakingly ambitious project of self-organization, a thoroughly centered self, integral and consistent. In this passage, the philosophical project was a task of concentration, which provided a spatial metaphor for the philosophical self as tightly located. However, concentration also provided a description of the mental pattern of the philosophical self. The passage was riddled with the language of mental absorption: not forgetting, calling to mind, recollecting, not losing sight, keeping in view. Elsewhere, Shaftesbury's urge to concentrate found support in stoic discussions of *prosokhē*, "attention."[10]

---

[8] Shaftesbury's notebooks (P.R.O. 30/24/27/10) are filled with "rules" to match their imperative diction: "Endeavour now at this Season, & in the midst of this, to recall any of those principall Rules" (p.107 [f.55r]; also, pp.83, 96, 188–190 [ff.43r, 49v, 150v–151v]). One eccentric product of Shaftesbury's regimen was an actual table of moral practice, a Shaftesburian decalogue, lifted from the works of Marcus Aurelius and Epictetus and intended as a cursory guide for his own ethical life: P.R.O. 30/24/27/10, pp.2–9 [ff.2v–6r], and P.R.O. 30/24/27/11 (sheets of vellum folded into a little booklet).
[9] P.R.O. 30/24/27/10, p.59 [f.31r]. This passage echoed repeated calls in Marcus Aurelius to self-recollection: IV.3, VI.11, VII.28, VIII.48.
[10] P.R.O. 30/24/27/10, pp.84, 167, 205, 207 [ff.43v, 85r, 159, 160]. Arrian gave the heading, "Of attention," to a chapter in which Epictetus urged the unflagging habit of attending to one's *proairesis*, moral personality. Epictetus warned that not paying attention deferred

Attentiveness, reflecting the late stoic concern with mastering one's own mental life, may seem a peculiarly intellective version of the will, but Shaftesbury did not use psychological terms in a systematic way.[11] Therefore, his procedures of moral rehabilitation addressed a psychology in which affective, intellectual, and voluntarist elements combined. His moral regimen was directed at both "Temper," the libidinal and temperamental dimension of personality, and "Ideas," the intellectual and discursive dimension.

Resignation and engagement

In discussing the training of the emotions, Shaftesbury invoked what he called "the Sovereign Precept," namely, "*to cutt off the orexis* [desire], and *to use strongly the ekklisis* [aversion]." The precept was, more or less, an Epictetan slogan, with which Shaftesbury was well acquainted.[12] What pruning desire and deploying aversion meant for Shaftesbury was "in a reall sence *Dejection, Mortification* and nothing less": "the depressing, extinguishing, killing that wrong sort of Joy & enliven'd Temper: the starving, supplanting that Exuberant, Luxuriant Fancy, the sapping & undermining of the Passions, ... and ye introducing a Contrary Disposition; vizt ye wean'd, allay'd, low, sunk; that wch creates a mean & poor Opinion of outward things."[13] Since the edifice of mind was raised on the emotions, the emotions had to be manipulated to provide a stable and uniform base. The goal was not eradicating desire but controlling it, replacing an untoward disposition with another more advantageous one. Shaftesbury's qualitative characterization of the emotions depicted two different emotional palettes, each with its concomitant mental outlook: one was florid and giddy; the other, sparse and somber. Emotional giddiness provided too fertile a ground for imagination and opinion. Since mental composure required a more ascetic emotional basis, the jungle of untrammelled and free-ranging desire had to be transformed into a more arid landscape through training.

While the passage just examined might suggest that Shaftesbury sought

---

"tranquil and appropriate living": Epictetus, *Discourses* IV.xii, II, 422–429; also IV.iii.7. Marcus Aurelius did not use the term *prosokhē*, but mental control was a major theme of his reflections: III.4, III.11, V.11, V.36.

[11] See Grean, *Shaftesbury's Philosophy*, pp.145–149, 221–226. Though Grean often discusses Shaftesbury as if Shaftesbury were writing a philosophical treatise on human psychology, his account of psychological language in Shaftesbury accurately indicates the changes in emphasis and the failures of system.

[12] P.R.O. 30/24/27/10, p.171 [f.87r]. The source was Epictetus, *Discourses* III.xii.16. Shaftesbury incribed the passage on the first page of the notebook, under the head *Askēmata*.

[13] P.R.O. 30/24/27/10, p.171 [f.87r].

emotional reduction at all costs, another passage depicted the two emotional palettes as extremes, each ineligible in its own way.

The Overthrow of all Character is from an over promising, or desponding View of Affaires adminsterd. tho' originally it is from ye first yt all ill arises. The first leads to a sort of Undertaking; ye other to a Resigning: both equally wrong. Matters having a little succeeded, Self-Applause arises, and hence Engagemt & Forewardness, beyond ye Measure & True Tone of Life. On the other side, Matters growing ill, or succeeding a little worse than ordinary, Self-Disparagement arises & thence Aversion to all Business, Love of Privacy, and violent Affection of Retreat & Obscurity .... Meer Pusilanimity! as ye other was Rashness & meer Madness.[14]

Here Shaftesbury endorsed indifference (*apatheia*) and equanimity (*ataraxia*) as accompaniments to engagements in the world. The would-be stoic sought the delicate balance of the worldly ascetic, in the world though not of it. He might teeter in either of two directions. On one side was optimistic and enthusiastic engagement, which responded volatilely to promising developments in the world. The precipitousness of such engagement disturbed moral peace drawing one's resources away from the interior domain of control. Moreover, "self-applause" accompanying this optimism suggested the unsound neediness of the self. On the other side was pessimism, which responded to unpromising developments with despair, disengagement, and, ultimately, hermetic retreat. Like the optimistic, this response precipitously violated evenness of temper. The "affectation" that accompanied it suggested that retreat could lead to the same inauthenticity as engagement.

The two emotional palettes were the bases of Shaftesbury's social and philosophical selves described in the last chapter. They also corresponded to the self's social options, engagement versus retirement, sociability versus isolation – options between which Shaftesbury himself gravitated over the course of his life. (Indeed, later in this study, these options will modulate again: in chapter 6, into options for the writing of philosophy, and in part II into models of cultural organization.) Neither in itself was satisfactory. Isolation, of course, violated the basic sociability of humans, since it embodied egoistic individualism. However, social engagement might degenerate into meretricious gregariousness and, in the end, an abandonment of the self and the loss of autonomy. These polar alternatives posed Shaftesbury with a recurring dilemma, which he repeatedly resolved by passing through its horns. Rational sociability or politeness aimed to evade the dangers of sociability without incurring those of isolation.

[14] P.R.O. 30/24/27/10, p.386 [f.249v].

If, as in the previous passage, the human temper was suspended between poles of expectation and dejection, the solution to such pendular movements was an object of training. Moreover, the very polarity of the emotions was the basis for a dialectical method. The principle of the regimen was a deliberate self-contrariness. The over-florid emotional palette had to be countered by the self-conscious pursuit of pallor and grayness, and vice versa. Echoing Epictetus, who had himself urged a regimen with this structure, Shaftesbury asserted that "the best Practice & Exercise is to go by Contraryes, just in the teeth of Temper, just opposite of Humour."[15] The recipe for balance was the deliberate setting in motion of a temperamental dialectic: in the face of good fortune, the calling forth of diffidence; in that of bad fortune, confidence.

Self-discourse

Something similar appeared in Shaftesbury's prescriptions for control of the ideational zone of human psychic experience, the zone of "ideas," "images," "fancies," and "appearances."[16] Moral fitness depended on entertaining the proper "images" and "fancies" with the correct meanings: "Safety, & Security" resided in "the aptness, readyness, vigour & piercingness of the right Images, Appearances, Rules & in the habit of the Mind this way."[17] One had to be sure that one was responding to the correct images. Moreover, they had to be able to take effect: they had to find a resonance in the mind, and the mind had to be habituated to respond.

Since it was easy for the self to entertain the wrong ideas and fancies or to invest the right ideas and fancies with the wrong meanings, Shaftesbury was concerned with "the right Use of Ideas & Appearances" or, in the Greek expression he adopted, *khrēsis phantasiōn*. The manipulation of ideas was a call to activate mental procedures to combat the force of false ideas and impressions. With this mental militia in the field, "hardly can any Appearance arise, hardly can there by any Object ever so remote or forreign but what the Mind will accommodate to itself, & turn to its own use." If the mind did not harness the force of ideas and impressions for its own use, then that force would buffet the mind in unpredictable and dangerous ways. Mental self-possession meant that true notions dominated, effecting the analogue between self and cosmic order: "The *daimōn*

---

[15] P.R.O. 30/24/27/10, p.366 [f.239v]; also p.386 [f.249v].

[16] These were Shaftesbury's English equivalents for *phantasia*, the term used by Epictetus (the Latin *visum*), though *dogmata* (opinions) and *prolēpseis* (preconceptions) were also at issue.

[17] P.R.O. 30/24/27/10, p.96 [f.49v].

[soul] and *to daimonion* [the Divine power]. The *to hēgemonikon* [the ruling principle of the self] and *to theion* [the Divine]. Coppy & Originall."[18]

One important way that Shaftesbury figured the imposition of order on the inner world was aesthetic. The Mind, he wrote, was a kind of artist, subjecting its materials (ideas, images and so forth) to formal criteria.[19] However, as chapter 3 pointed out, Shaftesbury deployed other figures more prominently than that of the fine arts in elucidating the mental world. This is evident in his treatment of "inversion," a term which specified further the character of the *khrēsis phantasiōn*, that "right Modelling or Molding" of mental materials. Inversion transformed "Fancyes or Appearances" by "the wresting of them from their own naturall & vulgar sence into a meaning truly Naturall & free of all delusion & imposture."[20] For instance, the idea of wealth had to be "inverted" so that it no longer referred, as in everyday usage, to material riches but referred instead to wisdom. Inversion amounted to self-conscious transvaluation, strategically set against everyday linguistic practice, as a therapeutic tool in Shaftesbury's mental life. This notion of semantic transformation operating at the heart of the notebooks anticipated the transvaluative strategies used in Shaftesbury's published writing.[21]

Moreover, the idea of inversion recapitulated in the domain of ideas the sort of contrariness noted in Shaftesbury's treatment of temper. The technique of the moral life depended on the plasticity of meaning. The manipulation of ideas, fancies, and appearances was a matter of countering statement with counter-statement, thesis with antithesis: it was the deliberate effort of the mind and soul to move in a direction contrary to that of everyday opinion.

This dialectical characteristic is evident wherever in the notebooks Shaftesbury engaged in the activity of inversion, and he so engaged frequently. For example:

What is the Subject? is it Riches? or a Title? Is it a Female? Is it Renown & Credit? – *My Name will be famouse!* – amongst Whome? in what place? for how long? What if it were to reach to Asia? what if to continue a thousand years, or more?

[18] P.R.O. 30/24/27/10, pp.112, 128–129, 210 [ff.57v, 65v–66r, 161v]. Epictetus recorded that Diogenes had taught *khrēsis phantasiōn*, "power to deal with external impressions": *Discourses* III.xxiv.69, II, 206–207. See also Epictetus, *Discourses* I.xxvii and II.xviii regarding *phantasia*, impressions, and I.xxii regarding *prolēpseis*, preconceptions. For various transvaluative exercises, see P.R.O. 30/24/27/10, [f.221v] and subsequent pages.
[19] P.R.O. 30/24/27/10, p.191 [f.152r]; also, pp.112, 129–130, 241, 286 [ff.57r, 66r–v, 177r, 199v].
[20] P.R.O. 30/24/27/10, pp.112, 126 [ff.57v, 64v].
[21] See chapter 1 on the transvaluation of politeness and philosophy and chapter 8 on the transvaluation of enthusiasm.

88   Polite philosophy

Erostratus has a Name. Alexander has a Name. What is this to them, now at this time? What was it then during their life? What is Fame? – a certain Sound. – of what kind? of Trumpets, Timbrels, Drums? – No. but of Tongues. – of what Tongues? of such as are govern'd by reason, or that have any regular and steady Motion, or that are consonant to themselves? – No: but on the contrary, that are irrationally govern'd, Wild, incohaerent, inconsonant. What, therefore, is Fame?[22]

The passage illustrates the method of re-educating the self by wresting a word from its usual associations and resituating it. The passage presupposed the attractiveness of fame in everyday usage, against which it offered a series of alternative and antagonistic meanings. In place of fame's attractions were set its finitude, perishability, insubstantiality, and irrationality. What makes this sort of operation dialectical is that, when successful, the opposition moved the mind. Whether in the thinking or the writing or the reading and rereading, the process had value as persuasion.

Equally important, this dialectical process was represented discursively. The movements of the mind were given the form of verbal interchange among voices. This passage was a textual version of an inner discussion, though its exact dynamics may be unclear. Not a dialogue of equals, the discussion was rather like a Socratic dialogue, in which one voice was persuasively interrogatory and the other was passively indicative. In fact, a reading of the passage suggests not so much dialogue as forensic speech mimicking the rhythms of dialogue: a rhetorical juggernaut of question and answer, moving ineluctably toward a conclusion. Whatever the exact parameters, the passage presumed a discursive situation, a situation of speakers and listeners. In other words, Shaftesbury figured the inner world as a realm in which the conditions and capacities of discourse were applicable.

The discursivity of the inner life can be inferred from other passages in the notebooks that are similar to the one about "fame."[23] However, Shaftesbury himself was quite explicit about his intent in this regard. Elaborating on the techniques of *khrēsis phantasiōn*, Shaftesbury wrote:

There is nothing more usefull in the management of the *Visa* [images] or yt helps to fight more strongly agt ye striking Imaginations, than to learn a sort of custome of putting them into words, making them speak out & explain themselves as it were *viva voce*, and not tacitely & murmeringly; not by a Whisper & indirect Insinuation, imperfectly, indistinctly & confusedly, as their common way is.[24]

Here was an exhortation to actuate an inner world of conversations and speeches. Shaftesbury demanded a logocentric effort to translate dis-

---
[22] P.R.O. 30/24/27/10, p.111 [f.57r]. Cf. Marcus Aurelius on fame: IV.3, IV.19, VI.16, VIII.37.
[23] See, for instance, P.R.O. 30/24/27/10, pp.96, 274 [f.49v,193v].
[24] P.R.O. 30/24/27/10, p.97 [f.50r].

positions, affections, appearances, and ideas into words so that inner discourse could proceed. The power that the mind could obtain over the fancies and appearances was a function of the degree to which the fancies and appearances could be forced into discourse. Shaftesbury continued:

> These are the Dialogues that are to be studdyed, & dwelt upon, written, meditated, revolv'd. These are the Discourses we should be vers'd in . . . Let me learn to reason & discourse thus with my own Mind: that I may be no longer inconsistent with my Self & my own Reason, and live in perpetuall Disorder & Perplexity. Let me examine my Ideas, challeng & talk with them thus, before they be admitted to pass. *Idea! wayt a little. stay for me, till I am ready: till I have recollected Myself: Come on. Let us see. What art Thou? from Whence?*[25]

Shaftesbury introduced speech into the inner world as a means of restoring health. The fundamental method of moral rehabilitation, the unlearning and relearning that constituted the reformulation of habits, was discursive. The "Art" of *khrēsis phantasiōn* was ultimately an art of discourse: "This is the right Use of Ideas & Appearances . . . This is the Art & Method to be learnt: how to put these into Words; so as to reason with them: force them to speak; hear their Language & return them their answer. This is ye Rhetorick, Eloquence & Witt wch we should affect."[26]

This depiction of the discursive operations of the philosophical mind was the heart of Shaftesbury's notebooks. The personal crisis to which the notebooks bore witness was a crisis of sociability. The central problem was not substituting sociability for egoism (the problem posed in *An Inquiry Concerning Virtue*) but constituting a moral self out of ineluctable sociability. Moreover, a highly important and characteristic way in which this problem of sociability presented itself was discursive. Therefore, autonomous selfhood depended on one's having a clear and distinct inner voice: "Who governs, or What? . . . Learn by ye Voices. Who speaks with a high Tone? who decides & gives Judgment? Who has ye Talk? ye Last Word?" Such a voice was required to engage and establish stable relations with the voices of the world outside one. He put it succinctly: "*Am I talk'd with? Or do I talk?*" The inner voice was a necessity for moral action: "for something still there is yt talks within and leads that very Discours wch leads in Action & is wt we call *conduct.*"[27]

---

[25] P.R.O. 30/24/27/10, pp.110–111 [ff.56v–57r].
[26] P.R.O. 30/24/27/10, p.112 [f.57v]. One of the appeals of the later Roman stoic texts was their own self-discursive properties. As Mikhail Bakhtin pointed out, Marcus Aurelius and Epictetus were "masters" of the genre of soliloquy, which aimed at "the discovery of the *inner man* – 'one's own self,' accessible not to passive self-observation but only through an *active dialogic approach to one's own self*": *Problems of Dostoevsky's Poetics*, trans. Caryl Emerson (Minneapolis: University of Minnesota Press, 1984), p.120. The texts of each provided models of philosophy as discursive action.
[27] P.R.O. 30/24/27/10, p.275 [f.194r].

Inner discourse was the most conspicuous feature in the project of self-construction to which the notebooks were dedicated. Though they recounted the liabilities that accompanied the plasticity of the human self, they also sought to convert that very plasticity into a resource of selfhood. The essence of philosophy was self-making and self-transformation. Moreover, this deeply discursive interpretation of philosophy shaped Shaftesbury's notion of philosophy as public discourse. Since the point of all moral reflection was the creation of the moral self, ethical insight without existential realization was sterile. The philosophical process involved prying the autonomous self from its adhesion to the social. Its success depended on its capacity to construct and activate the autonomous self. This was the informing goal of Shaftesbury's later published writings, of *Characteristicks* as a whole. Its informing means were discursive.

5 Philosophy in society

"Character"

The word "character" encapsulated Shaftesbury's answer to the problem of the self, since it referred to the qualities of consistency, unity and autonomy, founded on well-developed interiority, that defined the philosophical being and moral actor.[1] The term's etymology, of which Shaftesbury was well aware, suggested its purchase. The noun could be traced to a complex of ideas arising from the Greek verb, *kharasso*, meaning, among other things, "to sharpen," "to brand," "to stamp," and "to engrave."[2] Thus, the Greek *kharaktēr* had the capacity to relate contrasting ideas: while the term presupposed the malleability of the object stamped, it also implied the stability of the stamp on the object; while it referred to the outward appearance, it might also refer to an underlying pattern.

This capacity of the word *kharaktēr* to coordinate the self's plasticity and durability as well as its interior and exterior manifestations was evident in an Epictetan injunction, favored by Shaftesbury: "Lay down for yourself, at the outset, a certain stamp and type of character [*kharaktēra kai tupon*] for yourself, which you are to maintain whether you are by yourself or are meeting with people."[3] While assuming that the self must model itself, the injunction also insisted on the durability of character.

---

[1] Though Shaftesbury sometimes used "character" as an equivalent of "self" (P.R.O. 30/24/27/10, pp.134, 142, 369, 386 [ff.68v, 72v, 241r, 249v]), he elsewhere assigned it special status as the ideal of selfhood, "our very true & genuine Selves" (P.R.O. 30/24/27/10, pp.59–62, 220 [ff.31r–32v, 166v]).

[2] The sense of sharpening led to several other words (*kharax, kharaktes*) associated with stakes, fences, and palisades; it suggested the materials with which boundaries are established, an apt sense for Shaftesbury's interest in "character." The other sense of the verb *kharasso*, making an impression of one sort or another, led to the word *kharaktēr*, which had several senses: the performer of the action, the engraver or the one doing the stamping; the instrument responsible for the action, the die, the stamp, the branding iron; and the impression itself, the mark engraved, stamped, branded. By extension, it became also the distinctive mark or pattern of a person or thing.

[3] Epictetus, *Encheiridion* 33.1, II, 516–517. Cf. P.R.O. 30/24/27/10, pp.2, 134, 362 [ff.2v, 68v, 237v].

Moreover, modeling pertained to and related both the form of the inner life and the shape of self-presentation. "Character" expressed both the drive for a well-modeled inwardness and the recognition that ineluctably the self was also a social entity. In Shaftesbury's central project of forming "character," the modeling of an outward self was as important as constructing the inward one.

Thus, the modeling of the outward self was another arena in which Shaftesbury carried out his exertions and exercises. Daily life offered dense possibilities for moral courage, since the challenge to the moral athlete resided not just in great occasions and heroic circumstances but "in that wch every minute offers & gives opportunity. Eating. Talk. Story, Argument, the common Entertainment, Mirth & Laughing, Voice, Gest, Action, Countenance."[4] Thus, far from confining himself to the motions of the mind, Shaftesbury was concerned with sheer physicality and considered such aspects as the pose of the body, the gestures of the limbs, and the mien of the face. Among the most striking because unexpected elements in Shaftesbury's notebook writings is this concern with outer deportment.

While Shaftesbury assumed that the external character was the public revelation of the inner self, his reflections resisted the notion of any easy transparency or direct translatability between inner and outer. This opaqueness of the inner self served to protect it from the pity or ridicule of others: "Take care however not by thy own Fault to give occasion to this Pitty or this Sport, by exposing anything (as it must be exposed, if discovered & directly ownd)."[5] This opaqueness was also a form of courtesy to others, an acceptable "Dissimulation" that "hides what passes within, and accommodates our manners to those of our Friends and of people around us, as far as this with safety can be allow'd."[6] Finally, insisting on such dissimulation helped to blunt the standing temptation of the self, first noted in chapter 3, to make itself an object of display for others. Since philosophical rigor could easily degenerate into showmanship on a higher plateau, Shaftesbury instructed himself: "Be severe over thy Self; but appear so as little as may be, with safety.... Nor is inward Severity (in ye thwarting either of Joy or Greif) so very hard to be hid, if honestly meant. But suffer it once to aim at Appearance, let it but seem to want Wittnesses, & see presently how nauseouse & offensive!"[7]

Thus, public demeanor was not a simple window on the inner self but a

---

[4] P.R.O. 30/24/27/10, p.71 [f.37r].
[5] P.R.O. 30/24/27/10, p.192 [f.152v].
[6] P.R.O. 30/24/27/10, p.72 [f.37v]; also p.388 [f.250v].
[7] P.R.O. 30/24/27/10, pp.388–389 [ff.250v–251r].

more complicated and mediated construction, requiring an "Involution, Shaddow, Curtain."[8] This was an important move in Shaftesbury's effort to promote moral seriousness while assaulting self-solemnity.

Self-presentation

More specific directives regarding "*the Character* I am to maintain"[9] appear inside the front cover of the first of the *Askēmata* notebooks, where Shaftesbury transcribed several passages from Epictetus.

One reiterated the warning against theatricality: "all the methods which are applied to the body by the persons who are giving it exercise, might also themselves be conducive to training, if in some such way as this they tend toward desire and aversion; but if they tend toward display, they are characteristic of a man who has turned toward the outside world."[10] But even the philosopher was settled into relations with others, as another passage made clear. After reiterating the imperative to train, Epictetus said:

No, that's not our way, but we wish to live like wise men from the very start, and to help mankind. Help indeed! What are you about? Why, have you helped yourself? But you wish to help them progress. Why, have you made progress yourself? Do you wish to help them? Then show them, by your own example, the kind of men philosophy produces, and stop talking nonsense. As you eat, help those who are eating with you; as you drink, those who are drinking with you; by yielding to everybody, giving place, submitting – help men in this way, and don't bespatter them with your own sputum.[11]

Though self-mastery came first, a philosophical commitment implied an interest in others' moral condition. However, any edification had to proceed by example rather than explicit tutelage.[12] The only persuasive argument for philosophy was the philosophical life. In other words, philosophical practice had communicative value while theoretical recipes were worthless.

Together, these two Epictetan passages indicated the double activity of the philosopher in society. While he had to protect and preserve his philosophical integrity, he also had to do what he could to expand the scope of philosophy in the world. The essence of philosophy may have been self-knowledge and self-command, but philosophy had to overflow the bounds of the personal, becoming a public activity, edifying more

---

[8] P.R.O. 30/24/27/10, p.362 [f.237v].
[9] P.R.O. 30/24/27/10, p.143 [f.68v].
[10] Epictetus, *Discourses* III.xii.16, II, 87.
[11] Epictetus, *Discourses* III.xiii.23, II, 95.
[12] It is hard not to notice here that Epictetus's own form of instruction was often highly injunctive.

than the individual consciousness. The philosopher was poised between an autonomy that was most secure when the philosopher was in isolation and an edificatory responsibility that necessarily put him in contact with others and, so, at risk. In this precisely poised position, the philosopher's means of relating to others were constrained in ways indicated by the Epictetan transcriptions. Warning against display and injunction, the passages together suggested bad models of social interaction.

Shaftesbury captured the basic principles of these models once when he warned himself to be "neither a Reformer nor an Entertainer."[13] The "entertainer" was a sociable being, giddily displaying himself for others. The standard by which he oriented himself and exercised his powers of choice was the opinions of others. Occupying a stoic anti-world, the "entertainer" embodied a facile sociability, what I will call a hypersociability, that prevented autonomy. However, the "reformer" occupied an equally dangerous situation. He did not necessarily pander to others nor did he overtly sway according to others' opinions. However, his autonomy was accompanied by aloofness and superiority. His isolating condescension made him an embodiment of unsociability.

Facile sociability was treacherous because it was propelled by a desire for and promise of proximity or "familiarity". Since the quest for "familiarity" involved seeking others' affection and esteem, it conduced to the betrayal of one's integrity.[14] Consciously echoing the courtesy books, Shaftesbury listed the techniques of agreeableness ("*Imitation, Gest, & Action in Discourse; different Tones of Voice; alterations of Countenance; odd & humoursome Turns of Speech, Phrases & Expressions*") in order to question their implications:

Consider what a mean & contemptible state, that mind is in, at that instant when it gos about any thing of this kind: what it aims at: what its End & Scope is: how it looks upon it self when it fails, & is disappointed: what kind of Joy it has, when it succeeds: and what sort of Minds are those wch partake with it in this way, & are the ablest in this Art: what Morralls, Manners, Life this brings along with it.[15]

Sociability of this sort led to philosophical disorientation, since its ends and means were determined by philosophically extrinsic standards set by unphilosophic others.

Shaftesbury's horror of the hypersociable personality led him to enjoin the importance of a reserved manner. He proposed being "Sincere, Just,

[13] P.R.O. 30/24/27/11, p.5 [f.4v].
[14] P.R.O. 30/24/27/10, pp.124–125, 133–134, 362 [ff.63v–64r, 68r–v, 237v]. In P.R.O. 30/24/27/10, p.124 [f.63v]: "must not I (if this familiarity be aim'd at) prostitute myself in the strongest manner, & be a Hippocrite in the horridest degree?.... why lay this stress on their good opinion & Esteem?"
[15] P.R.O. 30/24/27/10, pp.68–69 [ff.35v–36r].

Modest & duly reserv'd," which might appear "Dull, silent & unentertaining" and thereby risk "the Esteem of Friends." This striving toward an inobtrusive register was evident throughout the notebooks. For instance, he urged that "Countenance" be "*Low, Meek, Simple.*" He set this humble standard against more conspicuous styles of countenance: "Mimickry. Imitation. Humouring. Acting.," which he labelled "Detestable" and "Monstrouse." Similarly, personal gesture and movement should be "Chast, still, quiet, Grave." One ought to eschew the contrasting "open, loose, indecent boisterouse Way" and encourage a style rather more "seriouse, slow, doubting, undecisive." Even qualities of voice (tone, timbre, "*Prununciation & Accent*") came in for formal diagnosis and prescription.[16] Throughout, the theme was reduction, minimization, and movement away from the sharp, bright, and highly contrasting, away from what, in a loose sense, can be called the dramatic. This drive bespoke a suspicion of socializing, as if, left to itself, the social self would trade off its integrity in an orgy of interaction.

However, Shaftesbury also wanted to avoid the sort of unsociability to which the abhorrence of hypersociability might drive one. While vivacious hypersociability often corresponded to a vacuous inner life, grave unsociability self-consciously sought external expression for the gravity of the inner life, using outward forms to insist on its inner seriousness. It therefore issued in a very different sort of engagement with others than that which issued from hypersociability. Not amusing or entertaining, it sought rather to discipline and reform: it did not jest but rather enjoined; it did not pander but instead sermonized. What it shared with hypersociability was "affectation." When the self-consciously morally serious person insisted on acting out seriousness, this was its own form of pandering to an audience, its own form of insincerity, liable to smugness, self-righteousness, and self-superiority.

Shaftesbury insisted that solemnity and gravity within did not require "any industriouse Affectation of Gravity" outside. Moral autarky ought not to dictate social uncouthness. While an openness and familiarity that pandered to others at the expense of the moral character was obviously self-subverting, so too was the grave stance that rebuked and taught and was ultimately "Tyrannical & Barbarouse."[17]

[16] Shaftesbury's most specific remarks on the physical aspects of social performance appear as an "appendix" to his table of moral rules, referred to in the last chapter: P.R.O. 30/24/27/10, p.3 [f.3r]; P.R.O. 30/24/27/11, p.5 [f.4v]. On the voice: "Remember Him of whome it was said yt he spake not any word higher than another. Remember therefore: Neither the Flashy Suddain Precipitant Way: nor the Animated; nor the Loud: nor the Emphaticall: But the Still, Quiet, Backward, soft Deliberate: and so as to be rather remiss & Life-less than lively in that other manner" (P.R.O. 30/24/27/10, p.3 [f.3r]).

[17] P.R.O. 30/24/27/10, p.363 [f.238r].

Seeking a style of sociability that was neither so sociable that it sacrificed integrity nor magisterial in a way that repelled others, Shaftesbury urged a middle position that would honor the claims of both autonomy and sociability. He once defined it this way: "The Perfection of Carriage & Manners, is between the Ruggedness of one who cares not how he gives offense, and the Suppleness of one who only studdyes how to please. and this is Simplicity. for, Affectation is as well on the one side as on the other."[18] The correct demeanor was a mean between the poles of unsociability and the hypertrophy of sociability. At both poles, Shaftesbury judged, behavior degenerated into "affectation."

His solution was a "simply & (in appearance) humble, mean, cold, insipid Character: this middle Genius, partaking neither of hearty mirth nor Seriousness." Or, as he wrote elsewhere: "a Mirth not out of the Reach of wt is Gravest. a Gravity not abhorrent from the use of that other Mirth. In this Ballance seek a Character." This mixture of "Jest" and "Earnest" constituted a "soft Irony" defining the social self at its best, a social self suitable to the philosophical self: "such a Tenour as this, such a Key, Tone, Voice, [is] consistent with True Gravity & Simplicity, tho' accompany'd with Humour & a kind of Rallery."[19] Irony presupposed aloofness and distance, a certain manipulating of effects. It allowed the simultaneous establishment of the proper distance between social and philosophic self and of the proper distance between the philosopher and others. While it allowed the maintenance of essential gravity and simplicity, it mitigated this seriousness with humor and raillery.

In addition to an emphasis on morals and on conversation, the ironic stance, which Shaftesbury first developed as a strategy of personal survival, became a determining norm in the writing of *Characteristicks*. Its politeness was, in part, its attempt to purvey serious moralism without a display of seriousness. Before turning to *Characteristicks*, however, the poles of sociability discussed here have a further relevance which must be explored.

The paradigm of conversation

In "Sensus Communis," Shaftesbury wrote:

If the best of our modern Conversations are apt to run chiefly upon Trifles; if rational Discourses (especially those of a deeper Speculation) have lost their credit, and are in disgrace because of their *Formality*; there is reason for more Allowance in the way of *Humour* and *Gaiety*. An easier Method of treating these Subjects, will make 'em more agreeable and familiar. To dispute about 'em will be

---

[18] P.R.O. 30/24/27/10, p.67 [f.35r].
[19] P.R.O. 30/24/27/10, pp.362–366 [ff.237v–239v].

the same as about other Matters. They need not spoil good Company, or take from the Ease or Pleasure of a polite Conversation.[20]

This passage recast the alternative social stances we have been discussing as forms of discourse. The hypertrophic mode of sociability was embodied in conversations of a lively but vacuous character while the unsociable mode was embodied in rational discourses of such formality that they were disagreeable. Mediating between them was substantive polite conversation, which was both sociable and rational, polite and philosophical – the discursive practice embodied by Palemon in the Park.

In "Sensus Communis," Shaftesbury indicated the parameters of the practice by reflecting on a "late" conversation, at which both the Shaftesburian narrator and the addressee were present. The conversation was "of a free kind," and its participants were persons "whom you fancy'd I shou'd in great Gravity have condemn'd." Grave condemnation characterized unsociability, but it appears that the opportunity for gravity was missed here, since the speaker continued:

'Twas, I must own, a very diverting [conversation], and perhaps not the less so, for ending as abruptly as it did, and in such a sort of Confusion, as almost brought to nothing whatever had been advanc'd in the Discourse before ... A great many fine Schemes, it's true, were destroy'd; many grave Reasonings overturn'd: but this being done without Offence to the Partys concern'd, and with Improvement to the good Humour of the Company, it set the Appetite the keener to such Conversations. And I am persuaded, that had *Reason* herself been to judg of her own Interest, she wou'd have thought she receiv'd more advantage in the main from that easy and familiar way, than from the usual stiff Adherence to a particular Opinion.[21]

Although this conversation was substantive (dealing in "fine Schemes" and "grave Reasonings"), it was also diverting. Indeed, the "diverting" was, from the outset, being given normative weight, and in a double sense. For this conversation was, in the first place, pleasant: the ambience was sociable and the chat, all "without Offence," all to the benefit of good humor. However, it diverted its participants as its own contents were diverse and filled with diversions. Abrupt ending, apparent confusion, were not hindrances to the intellectual value of the discussion. (A bit later it was remarked: "*Vicissitude* is a mighty Law of Discourse, and mightily long'd for by Mankind."[22]) On the contrary, reason was well served by such a conversation: because it was critical, it undermined unwarranted assertions; because it was open-ended, it illuminated many areas; and because it was amiable, it encouraged further discussions of a similar sort.

[20] "Sensus Communis" I.vi, I, 77 (Robertson, I, 54).
[21] "Sensus Communis" I.iv, I, 68–69 (Robertson, I, 48–49).
[22] "Sensus Communis" I.iv, I, 70 (Robertson, I, 49).

98   Polite philosophy

Such a conversation had other virtues as well. For one thing, it was free:

'Tis the Habit alone of reasoning, which can make *a Reasoner*. And Men can never be better invited to the Habit, than when they find Pleasure in it. A Freedom of Raillery, a Liberty in decent Language to question every thing, and an Allowance of unravelling or refuting any Argument, without offence to the Arguer, are the only Terms which can render such speculative Conversations any way agreeable.[23]

As Robert Voitle has pointed out, the opening sentence here encapsulated the destination toward which early modern understandings of reason were tending: away from scholastic notions of right reason, toward modern philosophical notions of empirical and discursive reason.[24] However, the passage also traced rationality, via agreeableness, to freedom. The freedom at stake here was freedom to question and even to ridicule. Such discursive or intellectual freedom was not a legal entitlement or a politically sanctioned domain of latitude but, rather, the precondition of rational interchange, a convention for the operation of conversation.[25]

These passages gave intellectual and discursive freedom a specifically conversational setting. However, such conversation had other commendable qualities. Conversation presupposed activity on the part of participants. If reason was a habit actuated in the practice of conversation, conversers were agents: they resisted the passivity of mere listening ("*Semper ego Auditor tantum!* is as natural a Case of Complaint in Divinity, in Morals, and in Philosophy, as it was of old, *the satirist's*, in Poetry"); indeed, their engagements were agonistic ("A free Conference is a close Fight").[26] Attached to their activity was a kind of equality. If not equally endowed with reason or wit, participants in conversation were equal in their capacity to deploy what they had of them. Moreover, conversation distributed equally the pleasures of discourse among its participants.

It is not far-fetched to think of the conversation here represented as an ideal speech situation in Shaftesbury's scheme.[27] Ideal conversation was a

---

[23] "Sensus Communis" I.iv, I, 69 (Robertson, I, 49).

[24] Robert Voitle, "The Reason of the English Enlightenment," *Studies on Voltaire and the Eighteenth Century*, 27 (1963), 1735–1774.

[25] This freedom was not license (and not "absolute") since it was qualified by the avoidance of "offense." However, it is important to note that this discussion assumed that ideal conversation depended not only on not *giving* unnecessary offense but also on not *taking* unnecessary offense. Thus, decency was a restraint on all participants, on speakers and listeners, on critics and defenders.

[26] "Sensus Communis" I.iv, I, 70 (Robertson, I, 49–50).

[27] It seems appropriate to borrow the language of Jürgen Habermas here, since a pivotal part of his project, as it was of Shaftesbury's, is an ethics and politics of discourse. Habermas's early concern to define the eighteenth-century public sphere (in *The Structural Transformation of the Bourgeois Public Sphere*, mentioned in the introduction, pp.13–14 above) has led him, via a "linguistic turn," to a theory of communicative

moral framework for public interchange, since its conventions embodied the norms of freedom, equality, activity, and pleasure. In allowing individuals to become more rational and more autonomous, it fit into an emancipatory program. At the same time it was a model of intellectually productive discourse since it provided the best conditions for the advancement of reason.

This ideal speech situation also provided a standard against which the sterility of distorted communicative patterns could be measured. These patterns corresponded to the alternatives of unsociability and hypersociability.

One alternative to ideal conversation forced individuals into silence, making them unwilling listeners.

In matter of Reason, more is done in a minute or two, by way of Question and Reply, than by a continu'd Discourse of whole Hours. *Orations* are fit only to move the Passions: and the Power of *Declamation* is to terrify, exalt, ravish, or delight, rather than satisfy or instruct ... To be obstructed therefore and manacled in Conferences, and to be confin'd to hear Orations on certain Subjects, must needs give us a Distaste, and render the Subjects so manag'd as disagreeable as the Managers.[28]

An oratorical situation is described here, in which one participant appropriated discourse to himself. This monopoly replaced the shared exercise of speech among conversants with the inherently unequal relation between orator and auditor. The price paid by auditors for one person's having appropriated discourse was a loss of activity and a kind of bondage. Gravity replaced lightness; discomfort replaced pleasure; dogmatism replaced skepticism. Reason was less efficiently served in the oratorical situation not only because criticism was silenced but also because auditors were more likely to be repelled than convinced.[29] Oratory lacked the emancipatory potential of conversation since it was an authoritative regime.

The orator, characterized in "Sensus Communis," was the same figure as the "reformer" against whom Shaftesbury had warned himself in his notebooks: the "reformer" sanctimoniously brought his self-seriousness

action, in which an ideal speech situation (with parameters much like Shaftesbury's) provides a model not only for the pursuit of truth but also for a just form of human life. See Anthony Giddens, "Jürgen Habermas," in Quentin Skinner, ed., *The Return of Grand Theory in the Human Sciences* (Cambridge: Cambridge University Press, 1985), pp.121–139.

[28] "Sensus Communis" I.iv, I, 70 (Robertson, I, 49–50).
[29] Cf. "Miscellany" II.iii, III, 97–98 (Robertson, II, 217): "an abundancy of forc'd Instruction, and solemn Counsel, may have made Men full as averse to any thing deliver'd with an Air of high *Wisdom* and *Science*; especially if it be so *high* as to be set above all human Art of *Reasoning*, and even above *Reason* it-self, in the account of its sublime Dispensers."

to bear on others in a way that tended toward offensiveness and affectation. However, in the published writings, the characterization had a wider cultural relevance. If Palemon in the Park was the hero of discourse, its villains were all those grave and rigid authoritarians over speech and mind (formalists, dogmatists, scholastics, academics, magisters, pedants) attacked in *Characteristicks*. Such terms referred to the institutional guardians of oratory in the early eighteenth century, namely, the Church and the university. If, for Shaftesbury, conversation was the paradigm of discourse, the sermon and the lecture exemplified the distortion of discourse. Thus, his models of social character and of speech situation found their way into a cultural criticism, which it will be the task of part II to explore.

Of course, replacing oratory with conversation was not enough, since there was plenty of conversation in society already. Its fault was its triviality. Since conversation was usually composed of acts of mutual flattery and display among hypersociable beings, it was bound to degenerate into inanity. This inanity was a serious matter, since such conversations constituted the social and intellectual environment of the English elite. Thus, Palemon's conversation in the Park was characterized by Philocles as "that unseasonable Conversation, so opposite to the reigning Genius of *Gallantry* and *Pleasure*."[30] Modern conversation, according to Philocles, was divorced from matters of substance. Philocles, pursuing the requirements of polite conversation by analogy with painting, said that a painting required muscling as well as color and drapery; conversation, meanwhile, required reason and learning as well as playfulness and dalliance.[31]

Inspired by antiquity, Philocles envisioned forms of elite life other than the prevalent one. Then, "Reason and Wit had their *Academy*, and underwent this Trial; not in a formal way, apart from the World; but openly, among the better sort, and as an Exercise of the genteeler kind. This the greatest Men were not asham'd to practise, in the Intervals of publick Affairs, in the highest Stations and Employments, and at the latest hour of their Lives."[32] Here Shaftesbury cast his project for the elite in accord with the spirit of Hellenic revivalism. The Greek world of his imagination inspired his attempt to give ballast to the discourse of the gentleman. Thus, having freed gentlemen from the thralls of discursively untoward institutions, he would cultivate them in conversible ways that conduced to a rational and civilized life.

The tool for this project was *Characteristicks of Men, Manners, Times,*

[30] "Moralists" I.i, II, 183 (Robertson, II, 4).
[31] "Moralists" I.i, II, 186–187 (Robertson, II, 5–6).
[32] "Moralists" I.i, II, 191 (Robertson, II, 9).

Opinions. In his notebooks, Shaftesbury defined his ideal of social behavior as a middle position between frivolous sociability and frigid gravity. For his own person and for society at large, he aspired to a synthesis of sociability and philosophical seriousness. As such social norms governed his notion of the philosophical undertaking, so they shaped his conception of philosophical writing.

6 Philosophical writing

Philosophy as advice

Shaftesbury's "Soliloquy" had the subtitle, "Advice to an Author," linking his essay to that broad genre of literature published in early modern Europe under the denomination of "advice." Though advice literature ranged from guides on governance for princes to handbooks on social punctilios for the upwardly mobile, much of it concerned the means and goals of a satisfactory life. The genre was the chief vehicle for the dissemination of the language of "politeness" in the seventeenth century.[1] Since Shaftesbury was engaged in raising that concept to new complexity and centrality, it was fitting to pay the genre tribute in this essay's title. More generally, Shaftesbury's project was deeply related to the advice genre since his writing covered behavior, morals, and politics, and was ethical and pragmatic in orientation. However, because advice literature was didactic, its style was direct, indicative, and unambiguous. Inserting "advice" in his title, Shaftesbury evoked the genre as a foil for the discursively complex activity that "Soliloquy" both enunciated and instantiated.

"Soliloquy" commenced with a meditation on *"the Way and Manner of advising"* itself. According to a commonplace, Shaftesbury wrote, no one is better for the advice he receives. Suggesting that it is one thing for an advisor to proffer advice but quite another for an advisee to absorb and follow it, the commonplace posed the problem of persuasion, the most elementary of rhetorical quandaries. Indicating effective vehicles for the practice of advising and embodying them in his own text were central tasks of Shaftesbury's mature project. He was convinced that "there is a certain Knack or *Legerdemain* in Argument, by which we may safely

---

[1] Such literature is the basis for the discussion of the language of "politeness" in the Introduction, pp.3–8. For politically oriented advice literature, see Quentin Skinner, *The Foundations of Modern Political Thought* (Cambridge: Cambridge University Press, 1978), I, 213–221, and Dena Goodman, *Criticism in Action: Enlightenment Experiments in Political Writing* (Ithaca: Cornell University Press, 1989), pp.6–7.

proceed to the dangerous part of *advising*, and make sure of the good fortune to have our Advice accepted, if it be any thing worth."

Thus, Shaftesbury admitted the validity of the commonplace not as a condition inherent in all advising, but only as a description of the ordinary fate of advice under the "strangely inverted" conditions in which it is usually offered: "That which we call'd *giving Advice*, was properly, taking an occasion to shew our own Wisdom, at another's expence. On the other side, to be instructed, or *to receive Advice* on the terms usually prescrib'd to us, was little better than tamely to afford another the Occasion of raising himself a Character from our Defects." In other words, though advice appeared to be a generous act, it was usually a self-advancing ploy on the advisor's part. In the plainest of terms, Shaftesbury characterized it as an opportunity for the advisor "to gain a Mastery" over the other.[2]

Advising as usually practiced, then, corresponded to the unsociable pattern of discourse examined in the last chapter, a speech situation governed by the human instinct for power, in which the advisor sought to dominate the advisee and the advisee sought to fend off incursions on his autonomy. While the opening of "Soliloquy" confirms the significance, explored in chapter 5, of paradigmatic speech situations in Shaftesbury's writings, this material takes on a new relevance here as a lens to view not only social relations but the relations between authors and readers. According to Shaftesbury, authors as "profess'd *Masters of Understanding* to the Age" were themselves advisors. Since Shaftesbury cast himself here as an advisor to authors, "Soliloquy" was centrally concerned with the rhetoric of morals. Calling himself "*a Language-Master*,"[3] he pointed to the intersecting character of his ethical and discursive concerns. Since discursive reflection was linked to ethical investigation, the clarification of the strategies of discourse clarified the principles of morals. As he himself wrote of "Soliloquy": "His pretence has been to *advise Authors*, and polish *Stiles*; but his Aim has been to correct *Manners*, and regulate *Lives*."[4]

That "certain Knack or *Legerdemain* in argument" which Shaftesbury proposed as the key to sound advising had its origins in his earlier reflections. Indeed, "Soliloquy" presented, in a polished form, many of the ideas that Shaftesbury had explored in his notebooks. What there applied to personal psychology was applied here to authorial technique. In "Soliloquy" as in the notebooks, the reference point for moral discussion was self-knowledge. Since authors sought to lead readers to the moral

---

[2] "Soliloquy" I.i, I, 153–155 (Robertson, I, 103–104).
[3] "Soliloquy" I.i, I, 155 (Robertson, I, 104).
[4] "Miscellany" III.ii, III, 187 (Robertson, II, 272).

life, authors themselves had to seek self-knowledge: "He who deals in *Characters*, must of necessity know *his own*; or he will know nothing."[5] Moreover, as self-discourse was the foundation of moral character in the individual, so it had to be foundational for the moralist author. In the most summary form, Shaftesbury's "advice to an author" was: "soliloquy!" – the inner discourse developed and practiced in his notebooks.[6]

Furthermore, while self-discourse was required for the author to develop moral insights of any worth, it also had an important role to play in the establishment of his authorial character. In the absence of self-discourse, the author's behavior towards his readers assumed the pernicious and unpolite patterns, broached in earlier chapters. On one hand, self-discourse was a remedy to textual vacuity. Reformulating ideas from the notebooks, Shaftesbury asserted that such intellectual fatuousness could be impeded by a developed interiority. Solidity of thought was a function of the inner reflection that preceded its writing, for "'tis the hardest thing in the world to be *a good Thinker*, without being a strong *Self-Examiner*, and *thorow-pac'd Dialogist*, in this solitary way."[7] On the other hand, excessive seriousness was also related to failings in self-discourse. The dogmatist's self-silence and self-ignorance cast doubt on the truth of his vaunted moral knowledge.[8] Moreover, his very stance was an impediment to the spread of moral wisdom since the failure to engage in self-discourse cut him off from the sources of moral persuasiveness. All dogmatism, seeking to dominate, was the death of self-discourse. It was an authoritarian mode, inherently hostile to the moral life.

By contrast, true moralism was engaged not in suppressing inner discourse but in nurturing it. "And, this in our default, is what the *Moralists* or *Philosophers* endeavour to do, to our hand; when, as is usual, they hold us out a kind of *vocal* Looking-Glass, draw Sound out of our Breast, and instruct us to personate our-selves, in the plainest manner."[9] Teasing an inner discourse out of the mind was what the self-knower wanted. The genuine philosopher, having already engaged in the self-

[5] "Soliloquy" I.ii, I, 189 (Robertson, I, 124).
[6] "Soliloquy" I.ii, I, 171 (Robertson, I, 113). The features of this inner discourse, as well as some of the expressions in which it was formulated, were the same in both "Soliloquy" and the notebooks: the inner world was figured as a world of voices; self-discourse was the means of self-knowledge and of self-possession; self-discourse had as its object the control of both humor and fancy in order to create a uniform self, autonomous of unreliable shifts of temper or changing influences from outside.
[7] "Soliloquy" I.i, I, 168 (Robertson, I, 112).
[8] "Soliloquy" I.ii, I, 173 (Robertson, I, 115).
[9] "Soliloquy" I.ii, I, 171 (Robertson, I, 113–114). A "*vocal* Looking-Glass" is, literally, an echo, one would think. But that is not what Shaftesbury wanted the image to mean. Rather, this "glass" had to be a voice to the self from the text that operated as an inner voice did, initiating the process of self-discourse.

discoursing route to self-knowledge, aimed to provoke such verbalization in others. One way he did it was by teaching the value of self-knowledge and by telling explicitly what the pursuit of self-knowledge consisted in ("instruct us to personate our-selves, in the plainest manner"). He also offered "a kind of *vocal* Looking-Glass." This could only be his works themselves as they were exemplary of the process of self-inquiry. In other words, the particular modes of discursivity that the philosopher displayed in his work ought to mirror the interior discursive processes that Shaftesbury urged on all self-knowers.

Of course, this was the ideal. The reality was rather different since, as Shaftesbury wrote in "The Moralists": "It may be properly alledg'd perhaps, as a Reason for this general Shyness in *Moral Inquirys*; that the People to whom it has principally belong'd to handle these Subjects, have done it in such a manner as to put the better Sort out of countenance with the Undertaking."[10] Since Shaftesbury had confidence in the potential of the "better Sort" as an audience for moral discussion, the absence of such a philosophical public was the fault of moralists and the manner in which they pursued their activity. In short, their deformed discourse had alienated the audience for ethical discussion.

One object of this criticism, as shown in chapter 2, was modern philosophy. While the orientation of modern philosophy was speculative, abstract, and systematic, true moral philosophy had to be concrete, practical, and useful. However, "Soliloquy" had other targets in view, especially two sorts of moralist writers who came in for specific criticism.

One sort were "the Writers of MEMOIRS and ESSAYS." Predictably, their "frothiness" arose from deficiencies of interiority. Their self-discourse was hobbled since, "tho they are often retir'd, they are never *by themselves. The World is ever of the Party. They have their Author-Character* in view, and are always considering how this or that Thought wou'd serve to compleat some Set of *Contemplations*." Such authors' awareness of the audience foiled any developed interior discourse. Not having contended adequately with their own selves, such authors extruded their own self-confrontations into the public realm, making themselves the subject of their writing: they "exhibit on the Stage of the World that *Practice*, which they shou'd have kept to themselves."[11] Having failed to create an

---

[10] "Moralists" I.i, II, 185 (Robertson, II, 5).
[11] "Soliloquy" I.i, I, 163–164 (Robertson, I, 108–109). In referring to their "Meditations, Occasional Reflections, Solitary Thoughts or other such Exercises," Shaftesbury referred to a small bibliography of gentlemanly Restoration essayists, including: Henry Tubbe, *Meditations Divine and Moral* (1659); Joseph Henshaw, *Meditations, Miscellaneous, Holy and Humane* (1658); Sir Matthew Hale, *Contemplations, Moral and Divine* (1682); Sir William Killigrew, *Mid-night Thoughts* (1682); Sir Thomas Culpeper, *Essays or Moral Discourses* (1671); and Robert Boyle, *Occasional Reflections upon Several Subjects* (1665).

autonomous self through processes of self-discourse, they displayed the self before others in hopes of some gratification. The discursive situation of such texts was therefore theatrical, pandering, and inauthentic.

Shaftesbury was even more strongly critical of the textual unsociability of another class of writers: "Candidates for Authorship ... of the *sancti-fy'd* kind," namely, clerical writers. Like the gentlemanly essayists, the clerics suffered deficiencies of interiority: "These may be term'd a sort of *Pseudo-Asceticks*, who can have no real Converse either with themselves, or with Heaven; whilst they look thus a-squint upon the World, and carry *Titles* and *Editions* along with 'em in their Meditations." Their inner ear was too cocked to the voice of the world for their inner voice to engage in an authentic and autonomous inner discourse. As a result, their works, exposing inner discourse to the public, had a similar prematurity to those of the essayists.[12]

However, the failure of the clerical writer to engage sufficiently in self-discourse had more extensive consequences, since "A *Saint*-Author of all Men least values Politeness." The cleric's inability to criticize himself or engage in self-discourse made him resistant to the disciplines imposed by polite conversation. Shaftesbury specified the exact form of clerical impoliteness, writing "where, instead of Controul, Debate or Argument, the chief Exercise of the Wit consists in uncontrolable Harangues and Reasonings, which must neither be question'd nor contradicted; there is great danger, lest the Party, thro this habit, shou'd suffer much by Cruditys, Indigestions, Choler, Bile, and particularly by a certain *Tumor* or Flatulency, which renders him of all Men the least able to apply the wholesom *Regimen* of Self-Practice."[13] Since the clerical mode of discourse was argumentative, authoritative, and domineering, the clerical writer was little more than a textual bully, whose aggressiveness was morally sterile. Unfamiliar with inner conversation, the clerical writer produced a discourse foreign to conversation and its benefits.

The great problem posed by these clerical and moralistic writers, from Shaftesbury's standpoint, was their influence over readers of the "better sort." Shaftesbury wrestled with the traits of moral suasion because he cared about its readership – the well-bred, polite elite, his own class. However, bad moralism left no room for the good, and the difference mattered greatly: "Whatever Company we keep; or however polite and

---

On the pursuit of moral edification through essayistic self-revelation, see Robert Adolph, *The Rise of Modern Prose Style* (Cambridge, Mass.: The MIT Press, 1968), pp.129–130ff.

[12] "Soliloquy" I.i, I, 164–165 (Robertson, I, 110). These remarks recall the preface to the edition of Benjamin Whichcote's sermons, which pointed up the contrast between the supposed humility of the clerics and the eagerness of many to achieve a literary celebrity through published sermons and polemics.

[13] "Soliloquy" I.i, I, 165–167 (Robertson, I, 110–111).

agreeable their Characters may be, with whom we converse, or correspond: if the *Authors* we read are of another kind, we shall find our Palat strangely turn'd their way."[14]

Shaftesbury's observation that modern discourse tended, unfortunately, to either frigid oratory or frivolous conversation had a direct parallel in his complaints about the reading matter of the modern elite.[15] Just as Shaftesbury wanted to develop a character between those of the "Reformer" and of the "Entertainer," so he wished to insert his own writing between the categories in which the reading of the polite now fell. He eschewed both the frivolous and the formal. While providing readers with matter of intellectual and moral substance, he sought to evade the traps of didactic writing. He wished something both rational and sociable, philosophical and polite. Of course, the writer-reader relationship will always have something of the "magisterial" in it: the reader may respond to the writer, but the writer is absent. However, this magisterial inertia can be either sustained or interrupted by the stylistic idiom. Manifestly, Shaftesbury sought to mitigate the authoritative tendency of writing by seeking a discursive mode. As the self-discourse of the writer was necessary for his knowledge of character, so the discursive qualities of the text were necessary for the moral transformation of the reader.

The "Socratick History"

While *Characteristicks* was Shaftesbury's grand endeavor in discursive philosophy, another unrealized project revealed much about his ambitions for philosophical writing. This was to be a "Socratick History," as he called it, a series of translations from the chief ancient sources on the life of Socrates, set among introductions, explanatory essays, and notes by the third earl.[16] Though he did not complete the project, Shaftesbury had filled a notebook with reflections which indicate not only his moral and civic concerns but also his formal criteria for philosophy.

---

[14] "Soliloquy" III.iii, I, 341–342 (Robertson, I, 220–221).
[15] "Soliloquy" III.iii, I, 343–344 (Robertson, I, 221).
[16] The notebook is P.R.O. 30/24/27/14. Neither Stanley Grean nor Robert Voitle comments on this project. Shaftesbury envisioned a work parallel to Machiavelli's *Discourses* on Livy. As the ancients excelled the moderns "in Policy & Governmt," so they were also excellent in knowledge of "Morralls." While the Machiavellian commentaries were among the finest works of the moderns, the moral achievement of the ancients ("this History of Xenoph [i.e. the *Memorabilia*]: & wt attends it") had not yet found its special interpreter: P.R.O. 30/24/27/14, p.59. Another notebook contains a design for an edition of Arrian's account of Epictetus. This notebook, P.R.O. 30/24/27/16, also suggests that the project would both address a scholarly audience and suit the "less Critical and learn'd" (p.1).

Shaftesbury saw the project as a vindication of the active ideal of philosophy, embodied in the Xenophonic version of Socrates, as against the contemplative ideal, embodied in the Platonic version. According to Shaftesbury, "the Substance of the genuine socratick Philosophy was Action & Capacity, how to be useful in the World, a good Patriot, a good Friend, a good Economist & towards a Family etc."[17] In Shaftesbury's reading, Xenophon presented Socrates as a philosophical tutor who applied wisdom to the range of relations in which the social individual was engaged. By contrast, Shaftesbury criticized Plato for "drawing Socrates into Metiphysicall & Theological Notions," which Shaftesbury perceived as suiting Plato's philosophic purposes but not as representing Socrates historically. The historical Socrates was a civic philosopher integrating thought and action.

Though the Socratic notebook elucidates Shaftesbury's appraisal of Socrates, it also indicates the design for Shaftesbury's own book about Socrates. Since the life of Socrates raised "the great questions of Vertue agt the Vitiouse," Shaftesbury's project aimed at moral edification. His preface would have pointed out that his own experience of reading the Socratic literature afforded "profitable Delight & as helping to correct my Faults make me ... in love with Vertue." His own edition would extend the benefits of this material, especially to those who otherwise lacked access to it, for instance, on account of their ignorance of classical languages.[18]

Therefore, Shaftesbury's anticipated audience was inclusive. This general audience was itself diverse, but its most significant component was "the Polite," a group whose susceptibility to moral edification Shaftesbury sought to touch. Such people ("not Schollars or Learnd but Lovers of Nation & Language") determined the strategies that Shaftesbury adumbrated in his notes, for this group, despite its lack of learning, had to be able to grasp the material.[19]

However, while his aspirations to moral persuasion pushed him towards making the book agreeable to a polite readership, the extent of his own reading pushed him towards making the book a record of accurate scholarship.[20] The tension between scholarship and politeness

---

[17] P.R.O. 30/24/27/14, p.145.
[18] P.R.O. 30/24/27/14, pp.1, 59, 76.
[19] P.R.O. 30/24/27/14, pp.53, 76.
[20] The heart of the project was a translation of Xenophon's writings: the *Memorabilia*, his version of the *Apology*, the *Economics*, and the *Convivium*. Other texts to be included were Diogenes Laertius's life of Socrates, Aristophanes' *Clouds*, the Table of Cebes, and various pieces by Plato. A prospective table of contents appears on sig. 2v–4v. Shaftesbury considered including translations of letters between Socrates and Xenophon, together with an appraisal of their genuineness (sig. 3v). These primary pieces were to be embedded in commentary by Shaftesbury, whose references in this notebook spanned

repeated the tension between philosophy and politeness since both philosophy and scholarship were liable to divorce intellectual pursuit from practical moral interest. In Shaftesbury's view, this divorce resulted in useless intellection, which, to make matters worse, was likely to be poorly written. Since the world of practical social activity with which politeness was associated was mindless and immoral without intellection, it was crucial to keep in harness both elements in the polarity.

The Socratic notebook provided considerable evidence of Shaftesbury's effort to handle these contrary pressures. Repeatedly invoking the needs of a diverse, general audience, he insisted that his discourses were not to be "of a Critical Character, but Morrall, Polite & if possible or as much as is possible, entertaining & Eloquent." Therefore, scholarly controversies about Xenophon's life ("all of this kind wch is Criticall") had to be confined to notes and margins.[21] Such controversies were of interest to Shaftesbury, since Xenophon's character, and hence eligibility as a model of the polite philosopher, were at stake: was he a passionate thrall of young men? why was he banished by the Athenians? did his stay among the Persians make him a monarchist?[22] Nonetheless, the apparatus rather than the body of the text had to bear the burden in order "that those who less regard wt is Criticall may not be troubled with it, & that the Life it self may be writ politely & elegantly without the load of such disputes & difficultyes of Authors."[23]

Even the critical notes were to be written with a sensitivity to the general audience. Thus, he proposed a double-tiered apparatus: "To place in the Pages of the Text no other Notes besides wt will be agreeable & pleasant to the Reader; wt will not have the Air of Pedantry & wt will pass with the Polite people entertain them & adorn the Text. The rest viz: the Criticall Notes & Greek, by themselves at the end, in a small print." Moreover, the notes, at least the ones on the pages of the text, could not be in the " common & Dry way of Commentators"; rather, he instructed himself, "begin every Note (as far as possible) as a Discourse or beginning of a Work," i.e., in an engaging and discursive way. It was better to sacrifice precision in references than to impede the discursive flow and "make it look like meer learning & heaps of Authors."[24] In the battle to control the form of the work, it is clear that the rhetorical demands of

   both ancients (Apuleius, Plutarch, Suidas, Aelian) and moderns (Thomas Stanley's history of philosophy, Cudworth's writings, Henry More's *Enchiridion ethicum*).
[21] P.R.O. 30/24/27/14, pp.108, 147. He called this "Mr. Bayls way" with reference, presumably, to the *Dictionary*'s famous footnotes.
[22] P.R.O. 30/24/27/14, pp.6, 68–69.
[23] P.R.O. 30/24/27/14, p.147. Adequate discussion of the order of the Platonic dialogues posed another problem of balancing critical accuracy and polite readability (p.76).
[24] P.R.O. 30/24/27/14, pp.75–76.

addressing a polite audience won out over the analytic demands of presenting scholarly material.

Meanwhile, the entire manner of the discourses themselves was geared to engaging the interests of the general readership. Shaftesbury cited Plato's *Apology* as an instance of "that Air of Negligence & good Humour" which his commentaries were to imitate. He would leaven his passages with frequent citations from Horace, "because he is now so much in esteem, & by this there will appear an Air of Gallantry & Humour." The writing itself was "upon no account to depart from the Purity of the English Tongue & wt is polite."[25]

As elsewhere in his writing, Shaftesbury invoked simplicity as a normative and stylistic standard. One aspect of simplicity was brevity. Concision in expression would produce an apothegmatic effect which would, in turn, enhance quotability. Quotability meant that the ethical message would more easily circulate among polite readers. However, another reason "to be short in everything" was to leave "more to be thought than what is explicitly in so many words related, but this, with simplicity & without affection of Mistery, & deep Thought." The simplicity of concision, thus, authorized an elliptical style, aiming to provoke thought. Shaftesbury warned himself against excess explanation, which would reduce the autonomous processes of the thinking reader.[26]

He also warned against superfluous assertiveness: his "ordinary way" throughout the work was to be that "of Diffidence & Undeciding." He called this manner "Xenophontick Style" and "Xenophon's Simplicity," and he enjoined it in operative maxims for the work: "To shun absolutely the Dogmatick style, & in every thing (as it were) to doubt"; "To avoid every thing that has so much as the air of Controversy."[27] The maxims were elements of a stylistic program aiming to reduce the intimidating traits of the discourse, to make the discourse more accessible to the reader, and finally to propel more effectually the thought of the discourse into the mind of the reader.

Thus, this projected work was meant to be both moral, that is, philosophical, and polite. Its politeness, which would make it a pleasurably attractive piece of reading, was a function of a polite authorial stance. The author wrote in an agreeable English. He punctuated the discourse with

---

[25] P.R.O. 30/24/27/14, pp.50, 52, 75. Shaftesbury thought that, if he were to reproduce the "Beauty of Style" of Xenophon and Plato, he had better read "some of the most eloquent & even Luxuriant of our English Writers," such as Dryden in his prefaces and Charles Davenant in his essays; reading some of the "politer Novells as *Dutchess of Cleves* or those best translated or wrote in English" might help him better frame the dialogic elements of the Socratic writings (p.52).

[26] P.R.O. 30/24/27/14, pp.52–53, 74.

[27] P.R.O. 30/24/27/14, pp.48–49, 52, 132; also, pp.76–77.

humor. He preserved moral scale, eschewing, at one end of the spectrum, excess detail and elaboration and, on the other, mysterious depth and abstraction. He consistently avoided the temptations of didacticism, dogmatism, and authority. Instead, he was diffident and unassuming. Adopting a somewhat distanced stance toward the material, he had a risible irony about him.

Such an authorial stance amounted to an imitation of the ancient sources as Shaftesbury perceived them. Xenophon's writings and, to a lesser extent, Plato's had been written in the polite manner which, Shaftesbury said, his work was intended to reproduce. Thus, he conflated the polite and the antique. Socrates was the original not only for the picture of the moral philosopher represented in Plato and Xenophon, but also for the dialogic and ironic authorial manners of the texts by Plato and Xenophon that depicted him. In a continuation of this series, Socrates was Shaftesbury's model both of the moral man and also of the authorial persona that shaped the projected "Socratick history."

Characteristicks

If in the case of the "Socratick history" our evidence consists mostly of statements of intention and design by Shaftesbury, *Characteristicks* confronts us with a completed work, the textual embodiment of Shaftesbury's project in polite philosophy. Since polite philosophy was moral philosophy in a discursively self-conscious mode, *Characteristicks* was a field for the deployment of discursive strategies.[28]

Aside from "Miscellaneous Reflections," which was written for *Characteristicks*, the rest of its contents had already appeared: *An Inquiry Concerning Virtue* had been published as early as 1699 while the other essays were published between 1708 and 1710.[29] Though *Characteristicks* was an expedient reassembling of previously published writings with a unifying gloss, it was also an apt vehicle for Shaftesburian philosophizing. When *Characteristicks* is viewed as a whole, what is striking is its suitability to express the principles that Shaftesbury had adopted in his philosophic development and had previously enunciated in his then separate writings.

We have seen how Shaftesbury, confronting personal crises, cast the project of self-knowledge in the form of self-discourse and how this choice

---

[28] Politeness as a discursive strategy is an important theme in Peter France's essays on eighteenth-century French literature, *Politeness and Its Discontents* (Cambridge: Cambridge University Press, 1992).

[29] On the components of *Characteristicks* and its publishing history, see Introduction, pp. 16–20 above.

resonated through his work. He endorsed a sociability that, by instituting conversational conventions, maximized the possibilities for self-discourse. He also made the wisdom and the persuasiveness of the writer depend on the processes of self-reflection and self-discourse. In turn, he insisted that the persuasive text also had to be, in its way, self-reflective and self-discoursing. Shaftesbury was anxious for his master text to create the scene of reasoned conversation as a way of inducing it in readers. This was what it meant for the text to be "a kind of vocal Looking-Glass" for its readers. What follows is not a synopsis but rather a guide to some sorts of discursivity which Shaftesbury sought to build into his own work.

Intrinsic to the evolution of *Characteristicks* was a diversity that became a source of value in the work. The very diversities of the work as a whole, compounded by the kinds of diversity within the components, encouraged the discursivity towards which Shaftesbury aimed. This diversity can be pursued through two of its aspects, genre and voice.

Characteristicks was a generic conglomeration, the title of each component calling attention to its literary kind. Of course, Shaftesbury wrote in an age when intellectual products were well labelled: titles were long, segmented and highly informative confections. However, by his titles, Shaftesbury was signalling the interest that inhered in *Characteristicks*' generic diversity.[30] One effect of generic diversity is to throw the task of locating unity upon the reader. A work with a regular form (a piece of expository philosophy such as Locke's *Essay on Human Understanding*, a religious treatise in a scholastic or analytic form such as Cudworth's *True Intellectual System*, a political work that seeks to follow deductive procedures such as Hobbes's *Leviathan*) seeks to convince on the basis of its comprehensive coverage of the problems it assumes to address. Its comprehensive and unifying aspirations are made palpable in its mode or organization.[31] Though the reader may not be convinced, the work, nonetheless, offers itself as a complete, orderly treatment. *Characteristicks* did not operate in this fashion. Its organization, its order, its principles of hierarchy and subordination, were much more matters for the reader to determine. Thus, the composite form of *Characteristicks* supported Shaftesbury's project of increasing the autonomous functioning of the reader's mind by reducing the authoritative character of the author.

---

[30] If anything, the titles exaggerated the diversity of the genres. Though they indicated that *Characteristicks* included a letter, an essay, an advice, an inquiry, a philosophical rhapsody, and miscellaneous reflections (or miscellanies), the components of the first volume (letter, essay and advice) and of the last (miscellanies) were all extended and discursive essays.

[31] See the discussion of the multiple significances that may attach to "discontinuous" forms used by early modern writers in Oscar Kenshur, *Open Form and the Shape of Ideas* (London: Associated University Presses, 1986).

Another implication of the generic diversity of *Characteristicks* was that truth enjoyed some specific and crucial relationship with variety. In the same way that, Shaftesbury wrote, conversations generated truth through a plurality of contributions, his work could be understood as generating truth through its own diversity. Though it contained pieces labelled "miscellanies," *Characteristicks* was itself precisely such a miscellany, and his remarks (discussed below) valorizing the miscellaneous were applicable to the entire work.

This miscellaneous character was not just a matter of genre but of voice as well. By virtue of its composite character, *Characteristicks* was not a monologic discourse.[32] The most obvious vocal rupture in the text occurred between the first two volumes and the third, for the "Miscellaneous Reflections" were introduced by and ascribed to a voice distinct from the author of the preceding treatises. "Miscellaneous Reflections" offered itself then as a commentary by someone other than the author. Inserting such a commentary established an ironic distance within the text, qualifying the authority of the first two volumes. If the voice of the third volume qualified the authority of the first two, the reader was encouraged to adopt a serial relationship with both these voices. Reminded by the text itself of the open-ended quality of intellectual debate, the reader found his intellectual autonomy affirmed.

However, even within the first two volumes, vocal differentiation was an important device, contributing to the discursive character of the work. The distinctions among the voices in which several components of *Characteristicks* were articulated created the impression that the components were not all derived from the same source, making the text, in a way, an imitation of discourse in society.

As chapter 2 indicated, the *Inquiry* was in the voice of a philosophical reasoner. This voice pursued the task of logical investigation in a cool and understated way, not calling attention to itself but aiming rather to be taken for granted. However, in its aspiration to convey the authority of reason, the "inquirer" was alone in *Characteristicks*, surrounded by other voices, which were more sociable than the grave reasoner of the *Inquiry*. The "letter-writer" (of *A Letter Concerning Enthusiasm*), the "letter-writer-cum-essayist" (of *Sensus Communis*), and the "advisor" (of *Soliloquy*) were all more casual than "the inquirer." Frequently digressing, their texts lacked formality. Like the voice of the "reflector" of the third

---

[32] For a definition of this expression, see chapter 2, note 6. For a very different interpretation of authority in Shaftesbury's writings, see Robert Markley, "Sentimentality as Performance: Shaftesbury, Sterne, and the Theatrics of Virtue," in Felicity Nussbaum and Laura Brown, eds., *The New Eighteenth Century* (New York and London: Methuen, 1987), pp.213–216.

volume, they frequently called attention to themselves as voices. By thus establishing their particularity as voices (as opposed to their anonymous authority), they confirmed the freedom of the reader in relation to the text, inviting the reader to question its authority.

A recognizable and self-exploratory voice is a defining feature of the essay as a form of writing. Shaftesbury's own comments on the nature of essayistic writing clarified his intentions in using it. He pointed out that "the SATIRICK, or MISCELLANEOUS of the polite Antients, requir'd as much *Order* as the most regular Pieces. But the *Art* was to destroy every such Token or Appearance, give an *extemporary* Air to what was writ, and make the *Effect* of Art be felt, without discovering the *Artifice*."[33] The "*extemporary* Air" summed up a stylistic desideratum and an important feature of textual discursivity. Shaftesbury frequently drew attention to the miscellaneous character of his essays. He contrasted the miscellaneous with the classical standards of order, decorum, and integrity and also with set discourses in divinity and in philosophy. Freed from "Exactness and Regularity," the essayist enjoyed "many greater Privileges by way of Variation, Interruption, and Digression."[34] Thus, the essay was, apparently at least, spontaneous and aleatory, free from formal constraints.

Finally, and most revealing, Shaftesbury called the essayistic "a more familiar Stile," appropriate to "pleasanter Reflections." Commenting on the subject matter of "Sensus Communis," he wrote: "WIT and HUMOUR ... will hardly bear to be examin'd in ponderous Sentences and pois'd Discourse. We might now perhaps do best, to lay aside the Gravity of strict Argument, and resume the way of *Chat*; which, thro Aversion to a contrary *formal manner*, is generally relish'd with more than ordinary Satisfaction."[35] Here Shaftesbury offered a clear equation of the essayistic, as the "way of *Chat*," with the discursive value for informality, raillery, liberty, grace, and, quite explicitly, pleasure. This conversational style was an alternative to "ponderous Sentences," "pois'd Discourse," "the Gravity of strict Argument," and "a contrary *formal manner*." The passage implied that Shaftesbury was in the process of moving from one style to another; but when really did Shaftesbury ever adopt "the Gravity of strict Argument" that here he could afford to lay it down? Contrary to the implication of the passage, "the way of Chat" was Shaftesbury's natural diction. This is not to say that he never adopted, or at least strove to adopt, "strict Argument." He had done so in the *Inquiry*; but, when that work appeared in *Characteristicks*, the "strictness" was mitigated

---

[33] "Miscellany" I.iii, III, 21–22 (Robertson, II, 169).
[34] "Miscellany" I.i, III, 1–6 (Robertson, II, 157–159); "Miscellany" II.iii, III, 113 (Robertson, II, 225–226); "Miscellany" II.ii, III, 82 (Robertson, II, 207).
[35] "Miscellany" II.iii, III, 97 (Robertson, II, 216–217).

because the text was handled ironically, surrounded by chatty comment that subverted the sorts of claims that the "strict" voice hoped to convey through its own idioms.

Shaftesbury's interest in discursivity found expression in other ways. The conversational ideal operated to validate certain genres and stylistic modes. For instance, Shaftesbury assigned a central significance to the letter as a polite genre since letters were a conversation at one remove from conversation itself. A "real *Letter*" was "not a precise and formal TREATISE, design'd for *publick* View."[36] If anything, however, this intensified the communicative burden that a letter bore. Speaking of Cicero, Shaftesbury wrote: "There was no kind of Composition in which this great Author prided or pleas'd himself more than in this; where he endeavour'd to throw off the *Mein* of *the Philosopher* and *Orator*, whilst in effect he imploy'd both his Rhetorick and Philosophy with the greatest Force." In the letter, philosophy and rhetoric were allowed to take leave of formality, but epistolary informality augmented philosophical weight and rhetorical force. It was no wonder that the Cicero depicted here by Shaftesbury saw letters as a summit of his communicative endeavors. The appeal of informality was its power to deploy order and method without bringing attention to them. Shaftesbury resisted the notion, wedded to the magisterial style, that formality must be patent. The letter was the perfect vehicle for polite philosophy: it accomplished its business without eschewing pleasure.

However, the summit of polite philosophy was dialogue, which brings us to "The Moralists." Among the components of *Characteristicks*, "The Moralists" was Shaftesbury's most fictive venture. Its main title referred to characters who inhabited it, while the sub-title of an early version of it, "a philosophical adventure," evoked its crafted plot.[37] This fictiveness meant that "The Moralists" added yet another voice to *Characteristicks*. The voice of "The Moralists" was that of Philocles addressing Palemon. The substance of the text was an account of several conversations arrayed in time in a receding fashion. The text opened with Philocles' exclamation, quoted in chapter 1, at Palemon's philosophical discourse "in such a

---

[36] "Miscellany" I.iii, III, 19–20 (Robertson, II, 167–8). In a note here, Shaftesbury explained that, though "A Letter Concerning Enthusiasm" was labelled a "*Treatise*" in the table of contents of *Characteristicks*, "'tis the Bookseller must account for it. For the Author's part, he considers it as no other than what it originally was." This is a characteristically conversational strategy: Shaftesbury was thawing the formality of the reader–author relationship by taking the reader into his confidence. On connections between the epistolary and the conversational in the eighteenth century, see Bruce Redford, *The Converse of the Pen* (Chicago and London: University of Chicago Press, 1986), pp.1–7.
[37] Though much shorter than the later version, the early version had the same sort of plotting and characterization as the later. For the plotting, see Horst Meyer, *Limae Labor* (Frankfurt-am-Main: Peter Lange, 1978).

Circle of good Company as we had round us yesterday, when we were in your Coach together, in *the Park*."[38] That discursive occasion reminded Philocles of an earlier one, on which certain remarks of Palemon's, again in a social circle, led to a long private discussion between Palemon and Philocles. Much of that discussion consisted of an account by Philocles of a series of discussions he had had at yet an earlier point with a changing assemblage of characters at a country house. Those discussions occurred over two days, largely under the auspices of Theocles, a philosophical mentor. Some of them were conversations among several people, some of them were dialogues between Philocles and Theocles. At the climax of these was a philosophical rhapsody by Theocles. Thus, from the inside out, we have a rhapsody at the center of a series of dialogues and conversations which were themselves recounted in a dialogue (sparked by a social conversation) which preceded a more recent social conversation. "The Moralists" was, in itself, then, populated with a range of voices, in a range of combinations, at a range of moments. Though not in a strict sense a dialogue, it was highly dialogic.

Shaftesbury assigned the highest prestige to dialogue, which he appraised as the perfect vehicle of philosophical training. He made a case for the *formal* as well as intellectual value of the dialogues. Dialogue, he said, elided prose and poetry, the philosophic and the literary. The Socratic dialogues of Xenophon and Plato "carry'd a sort of *Action* and *Imitation*." They were "either real *Dialogues*, or Recitals of such *personated Discourses*," and so registered character "according to the most exact *poetical Truth*." Their success at literary representation was central: "'Twas not enough that these Pieces treated fundamentally of *Morals*, and in consequence pointed out *real Characters* and *Manners*: They exhibited 'em *alive*, and set the Countenances and Complexions of Men plainly in view. And by this means they not only taught Us to know Others; but, what was principal and of highest virtue in 'em, they taught us to know *Our-selves*."[39] The essential operation of the dialogue to which Shaftesbury drew attention was its effectiveness in leading the reader to self-knowledge.

Shaftesbury elaborated this notion. Socrates, "the Philosophical *Hero* of these Poems," was shown off as "*a perfect Character*," albeit at times eccentric. Notwithstanding his centrality and idiosyncrasy, however, "the *Under-parts* or *second Characters* shew'd Human Nature more distinctly, and to the Life." It was in them that we might, "as in a *Looking-Glass*, discover our-selves." The text was a mirror that conduced to self-inspection.

[38] "Moralists" I.i, II, 182 (Robertson, II, 3).
[39] "Soliloquy" I.iii, I, 193–194 (Robertson, I, 127–128).

And, what was of singular note in these *magical Glasses*; it wou'd happen that, by constant and long Inspection, the Partys accustom'd to the Practice, wou'd acquire a peculiar *speculative Habit*; so as virtually to carry about with 'em a sort of Pocket-Mirrour, always ready, and in use. In this, there were *Two* Faces which wou'd naturally present themselves to our view: *One* of them, like the commanding Genius, the Leader and Chief above-mention'd; the *other* like that rude, undisciplin'd and head-strong Creature, whom we our-selves in our natural Capacity most exactly resembled. Whatever we were employ'd in, whatever we set about; if once we have acquir'd the habit of this Mirrour; we shou'd, by virtue of the double Reflection, distinguish our-selves into different Partys. And in this *Dramatick* Method, the Work of *Self-Inspection* wou'd proceed with admirable Success.[40]

The experienced reader internalized the figures of the Socratic dialogue so that the dialogue continued within. The self was broken down into different parts which then continued a discourse between them. Thus, the philosophical dialogue was not only a representation of dialogue, but it also disseminated dialogic initiatives within its readers.[41]

From the vantage we have now achieved, we can perhaps better understand Shaftesbury's ambivalence, noted in chapter 2, toward the *Inquiry Concerning Virtue*. There was a stylistic and methodological contrast between the *Inquiry* and the rest of the writing in *Characteristicks*. The contrast reflected an evolution that had proceeded within him, for he had rebelled against the notion of philosophical practice embodied in the original *Inquiry*. Written in the 1690s, the *Inquiry* antedated Shaftesbury's confrontation with the stoics and the years of his most intense self-examination, when his mature character was formed. It was written when Shaftesbury was still within Locke's field of intellectual gravity, when Shaftesbury seems to have been trying to work out his own positions in a Lockean way. The *Inquiry* was far more formal and orderly in its treatment of ethical issues than any of the highly discursive pieces Shaftesbury would later write. When the *Inquiry* appeared in *Characteristicks*, it remained different from all the other pieces because its occasion, motivation, and aspiration had been different. In the meantime, Shaftesbury had developed a notion of philosophical practice according to which

---

[40] "Soliloquy" I.iii, I, 195–196 (Robertson, I, 128–129).
[41] On the limits of Shaftesbury's attainments in this stylistic vein, see Jack Prostko, "'Natural Conversation Set in View': Shaftesbury and Moral Speech," *Eighteenth Century Studies*, 23 (1989–90), 42–61, especially 53ff. The eighteenth-century dialogue is treated in: Eugene R. Purpus, "The 'Plain, Easy, and Familiar Way': The Dialogue in English Literature, 1660–1725," *ELH*, 17 (1950), 47–58; Donald Davie, "Berkeley and the Style of Dialogue," in H. S. Davies and George Watson, eds., *The English Mind* (Cambridge: Cambridge University Press, 1964), pp.90–106; and the excellent discussion of Berkeley's use of dialogue in Peter Walmsley, *The Rhetoric of Berkeley's Philosophy* (Cambridge: Cambridge University Press, 1990), pp.61–126.

the practice deployed in the *Inquiry* subverted the very points that the treatise was trying to make.

Since the *Inquiry* had argued the case for human sociability, it had a place in *Characteristicks*; but one can understand the conflict for Shaftesbury. Here was a very literary philosopher who strove to develop a notion and practice of polite philosophy but who found himself, in the *Inquiry*, the author of a text that he could only characterize in terms hostile to politeness: formal, grave, methodical, dry, rigid. Perhaps the most resonant indication of the unpoliteness of the *Inquiry* was the statement, cited earlier, that it was offered "to the *patient* and *grave* READER ... who in order *to moralize*, can afford to retire into his Closet, as to some religious or devout Exercise."[42] Shaftesbury had to make sure the reader understood how unpolite the activity was that this essay demanded of the reader: a return to the closet, a rehabilitation of monkishness.

Shaftesbury ultimately dismissed the *Inquiry* as evidence of how little there was to be learned from formal philosophy. "The Moralists" was a contrast. Shaftesbury's own verdict on "The Moralists" was that it had to be, "according to his own Rules, ... reckon'd as an Undertaking of greater weight." "The Moralists," said Shaftesbury, was as "*Systematical, Didactick* and *Preceptive*" as the "formal" *Inquiry*, but its appearance was entirely different, something much more "fashionable": "It conceals what is *Scholastical*, under the appearance of a polite Work." Thus, "The Moralists" was a piece of polite philosophy. The exact purchase of politeness with respect to "The Moralists" was indicated in Shaftesbury's further comments:

It aspires to *Dialogue*, and carrys with it not only those Poetick Features of the Pieces antiently call'd MIMES; but it attempts to unite the several Personages and Characters in ONE *Action*, or *Story*, within a determinate Compass of *Time*, regularly divided, and drawn into different and proportion'd *Scenes*: And this, too, with variety of STILES; the *Simple, Comick, Rhetorical*, and even the *Poetick* or *Sublime*; such as is the aptest to run into Enthusiasm and Extravagance. So much is our Author, by virtue of this Piece, *a* POET *in due form.*[43]

"The Moralists" aspired to conversation at the highest level, in the form of philosophical dialogue. It also aspired to poetry and literary refinement. Finally, it sought to take advantage of all the stylistic possibilities of philosophy: the simple, the comic, and the sublime, though not the methodical.[44] "The Moralists" (and not the *Inquiry*) was the characteristic specimen of Shaftesbury's philosophical endeavor. It was the

---

[42] "Miscellany" IV.i, III, 191–192 (Robertson, II, 274).
[43] "Miscellany" V.ii, III, 284–286 (Robertson, II, 333–334).
[44] As discussed on pp.42–44 above, these were the styles that Socrates had encompassed and bequeathed to his successors.

epitome of *Characteristicks*, embodying the profound discursivity of intent that informed Shaftesbury's work.

This discursivity was the crux of politeness, and the model for discursivity was conversation, the locale from which its vocabulary and strategies radiated. Conversation was a structure of mutuality and equality. It addressed subject matter of mutual relevance, but it was at the same time disinterested. Propriety and decorum reined in self-concerned impulses. Its purpose was dialectical, but it was not bound by any urge to systematicity. In centering politeness in discursivity and discursivity in conversation, Shaftesbury inscribed gentlemanly sociability into his wide-ranging cultural and philosophical view.

We have seen that Shaftesbury's intellectual activity can be cast as a search for an adequate version of philosophy, whether as an introspective operation or as a social activity. In turn, this search had ramifications for philosophy as writing. In philosophical writing his discursive consciousness found the ultimate field for its operation. His consciousness of philosophy as sited in discourse led to a literary consciousness about philosophy and a most self-conscious practice as philosophical writer. The Shaftesburian text was the textual embodiment of a politely sociable philosophy.

Effective philosophical writing was a tool first for shaping men and then for shaping culture. As part II will show, Shaftesbury's cultural designs partook of characteristics deeply embedded in the project we have so far been examining: Shaftesbury was the ideologist for a culture that would be both philosophical and gentlemanly, moral and conversable – in a word, polite. And these texts were a lens for focussing that culture.

Part II

Polite Whiggism

7 From politics to cultural politics

"The hinge of the whole Work"

Characteristicks of Men, Manners, Times, Opinions first appeared in the early months of 1711,[1] though Shaftesbury subsequently made numerous revisions which were registered in the posthumous second edition of 1714. These early editions, published by the Whig printer John Darby, were works of high book art.[2] The paper was heavy, the typography was exquisite, the layout was careful and elegant, the ornaments were copious but restrained. These traits are not surprising in light of the labors Shaftesbury expended on the physical production of the book after he had written and revised the pieces comprising it.[3]

Nothing so well illustrates the deliberateness with which Shaftesbury approached his book-making as the graphical representations throughout the volumes. These were all dense and highly self-conscious emblematic messages, presented in immaculate and polished engravings with references to relevant passages in the text.[4] Among the most important of these was the engraving of the Triumph of Liberty, in which Liberty, reclining in a lion-drawn chariot, was represented as having subdued the passions and gained the adoration of the virtues. The Triumph was originally conceived in relation to a passage in "The Moralists" in which the philosophic Theocles painted in words "the Picture" of moral and political liberty.[5] Considering whether to use a small rendition of the pictorial triumph at the front of each of the volumes of the second edition, he wrote to his London agent: "You will object that this Devise of the Triumph of

---

[1] A letter of March 30, 1711, to John Somers indicated that by then volume III had already been printed (P.R.O. 30/24/22/4, ff.153–156).
[2] On this John Darby and his father (of the same name), see A. B. Worden, introduction to Edmund Ludlow, *A Voyce from the Watch Tower, Part Five: 1660–1662*, (Camden Fourth Series, volume 21, London: Royal Historical Society, 1978), pp.18–21, 25–26, 28, 39–40.
[3] See the papers of his last two years: P.R.O. 30/24/26/1, 30/24/26/3, 30/24/26/7.
[4] See Felix Paknadel, "Shaftesbury's Illustrations of *Characteristicks*," *Journal of the Warburg and Courtauld Institutes*, 37 (1974), 290–312.
[5] "The Moralists" II.ii, II, 252–254 (Robertson, II, 44–45).

Liberty is peculiar only to one Treatise viz The Moralists. But as that Piece and that very subject (moral and political) is the hinge and Bottom of all three [volumes] and of the whole Work it self, it will become every Title-Page."[6] This passage, identifying liberty as the key to *Characteristicks*, compactly sets an agenda for part II of this study.

Somewhat less explicitly, the passage also indicates a distinctive Shaftesburian approach to ethical and political questions. The fact that liberty would be presented in *Characteristicks* in both a verbal and a graphical form alerts us to Shaftesbury's sense of the fluid relationship between modes of representation: the sorts of persuasive tasks that a text undertook might also be the burden of other forms of expression. Shaftesbury's use of engravings exemplified the deployment of this insight, but so too perhaps, in a less simply iconographic way, did the impressiveness of *Characteristicks* as a physical artifact: the book in its specific physicality (and not just the text) was itself redolent of the politeness thematized in its words.[7]

However, Shaftesbury was less significant as a patron of ethically and politically motivated art than as an investigator of the connection between cultural forms and ethical and political meanings. That cultural forms were eligible for inclusion in a specifically political discourse was a matter about which Shaftesbury was quite explicit. When, at the end of his life, he retired to Naples, he wrote a friend that his "Conversation" with the local virtuosi concerned "Medalls & Pictures & Antiquitys." "I shall have papers now & then to enclose to you to forward," he promised. "I wish our Ministers in England may not take 'em for Politicks. They won't be much deceivd if they shoud break open my Letters in that Expectation. Whatever my Studdys or Amusements are, I indeavour still to turn them towards the Interests of Virtue & Liberty in general."[8] Even the study of artifacts had political implications, which, since Shaftesbury's virtuoso activities expressed Whig principles, the Tory ministry of Henry St. John and Robert Harley might judge unfavorably. The passage authorizes us to look for Whig meaning in the creations of his Naples years. However, it hardly mattered what Shaftesbury might or might not accomplish in the way of cultural politics during his final days in Naples, for *Characteristicks* had already made its acclaimed appearance.

---

[6] P.R.O. 30/24/23/8, ff.29–30, Shaftesbury to Thomas Micklethwaite, November 24, 1711.

[7] Another noteworthy instance of the interchange of verbal and non-verbal meaning in Shaftesbury's career was his commission for a painting, fulfilled by Paolo Mattheis, on the mythological subject of the choice of Hercules. Like Shaftesbury's "pictures" of Liberty, "the choice of Hercules" assumed both a visual and verbal form, since the aesthetics and semantics of the painting were plotted in Shaftesbury's essay, *A Notion of the Historical Draught of Hercules*.

[8] P.R.O. 30/24/21/200, Shaftesbury to Benjamin Furley, March 22, 1712.

Except for the first version of *An Inquiry concerning Virtue*, the components of *Characteristicks* were all written during the intense partisan controversies of Anne's reign. Shaftesbury was quite explicit about the Whiggish tasks that *Characteristicks* was intended to perform. Moreover, he presented himself as a cultural ideologist, conveying a politics of culture. It is odd, therefore, that *Characteristicks* has never been subjected to a sustained ideological examination. Part II is devoted to providing such an examination. Shaftesbury's cultural-political project was captured in the epigrammatic proposition: "All Politeness is owing to Liberty."[9] If the Whigs were the party of liberty and if politeness was the concomitant of liberty, then politeness could only be achieved under Whig auspices.

This chapter seeks to plot Shaftesbury's Whig dispositions against the patterns of post-1688 Whiggism. This task is especially important since Shaftesbury is usually seen in relation to the oppositional stance adopted by Country Whigs or commonwealthmen in the 1690s. Though, as we will see, he was associated with such circles, the circumstances that encouraged this association were short-lived. Changing political conditions and his own intellectual evolution led him toward the sort of legitimation of the post-1688 Whig regime expressed in *Characteristicks*.

Oppositionalist and legitimist Whigs

The Whigs had originated as a party of opposition in the 1670s, a Country party whose hostility to the Court was expressed in a defense of "liberty." However, after 1688, with new access to power, the Whigs had to confront their ideological inheritance with their new political circumstances. Their problem was that many of their inherited ideas were better suited for criticizing a regime than for legitimating one. This was especially true of the sophisticated version of the civic humanist tradition some of them had embraced since the 1670s.

Of course, there were several different political idioms, alive and well in the 1690s and long after, in which the Whig defense of liberty could be mounted. At the time of the Convention, the more conservative Whig position was expressed in the terms of the ancient constitution, which emphasized the continuity of the constitution and legitimated the Revolution as a return to constitutional normalcy after the diversion of James II's reign. This ancient constitutional Whiggism endured into the eighteenth century and can be found along with much else, in Edmund

---

[9] "Sensus Communis" I.ii, I, 64 (Robertson, I, 46).

Burke.[10] More radical Whigs of 1688 and 1689 spoke of contract and natural right, a language that presented the Revolution as an opportunity for constitutional revision. However, they failed to dominate events at that time and remained marginal for long afterwards. As John Dunn has pointed out, the work best expressing their ideas, John Locke's *Second Treatise*, was surprisingly uninfluential in political discourse in the decades immediately following the Revolution.[11]

Post-1688 Whig oppositionalism was not Lockean but rather in the civic idiom as it had been naturalized by James Harrington in the 1650s and later revised by Henry Neville in the 1670s. Shaftesbury's political thinking first arose within the civic idiom and, in the 1690s, he was close to writers, such as Walter Moyle, Robert Molesworth, John Toland, and Andrew Fletcher, who expressed it.

Our understanding of this civic tradition has been shaped by the work of J. G. A. Pocock.[12] According to Pocock, the civic writers defined liberty in terms of the virtuous participation of the citizen-like subjects in their government. Such participation was premised on a personal autonomy guaranteed by the possession of freehold land and expressed, crucially, in the bearing of arms. It is not hard to see then how the landed gentleman, the denizen of the Country, could be construed as the receptacle of civic virtue and, so, how the Country tradition was significantly classicized.

Pocock's interpretation of post-1688 political discourse places con-

---

[10] J. P. Kenyon, *Revolution Principles: The Politics of Party, 1689–1720* (Cambridge: Cambridge University Press, 1977), pp.2, 35–38; H. T. Dickinson, *Liberty and Property* (London: Weidenfeld and Nicolson, 1977), pp.70–80; J. G. A. Pocock, "Burke and the Ancient Constitution: A Problem in the History of Ideas," in *Politics, Language and Time* (New York: Atheneum, 1973), pp.202–232.

[11] Mark Goldie, "The Roots of True Whiggism 1688–94," *History of Political Thought*, 1 (1980), 195–236; Kenyon, *Revolution Principles*, pp.1–2, 5–20, 40, 43–50; Dickinson, *Liberty and Property*, pp.70–79; John Dunn, "The Politics of Locke in England and America in the Eighteenth Century," in *Political Obligation in Its Historical Context* (Cambridge: Cambridge University Press, 1980), pp.53–77.

[12] The most extensive treatment is *The Machiavellian Moment: Florentine Political Thought and the Atlantic Republican Tradition* (Princeton: Princeton University Press, 1975). The most up-to-date and also most pertinent to the eighteenth century is "The Varieties of Whiggism from Exclusion to Reform," in *Virtue, Commerce, and History* (Cambridge: Cambridge University Press, 1985). A usefully compressed account appears in "Cambridge Paradigms and Scotch Philosophers," in Istvan Hont and Michael Ignatieff, eds., *Wealth and Virtue: The Shaping of Political Economy in the Scottish Enlightenment* (Cambridge: Cambridge University Press, 1983), pp.235–245. The early eighteenth-century writers on whom Pocock relies to illustrate the tension between virtue and commerce include Andrew Fletcher, Charles Davenant, John Trenchard, and Thomas Gordon. This and the next several paragraphs summarize points made in a number of Pocock's works, especially "Civic Humanism and Its Role in Anglo-American Thought" and "Machiavelli, Harrington and English Political Ideologies" in *Politics, Language and Time*, pp.80–103, 104–147, and *Machiavellian Moment*, pp.386–395, 401–505.

siderable emphasis on the movement from Harrington's own thought to the neo-Harringtonianism of Henry Neville and his post-1688 followers. Harrington observed that the disruption of English political relations in the middle of the seventeenth century was rooted in a striking alteration in property relations: the decline of feudalism had transformed military capacity from a function of vassalage to one of landed proprietorship. Since military capacity was the basis of civic capacity, the effect was to redistribute political power from the monarch, who had relied on his noble tenants, towards the landholders in general. Extrapolating, Harrington invoked the principle that the distribution of property was the determinant of political authority. Assured that the new conditions called for adjustments in the constitution, he expected that the old order of a monarch, supported by Church and aristocracy, was ready to give way to a republic of freeholders. Though the real extent of citizenship in the Harringtonian polity is a debated matter, the fundamental Harringtonian insight was that historical conditions had brought about circumstances in which a republic of gentlemen could now be established.

If Harrington's politics was a response to the failure of monarchy in the Civil War, the neo-Harringtonian perspective was a response to the restoration of monarchy and to the irritated relations between monarch and elite when the romance of restoration faded. Among other things, Charles II had discovered secrets of parliamentary management, which were construed as a menace by the Whigs who opposed him. Though a gentlemanly republic was still a desideratum, Harrington's analysis required adjustment. Whereas Harrington had judged historical conditions favorable to a republic, it now seemed that historical conditions were obviating this possibility since liberty appeared to be in mortal combat with forms of constitutional corruption managed by the monarch. The neo-Harringtonian perspective, converging with some elements of the belief in an ancient constitution, came to yearn nostalgically for the glories of a "gothic" constitution.

According to Pocock, the neo-Harringtonian critique was useful for mounting opposition after 1688. The Whigs, having acceded to power, were branded as corrupt by both Tories and Country Whigs. However, post-1688 conditions necessitated a broadening of the neo-Harringtonian perspective. The civic model's fixation on land cast doubt on other forms of property which did not provide the same stability or autonomy as land. The critique of money focussed on particular innovations in the patterns of property-holding that seemed crucially hostile to the requirements of classical political virtue. The founding of the Bank of England and the funding of the National Debt produced forms of property which depended on the state and thus involved their holders in dangerous forms of political dependence. In addition, government bureaucracies were perceived to have increased in scale after the Revolution of 1688, adding to the prevalence of forms of property in which political dependence was implicit.[13] At its most developed, the civic commitment to landed virtue implied a critique of modern social and economic conditions.

This critique underwrote characteristic elements of the Country program, which sought to assure that the Court could not subvert liberty or virtue through force or more insinuating forms of influence. Since nothing could be more dangerous to the health of the polity than a large number of armed individuals dependent for a salary on the state, the Country opposed any standing army and yearned to revitalize country militias as the indigenous version of a citizen-army.[14] The civic model also provided reasons to bolster the autonomy of Parliament from undue influences from the Court by excluding placemen from Parliament, insisting on landed qualifications for admission, and legislating the frequency of parliamentary meetings rather than leave it to court discretion.[15]

As Pocock has pointed out, this pessimistic appraisal of the chances of liberty set an agenda for those who would apologize for the post-1688 Whig order. Defenders of a Whiggish regime obviously had to defend William III's plans for a standing army and fend off proposals that would limit the Court's ability to manage Parliament, but they also had to make a defence of modern conditions in England, conditions that the Whigs promised to dominate. According to Professor Pocock, "the Old Whigs identified freedom with virtue and located it in the past; the Modern Whigs identified it with wealth, enlightenment, and progress toward the future."[16] Defenders of the Whig regime needed to address the civic sense of the frailty of liberty and the momentariness of virtue. When we turn to Shaftesbury's political career, we will see that in the 1690s Shaftesbury

[13] These developments are discussed in: Howard Tomlinson, "Financial and Administrative Developments in England, 1660–88," in J. R. Jones, ed., *The Restored Monarchy, 1660–1688* (Totowa, New Jersey: Rowman & Littlefield, 1979), pp.94–117; Geoffrey Holmes, *Augustan England: Professions, State and Society, 1680–1730* (London: George Allen & Unwin, 1982), pp.239–287; and John Brewer, *The Sinews of Power: War, Money and the English State, 1688–1783* (London: Unwin Hyman, 1989), pp.25–134. For important qualifications on Pocock's account of the 1690s debate, see David Hayton, "Moral Reform and Country Politics in the Late Seventeenth-Century House of Commons," *Past and Present*, 128 (1990), 48–91.

[14] Among those who published against the standing army were John Trenchard, Walter Moyle, Andrew Fletcher, and John Toland. For the bibliography, see Lois G. Schwoerer, "Chronology and Authorship of the Standing Army Tracts, 1697–99," *Notes & Queries*, 211 (1966), 382–90, and J. A. Downie, "Chronology and Authorship of the Standing Army Tracts: A Supplement," *Notes & Queries*, 221 (1976), 342–346.

[15] Place was the main object of John Toland's *The Danger of Mercenary Parliaments* (1698), written, according to the preface to the 1722 edition, "in King *William*'s Time by Lord *Shaftesbury*'s Direction, and printed and dispersed privately at his Expence."

[16] Pocock, "Varieties of Whiggism," p.231.

was among those with a high level of civic anxiety. However, by the time he wrote *Characteristicks*, he aimed to present a vision of society in which liberty and virtue were less tenuous.

The defense of the Whig regime has tended to be neglected in the historical literature. Once upon a time, the name of John Locke was sufficient to evoke the character of political thinking in the period: with Locke as "political bible," the eighteenth century was simply rehearsing for nineteenth-century liberalism.[17] However, the revival of interest in eighteenth-century political discourse after the decline of Namierism changed this. It was research into oppositional writings that first demonstrated the varieties of Whiggism and the peripherality of Locke.[18] But the very focus on opposition tended to leave the resources of establishment Whig legitimation hazy or unexamined.

Thus, Isaac Kramnick described eighteenth-century opposition as the antipathetic response of the aristocracy and gentry to commercial developments undermining their social and political position. Robert Walpole, his regime, and its advocates embraced contemporary developments through "the emerging individualist and liberal ideology," founded primarily on the thinking of Locke. Aside from a mistaken sociology, Kramnick's was an attentuated version of establishment Whiggism. It is not at all clear that Lockean individualism was the main vehicle, let alone the only one, for the articulation of establishment Whiggism. Kramnick rested his case on selections from Walpole's periodicals and on the instances of Daniel Defoe and Bernard Mandeville. While important, these writers do not stand for the entirety of Whig establishment ideology for the first half of the eighteenth century. Kramnick included Richard Steele, but with little evidence to justify the inclusion. He omitted Joseph Addison and he used the third earl of Shaftesbury as a "precursor" of the earl of Bolingbroke (quite remarkably, in fact, as a patriarchalist).[19]

The one extensive account of Addison's social thinking rests on the same sociology as Kramnick's. In Edward and Lillian Bloom's *Joseph Addison's Sociable Animal*, Addison is a representative of the middle class, the new men, the moneyed interests. Every mention of trade in

[17] Leslie Stephen, *History of English Thought in the Eighteenth-Century* (originally published 1876; reprint edn, New York: Harcourt, Brace & World, Inc., 1962), II, 114.
[18] See Caroline Robbins, *The Eighteenth Century Commonwealthman* (Cambridge, Mass.: Harvard University Press, 1959).
[19] Isaac Kramnick, *Bolingbroke and His Circle: The Politics of Nostalgia in the Age of Walpole* (Cambridge, Mass.: Harvard University Press, 1968), pp. 106, 117, 188–204. John Cannon's *Aristocratic Century* (Cambridge: Cambridge University Press, 1984) deflates the quasi-Marxist sociology. Another study that treats establishment Whig thought only as a foil to oppositionalism is Bertrand Goldgar's *Walpole and the Wits: The Relation of Politics to Literature, 1722–1742* (Lincoln: University of Nebraska Press, 1976).

Addison's writing is taken as an indication of a middle-class insurgency and a conscious or unconscious "awareness of a submerged class rivalry."[20] However, the defense of trade did not constitute an attack on the prevailing social order in eighteenth-century Britain. Nor is it valid to interpret the politics of the *Spectator* as a simple expression of Lockeanism: that there are Lockean bits does not confirm anything about the *Spectator* as ideology.

An interpretation of establishment Whig ideology on its own terms is Reed Browning's *Political and Constitutional Ideas of the Court Whigs*, covering the 1720s to the 1750s. Neither Defoe nor Mandeville appear but John Hervey, Benjamin Hoadly, Thomas Herring, Samuel Squire, and Lord Hardwicke do. While insisting on its diversity, Browning is also concerned to demonstrate a fundamental unity of Court Whig thought, which was embodied, he says, in its Ciceronian qualities. This Ciceronian interpretation is an alternative to Kramnick's notion that Whig thought was a defense of a new bourgeois order based on Lockean possessive individualism.[21] Browning's Cicero offered the eighteenth century an ideal of citizenship without the specific anxieties inhering in narrower constructions of the civic ideal (what he calls the Catonic perspective): Cicero's entire stance was more pragmatic and so more adaptable to the circumstances of a complex society. He stands for a recognition that, if classical precedents were at all relevant to eighteenth-century Britain, then the model was the complex world of the late republic (when Rome was an empire, though without yet an emperor) rather than the earlier republic or a Greek city–state. Cicero seems eminently suitable to help legitimate rather than criticize an order that exists.[22] However, Browning's further argument – that Cicero not only had emblematic value but was a source of policies, principles, and philosophical underpinnings[23] – is far-fetched, since these aspects of Court Whiggery do not require a Ciceronian description. Nonetheless, Browning's account is important for making the question of establishment Whiggery central.

Other alternatives to civic humanism have emerged in the prodigious

[20] Edward A. Bloom and Lillian D. Bloom, *Joseph Addison's Sociable Animal* (Providence: Brown University Press, 1971), pp.11–12, 20, 21, 87–88, 114–117, 136.
[21] Reed Browning, *Political and Constitutional Ideas of the Court Whigs* (Baton Rouge: Louisiana State University Press, 1982), pp.73, 156n. Browning presents the work not as an alternative to Kramnick but as a corrective to the limitations of H. T. Dickinson's *Liberty and Property* and to the implications of J. P. Kenyon's *Revolution Principles* (see pp.ix–x, 15–16n, 176n, 234n, 251n). He criticizes Dickinson's overestimation of property as an element in Whig theory (see p.176n): the fact is that Dickinson, though he says that Locke is not the dominant influence on Whig thought between 1715 and 1760 (pp.10, 123–124), organizes his discussion precisely as if Locke were (pp.125–132, esp. 132).
[22] Browning, *Court Whigs*, pp.210–230.
[23] Browning, *Court Whigs*, pp.230–256.

amount of recent work on writers of the Scottish Enlightenment. For one thing, this work has re-established the importance of the natural law tradition. In its strongest formulation, the contention has been that the natural law tradition was the vehicle for the elaboration of a legitimist ideology for Whiggism, individualistic, commercial, and, in its way, liberal. In light of Shaftesbury's opposition to natural law thinking, examined in part I of this study, this is hardly a promising context for understanding him. However, mid-eighteenth-century Scotland has offered another alternative to civic humanism, in the form of manners and, indeed, politeness. Among others, Nicholas Phillipson has suggested: that the concern with manners and politeness was an important part of the response of eighteenth-century Scottish writers to their economic, social and political circumstances; that manners and politeness offered an alternative to the civic humanist paradigm for conceptualizing the exigencies of commercial society; and that Addison's writings were a *locus classicus* for the model and a source for its spread.[24] While Phillipson's work and that of others has examined the role of politeness in Scottish thinking, Addison himself and Steele have been relatively ignored from this ideological perspective. So too, of course, has Shaftesbury.

Shaftesbury's politics

Late in his life, Shaftesbury jotted some notes about his political persuasion, an "Acct of my Principles." He wrote that in the early 1690s he found himself "engag'd between two Partys equally pretending Service to ye Crown & Government & equall Merit in ye Revolution." The choice, he insisted, was a real one "notwithstanding Birth which I was resolv'd should not outweigh." Appearances initially favored the Tories: while the Whigs were proving themselves "corrupt," prominent Tories appeared "so Patriot-like." However, then came the bribery accusations against Henry Guy, Speaker John Trevor, and Thomas Osborne, now the duke of Leeds, which demonstrated "ye old Corruption of the old Raigns & Cheif of the Tory Party." The veil thus having been stripped from his eyes, "I chose therefore my Party & am a *Whigg*." However, he added: "But this ye Foundation of all. An Enemy to Corruption. This Monster to be subdu'd. Else nothing."[25]

---

[24] Nicholas Phillipson, *Hume* (London: Weidenfeld and Nicolson, 1989), pp.23–30, and other writings of Phillipson cited there.

[25] These notes appear at the end of a small almanac for 1711 (P.R.O. 30/24/24/13). His "corrupt" Whigs were Charles Mordaunt (later the third earl of Peterborough), Henry Booth (later the earl of Warrington), and Richard Hampden. All three had been exclusionists, who attached themselves to the Court after 1688 and received patronage.

This anecdote of political *Bildung* contains several noteworthy features. First, though Shaftesbury's was certainly a genealogy that disposed its heir in a particular political direction, he insisted on his independence. Second, the outcome of his choice was Whiggery of an unequivocal sort. But, third, he averred an enmity to "corruption," a statement that might qualify his partisanship. In sum, then, Shaftesbury presented himself in this passage as an independent-minded Whig with a horror of corruption.

This self-characterization provides a unity to Shaftesbury's career, but it also masks some significant shifts in his outlook. For Shaftesbury as for a generation of Englishmen, the years after 1688 were a period of political change and reassessment. As the Whig accession to court power put pressure on the very concept of Whiggism, so, similarly, a Williamite Court put pressure on Tory identity. In the well-known pattern, the Whigs became a court party while the Tories took over the Country traditions. However clear the overall pattern, the routes by which individuals adjusted to a complicated and often baffling reality were diverse, personal, and often obscure.

In Shaftesbury's case, Whig independence expressed itself, during the 1690s, in opposition to the Junto leadership of the Whig party in the name of the principles of the first Whigs. Characterizations of Shaftesbury's political stance have been based largely on this episode, when he participated in the Commons in the Parliament of 1695–98.[26] However, when he came to write *Characteristicks* between 1708 and 1711, his position had modulated. He was still concerned with the themes of virtue and independence, but his project in cultural ideology was very different from that of the Country ideology. Thus, his political career illustrates a significant interplay of Whig and oppositionalist elements.

Given Shaftesbury's Whig ancestry, the Revolution of 1688 was an

---

The Tories whom Shaftesbury temporarily admired were Sir Christopher Musgrave and the Tory lords, Nottingham and Rochester. Leeds, Trevor, and Guy were Court creatures with careers of varying significance under Charles II and James II. The drive against them was Country-led (but supported by Court Whigs since the objects were Tory). Aside from the DNB entries, see Henry Horwitz, *Parliament, Policy and Politics in the Reign of William III* (Manchester: Manchester University Press, 1977), pp.17–18, 52, 55, 72–74, 76, 93, 106, 146–172, and Dennis Rubini, *Court and Country* (London: Rupert Hart-Davis, 1968), p.54.

[26] Caroline Robbins places him in the lineage of *The Eighteenth Century Commonwealthman*, pp.88, 93–95, 128–133. For David Hayton, he is an "archetypal Country Whig": "The 'Country' Interest and the Party System," in Clyve Jones, ed., *Party Management in Parliament, 1660–1784* (New York: St. Martin's Press, 1984), pp.44, 52. For similar characterizations, see: Geoffrey Holmes, *British Politics in the Age of Anne* (London: Macmillan, 1967), p.221; J. H. Plumb, *The Growth of Political Stability in England 1675–1725* (London: Macmillan, 1967), p.138n; Voitle, *Third Earl of Shaftesbury*, p.209; Clayton Roberts, *Schemes and Undertakings: A Study of English Politics in the Seventeenth Century* (Columbus: Ohio State University Press, 1985), p.154.

event of immense positive significance: as it, in effect, excluded James Stuart from the throne, so it vindicated the movement which his grandfather had led. Shaftesbury's earliest extant political statements concern the Revolution, which he praised for having frustrated three great objects of Whig distrust – Stuart absolutism, Catholicism, and France.[27] This distrust was translated into the clearest touchstone of his Whiggism, his unambivalent hostility to the Tories, whom he portrayed as opponents of liberty and upholders of slavery. Tory slavishness expressed itself in affection for Monarchy and Court, for Church, and for France. At bottom, the Tories represented "a high & Absolute Court & Church-Interest" with a deep wish to return matters to their pre-1688 state.[28]

While his opposition to Toryism was patent, Shaftesbury's relations with Whiggery were complex. In *Characteristicks*, Shaftesbury wrote in a recognizably Whiggish vocabulary, interpreting the Revolution as an affirmation of an English liberty whose coordinates were balance in the relations of people and monarch, the rule of law (especially with respect to property), a Protestant succession, and a religious settlement (tolerating Dissenters and excluding Catholics from office).[29] In fact, Shaftesbury's writings are so choked with Whig disposition and assumption that it would be tedious to document in detail all the instances. Their overarching theme was the importance of liberty. Political liberty, he believed, was assured through a mixed and balanced constitution, in which Parliament representing the nation acted in cooperation with the Crown. Liberty was also secured in the rule of law and in legislation that guaranteed the liberties of the subject. In his view, liberty of worship within defined boundaries was a central liberty. It followed that Shaftesbury was suspicious of the established Church when it sought to enforce too rigorous a uniformity. It followed too that he was hostile to the memory of the Stuarts and to the example of absolutist France. On the other hand, he regarded the Dutch as firm defenders of liberty and so as natural allies of Britain. Absolute power and tyranny were his bugbears.

Nonetheless, Shaftesbury did not have much interest or confidence in the common Whig defenses of the Revolution. In *Characteristicks*, he

[27] P.R.O. 30/24/21/229, Lord Ashley to second earl of Shaftesbury, May 3, 1689.
[28] P.R.O. 30/24/20/15, Shaftesbury to Benjamin Furley, November 15, 1700. On Tory slavishness, see P.R.O. 30/24/20/53, Shaftesbury to Benjamin Furley, January 11, 1701 (redated). When the Duke of Gloucester died, Shaftesbury reported efforts by the "Partizans of Monarchy & *the Governmt of One*" to turn the development to Jacobite advantage: P.R.O. 30/24/20/13, Shaftesbury to Benjamin Furley, August 5, 1700. As for the Tories' gracious stance toward France, Shaftesbury described "the Tory & French Interest" as "one & the same": P.R.O. 30/24/20/19, Shaftesbury to Benjamin Furley, March 4, 1701.
[29] "Soliloquy" II.i, I, 216 (Robertson, I, 141). The passage would have been written about 1710.

dismissed political traditionalism, writing: "I think OLD ENGLAND to have been in every respect a very indifferent Country: and that *Late* ENGLAND, of an Age or two old, even since Queen BESS's days, is indeed very much mended for the better." Indeed, Shaftesbury wrote, "I think *Late* ENGLAND, since *the Revolution*, to be better still than *Old* ENGLAND, by many a degree."[30] The notion that England had undergone a growth in liberty over the centuries challenged the premises of ancient constitutionalism and other forms of political nostalgia. In these views, Shaftesbury anticipated those articulated by John Hervey in *Ancient and Modern Liberty Stated and Compared* (1730), which was certainly a modernist view of the history of liberty in England. Indeed, this passage links Shaftesbury with the mainstream of establishment Whiggism at the moment when that mainstream changed course from traditionalism to progressivism.[31]

Shaftesbury was no more attracted to the chief alternative Whig justification of the Revolution, based on rationalist ideas of natural law, right, and contract. As chapter 2 demonstrated, Shaftesbury took issue with Locke on account not of the argument's radical potential but rather of its implications for ethical theory, since it undermined natural sociability. If neither the ancient constitution nor contract was satisfactory to Shaftesbury, we will have to look for other approaches to the ideological justification of Whiggism.

Although *Characteristicks* embraced the Revolution unambivalently, Shaftesbury sympathized with those Whigs who felt that the Revolution had not gone far enough or that the security it was intended to have guaranteed was endangered once again by post-1688 developments. In 1708, he reflected on his activities in the 1690s as a campaign "against the injustice and corruption of both parties: each of them enflam'd against me, particularly one, because of my birth and principles; the other, because of my pretended Apostacy, which was only adhering to those principles on which their party was founded."[32] While his conflict with the Tories was a matter of principle itself, the conflict with the Whigs was a matter of interpreting the bequest of Whig principle and locating its authentic heirs. Here he wrote ironically of his own "pretended Apos-

---

[30] "Miscellany" III.i, III, 150–151 (Robertson, II, 249). See also "Sensus Communis" III.i, I, 108 (Robertson, I, 73) and P.R.O. 30/24/22/4, ff.65–67, Shaftesbury to Sir John Cropley, February–March 1708.

[31] On Hervey, see Browning, *Court Whigs*, pp.35–66, esp. 52–56; Robert Halsband, *Lord Hervey: Eighteenth-Century Courtier* (New York and Oxford: Oxford University Press, 1974), p.174; Kramnick, *Bolingbroke and His Circle*, p.134. On the pivot of Whiggism, see Herbert Butterfield, *The Englishman and His Past* (Cambridge: Cambridge University Press, 1944), pp.69, 81.

[32] Shaftesbury to Robert Molesworth, November 4, 1708, in *Letters to Molesworth*, p.13.

tacy," but he elsewhere referred to the "Apostacy" of the Junto and Court Whigs.[33]

Shaftesbury's flight from corruption was, institutionally, a flight from the Court. The Tories were reprehensible on account of their chronic affection for the Court. Meanwhile, the Whig tradition meant distance from the Court. At times, it appears that Shaftesbury envisioned a Whig party that would control English politics without being a party of the Court.[34] Not surprisingly, Shaftesbury frequently identified himself with the Country, using expressions such as "us of the Country Party."[35] He subscribed to the parallel dichotomies of Court and Country, corruption and virtue, slavery and freedom. For instance, in late 1700, he construed a place bill as "the great Stroak towards the Liberty of the Parlemts & a totall Reform" since it would have effected "lopping off at once one considerable Member of the Court-Body" (in this case, excisemen). Moreover, he hoped that this measure would "by parity of Reason & the Nature of the thing extend it self to the thorough Purgation of the Parlemt, & reducing it solely & wholly to the Country-Bottom."[36]

Shaftesbury did remain loyal throughout his life to certain elements of the Country program, both traditional and newly devised ones. His letters endorsed the constitutional salubrity of the Triennial Act of 1694, the Treason Trials Act of 1696, the Disbanding Bill of 1698–99, various bills specifying parliamentary qualifications, and balloting reform.[37] However, it was during his first period of active political engagement, when – still Lord Ashley – he served in William's third Parliament, that he appears most in the Country vein and, indeed, most radical.

Certainly, his parliamentary activities conformed to the pattern of the

---

[33] P.R.O. 30/24/27/10, p.291 [f.202r] (written 1704). Also: P.R.O. 30/24/27/10, pp.196–7 [ff.99v–100r]; Shaftesbury to Robert Molesworth, January 6, 1709, in *Letters to Molesworth*, p.22.

[34] See, for instance, P.R.O. 30/24/20/53, Shaftesbury to Benjamin Furley, January 11, 1701 (redated).

[35] P.R.O. 30/24/20/14, Shaftesbury to Thomas Freke (a Dorset gentleman and neighbor), September 10, 1700; 30/24/20/56, Shaftesbury to Benjamin Furley, February 22, 1701 (redated); 30/24/20/24, Shaftesbury to Benjamin Furley, May 9, 1701; 30/24/20/29, Shaftesbury to Benjamin Furley, July 21, 1701.

[36] P.R.O. 30/24/20/15, Shaftesbury to Benjamin Furley, November 15, 1700. See also: Shaftesbury to Robert Molesworth, January 6, 1709, in *Letters to Molesworth*, p.19.

[37] P.R.O. 30/24/22/2, ff.173–174, Shaftesbury to Sir John Cropley, February 18, 1706; 30/24/22/4, ff.65–67, Shaftesbury to Sir John Cropley, February/March 1708. In *Paradoxes of State*, discussed below, Shaftesbury listed many acts that had been passed or bills for which he had high hopes, in order to emphasize the degree to which the Country concerns had been addressed in the post-1688 order. The view that the 1688 Revolution had to be consummated in post-1688 legislation is also evident in P.R.O. 30/24/22/4, ff.102, Shaftesbury to Rowland Gwin, January 23, 1704. Gwin (1659–1722) served the British government in Hanover during Anne's reign and was a long-standing acquaintance of Shaftesbury.

Country Whig. Shaftesbury's maiden speech, in January 1696, supported the Treason Trials Bill, an issue that illuminates the currents of party transition at this time. Reforming treason procedure favored the rights of the accused and limited the prerogatives of the Crown in prosecuting. When the Convention Parliament debated reform, the Whigs were still mortified by the memory of the recent trials of William Russell and Algernon Sidney and so supported it. Though one component was enshrined in the Declaration of Rights, major reform was deferred. However, in the parliamentary sessions of the 1690s, the Court opposed any reform since, by then, those likely to benefit from treason trial reforms were Jacobites or other conspirators against William III. Meanwhile, Tories embraced the issue, though its passage in 1696 depended on the support of those whom Gilbert Burnet called "sour Whigs." Thus, while treason trial reform was not a standard Country issue, it might gain support from Whigs of an independent cast of mind. It is revealing that this was the issue on which Shaftesbury made his first parliamentary speech.[38]

Nor was this the only matter in connection with which he took a position against that of the Court Whigs, for, early in his parliamentary service, Shaftesbury gave enthusiastic support to the parliamentary qualifications bill of Sir William Williams, an old exclusionist. The qualifications of members were one aspect of a long-standing Country concern with parliamentary elections, growing out of a desire to guard the autonomy of members against manipulation by the Court.[39] The main function of Williams's bill was to raise the landed property requirements for knights and burgesses. Shaftesbury suggested amendments to Williams that underscored the demand that property be real estate and that insisted that members be resident in their shire or near the borough they represented.[40] In a contemporary letter, Shaftesbury characterized the measure as anti-Court and anti-prerogative, a view presumably shared by King William who ultimately vetoed it. Shaftesbury wrote that, though his support of the bill won him the disapproval of the ministers, he would always be for such measures, regardless of party. He thus struck the

[38] Samuel Rezneck, "The Statute of 1696: A Pioneer Measure in the Reform of Judicial Procedure in England," *Journal of Modern History*, 2 (1930), 5–26; Lois G. Schwoerer, *The Declaration of Rights, 1689* (Baltimore and London: The Johns Hopkins University Press, 1981), pp.94–96, 194, 226; Horwitz, *Parliament, Policy and Politics*, pp.137, 164; Voitle, *Third Earl of Shaftesbury*, pp.74–75. Burnet is quoted in Rezneck.

[39] G. E. Aylmer, "Place Bills and the Separation of Powers," *Royal Historical Society Transactions*, 5th series, 15 (1965), 45–69; Rubini, *Court and Country*, pp.114–117. On Williams's bill, see Horwitz, *Parliament, Policy and Politics*, pp.168, 177, 189.

[40] National Library of Wales, Canon Trevor Owen Mss. (papers of Sir William Williams), 202 ("Some amendments proposed by Lord Ashley"). I owe this reference to Dr. David Hayton of the History of Parliament Trust.

independent pose of the Country member while supporting the most characteristic of Country measures.[41]

The highpoint of Country politics in the 1690s occurred at the end of the Nine Years' War with the controversy over a standing army in peacetime, demanded by the King and his Whig ministers and abhorred by the Country gentlemen in Parliament.[42] Though there are no direct, contemporary statements by Shaftesbury about standing armies, he appeared in a 1698 list of those opposed to the army.[43] Moreover, he later attested to the risks that attached to supporting "the disbanding of the Army when there was such force abroad." By 1699, he was no longer in the Commons, having succeeded to his title, but his continuing influence against the standing army may be evident in the absence at that time of various Dorset members from crucial votes on disbanding.[44]

Our sense of Shaftesbury's politics in the later 1690s owes as much to his associations as to direct evidence. This is the period in which he enjoyed relations with various oppositionalist and mostly Whig writers.[45] He was the peer of some (Robert Molesworth, Walter Moyle, John Trenchard, Andrew Fletcher, Charles Davenant) and the patron of others (John Toland, William Stephens) – some of these men had views of a radical character, though it is easy to exaggerate their radicalism. In any case, they were a various lot. Their radicalism was most clearly reflected in their highly critical attitude toward institutional religion: they opposed priestcraft and urged toleration and some, at least, tended toward deism of one sort or another. They were also imbued with the Country Whig tradition and its concern with the liberties of the subject, the independence of Parliament, and the dangers posed by the monarch.

Blair Worden has characterized this group and its extensions as a two-tiered body of Whig critics.[46] On the one hand were the Calves-Head Whigs, more radical in their ideas, more deeply connected with the

---

[41] British Museum, Additional Manuscripts 4017, f.92, Shaftesbury to Thomas Stringer, February 15, 1696. Reintroduced the next year, the bill, first passed by the Commons and defeated in the Lords, was tacked to a fiscal measure. The tack was defeated but Ashley was among those voting for it: Horwitz, *Parliament, Policy and Politics*, pp.187, 189.
[42] Lois Schwoerer, *"No Standing Armies!"* (Baltimore: The Johns Hopkins University Press, 1974); Rubini, *Court and Country*, pp.131–156.
[43] I. F. Burton, P. W. J. Riley, and E. Rowlands, "Political Parties in the Reigns of William III and Anne: The Evidence of Division Lists," *Bulletin of the Institute of Historical Research*, Special Supplement No. 7 (November 1968), pp. 43, 33n. This list aimed to assess sentiments of members of the 1695–1698 Parliament because the army promised to continue to be an important question in the Parliament elected in 1698.
[44] P.R.O. 30/24/22/2, ff.173–4, Shaftesbury to Sir John Cropley, February 18, 1706; Hayton, "'Country' Interest and the Party System," p.54.
[45] Robbins, *Eighteenth-Century Commonwealthman*, pp.88–133; Worden, *A Voyce from the Watch Tower*, pp.18–55.
[46] Worden, *A Voyce from the Watch Tower*, pp.39–42.

tradition of London radicalism, and of a lower social provenance. On the other were the Aristocratic or Roman Whigs, the gentlemanly and highly literate men whose concern with corruption, edified by broad reading among ancient and modern political writers, took the form of a program for the moral-political education of the English political elite and for the strengthening of the institutions they were supposed to dominate virtuously. This account has the effect of putting distance between Shaftesbury and the more radical interests of men such as Toland and Stephens, with both of whom he would ultimately break.

His misgivings about the life of political engagement and perhaps the circles in which he moved led him to refuse to stand in the election of 1698. We have already seen the manner in which his notebooks articulated a personal crisis centering on the point at which the private and the public selves met. In the notebooks, he sometimes formulated his psychological tension as arising in the very scene of politics during "that whole Season from the first Apostacy of a certain Sett of Men [Court Whigs] to thy Retirement hither to Holland the first time," that is, precisely the period in which he threw himself into the politics of William's third Parliament. Politics was the exemplary arena of inauthenticity, of "Malignity hid under Humanity," of "fals Pitty expressed for Faults of others; affected Sorrow; Anger on the Publick account & for Mankind; the Quarrels engagd in for the commonwealth."[47] Rejecting the world of the politicos, he named names:

the Grave Legislators, Orators, Authors, Advisers & Politick Dealers, Aristotelians, Machiavellians, Memoire-Readers or Writers, Gothick or Antient Modellers, or Collectors; with all that Dinn of State Dogmatists, Prescribers, Moralizers, Exhorters, Praisers, Censurers, such as the D[avenan]t's, the F[letche]r's, M[oleswor]th's, J. L[ocke]'s etc:[48]

From the perspective of Shaftesburian introspection, the extroverted political confrontations of his former associates conduced to the faults of self-ignorance.

When he returned to politics in 1700, he was an earl and the political climate had changed. The character of William's fifth and sixth Parliaments was very different from that of William's third, when Shaftesbury had made a reputation as an independent Whig. Whiggism rather than independence was now the priority, especially in view of William's drift toward a Tory ministry in 1700 and 1701. That the Junto Whigs were themselves now outsiders encouraged Shaftesbury to unite with his fellow Whigs, notwithstanding his natural independence, and to rein in the

[47] P.R.O. 30/24/27/15, p.291 [f.202r].
[48] P.R.O. 30/24/27/10, p.305 [f.209r].

idiosyncrasies of his Country orientation. He now identified the Whigs as "our Party" and the impeached Whig Lords of 1701 as "our Friends."[49]

In 1701, concern with disbanding the armed forces had been entirely supplanted with concern about the French menace, in which Shaftesbury saw implicit the amalgamated threats of the Stuart dynasty, popery, and slavery. In letter after letter, he expressed a desire for a strong anti-French policy, insisting on the popular antipathy to the French and, so, on the Whig claim to govern. Similarly, he accused the Tory ministers of a pro-French and Jacobitical policy. The Tory dominance in the Commons bespoke a real reluctance on the part of the Tory constituency to support another war, but, in Shaftesbury's view, it was an "Unfair Representative" created by the maneuvers of the Court.[50] This Court was a malignant clique of Tories who connived to attack the Junto Lords, to recognize the Duke of Anjou as the Spanish heir, to convince the King that the English would not fight, to reduce the King's income, and to debilitate the navy. The Tories blocked all support for the Dutch and all attempts to curtail French power.

Then there was the honest party of the Country, which Shaftesbury conceived as the Whig and anti-Tory party. He wrote that the old Parliament had been dismissed because it was too much of the Country and because a less Country Parliament was desired. When the Parliament of 1701 supported anti-French measures, he said that its virtue was still intact.[51] What Shaftesbury failed to perceive was that increasingly the Country was becoming Tory. Thus, the sorts of Country measures that had led to the dismissal of the previous Parliament were *Tory* Country measures.[52] Shaftesbury's errors of political judgment reflected real tensions within the political landscape, but his position was increasingly at odds with current realities. He wanted to think that Country and Whig were identical. He knew that some Whigs had apostacized the Country for Court power in 1690s, but he did not yet perceive that the Country was abandoning Whiggery. His dual commitments, both to the constitutional reform program of the Country and to the foreign and religious policy of the Whigs, were not that widely shared. It took Shaftesbury quite a while before he recognized this development and ceased to identify himself with

---

[49] P.R.O. 30/24/20/22, Shaftesbury to Benjamin Furley, April 15, 1701.
[50] See Shaftesbury's letters to Benjamin Furley: P.R.O. 30/24/20/19, March 4, 1701; 30/24/20/20, March 25, 1701; 30/24/20/22, April 15, 1701; 30/24/20/23, May 6, 1701; 30/24/20/56, February 22, 1701 (redated). On the character of the Parliament of 1701, see Horwitz, *Parliament, Policy and Politics*, p.280.
[51] P.R.O. 30/24/20/56, Shaftesbury to Benjamin Furley, February 22, 1701 (redated).
[52] For instance, the resumption of William's grants of forfeited Irish estates: see Hayton, "'Country' Interest and the Party System," pp.60–63; Rubini, *Court and Country*, pp.69–92, 157–168.

"the Country." Yet, perhaps in 1701, we see his first inkling of what was happening when he wrote: "In short, our Adversarys have after 12 years mistake learnt their right Game, they act the Commonwealths-Men & herd with us. The Tares in our Wheat."[53]

Shaftesbury's understanding of the political landscape at this time was further evident in the one strictly political pamphlet he wrote. In late 1701, William dissolved the Parliament. In the new elections, Shaftesbury worked very hard to produce a Whig result in Dorset and adjacent counties in which he had influence. He was remarkably successful, taking great pride in having discomfited Sir Edward Seymour, the Tory magnate who traditionally dominated the south-west of England.[54] Moreover, Shaftesbury threw his energies into the proceedings of the new Parliament, working in concert with the Junto Lord Wharton and (then) Court Whig Lord Haversham.[55]

He also wrote *Paradoxes of State*, published in January 1702.[56] While the main context for the pamphlet was the continuing attack by the Tory/Country party on William's policy, the pamphlet also spoke to the past and continuing tensions in Shaftesbury's own political outlook. *Paradoxes of State* aimed to refute Country arguments by effacing all partisan differences, except that which it advanced as the one genuine issue in contemporary political life, policy toward France.

The first "paradox" was that, in fact, the interests of Court and Country were, under current conditions, the same. The distinction, he wrote, was rooted in the obnoxiousness of the Stuarts to Protestantism and liberty. However, 1688 returned a Protestant monarch to the throne. Moreover, the Bill of Rights and successive legislation (including various Country bills still being mooted) had secured English liberty.[57] Shaftes-

---

[53] P.R.O. 30/24/20/31, Shaftesbury to Benjamin Furley, August 26, 1701. Shaftesbury's confusion was very evident in his various attempts in his letters of 1701 and 1702 to make sense of the evolution of Robert Harley from Country Whig to Tory.

[54] Voitle, *Third Earl of Shaftesbury*, pp.210–213. On the local political background, William Speck, *Tory and Whig* (London: Macmillan, 1970), pp.11–12. The attempt to organize and effect "influence" can be observed in the ample Shaftesbury correspondence of the later part of 1701. Shaftesbury celebrated the victory in P.R.O. 30/24/20/49, Shaftesbury to Benjamin Furley, December 29, 1701.

[55] Horwitz, *Parliament, Policy and Politics*, pp.300–304; P.R.O. 30/24/20/52, Shaftesbury to Benjamin Furley, January 6, 1702.

[56] *Paradoxes of State, relating to the present juncture of affairs in England and the rest of Europe; chiefly grounded on His Majesty's princely, pious, and most gracious speech*. The 21-page pamphlet was printed for Bernard Lintott. According to P.R.O. 30/24/20/52 (Shaftesbury to Benjamin Furley, January 6, 1702), Shaftesbury had recently written the text, "wch I hastily drew up & sent to a Friend to have finishd." The friend was Toland: Worden, *A Voyce from the Watch Tower*, p. 45. On January 30, Shaftesbury reported that the pamphlet had appeared and sent copies to some Dutch friends (P.R.O. 30/24/20/55, Shaftesbury to Benjamin Furley).

[57] *Paradoxes of State*, p.2.

bury attributed the dissensions of the 1690s to the incompleteness of the Bill of Rights, but asserted that now the constitution was complete and liberty secure. The Country program having been enacted, the Court was now one with the Country.

The second "paradox" was that such differences as those between Whig and Tory and Williamite and Jacobite had been dissolved by circumstance into one "real Distinction ... between those that are in a *French*, and those that are in an *English* Interest." This argument thrust against the amalgamation of the Country and the Tory oppositions. It followed that the current configuration made it impossible for anyone to "continue an Enemy to the *Church* or *State* on the principle of *Liberty*." In fact, as the third paradox stated, "the most inveterat Enemies to civil *Liberty*, are those who wou'd now act the Part of *Commonwealthsmen*": "all the *republican* Pretences are quite out of Doors." The constitution, which created "the best, the most equal, and freest *Commonwealth* in the World," was no longer susceptible to a critique from the commonwealth or the Country perspective.[58]

In sum, the pamphlet bespoke Shaftesbury's discomfort with the direction of Country and commonwealth rhetoric and politics. The shift in the political configuration between the 1695–98 period and the 1700–1702 period had forced Shaftesbury, along with many of his contemporaries and fellow-travellers, to adjust to a situation in which the Court was regarded as necessary and the Whigs as the necessary incumbents of power at the Court. Though he remained loyal to the Country program of limitations on the Crown, his own ideological development was moving him away from Country commitments.

He was also moving away from direct political engagement. Anne's accession, which brought the Tories to power, left little for Shaftesbury to do. In addition, the congenital weakness of his health, exacerbated by over-exertion in the last Parliament of King William, had begun to exact a toll. From Wimborne St. Giles's, he exerted what influence he had over the elections in 1702, before breaking up his household at St. Giles and sojourning in Holland for most of 1703 and 1704.[59] His return, involving a long and rough crossing, left him seriously ill, a condition from which he

---

[58] *Paradoxes of State*, pp.3–4. The pamphlet also made a number of ancillary points: it attacked the High Church initiatives against the bishops; it commended toleration and comprehensive solutions to religious dissent; it denied that the anti-French policy could be condemned on the basis of taxes (pp.4–7, 18–19).

[59] P.R.O. 30/24/20/66, Shaftesbury to Benjamin Furley, November 1702; 30/24/22/2, ff.155–156, Shaftesbury to Burgess, January 22, 1705; 30/24/22/4, f.102, Shaftesbury to Rowland Gwin, January 23, 1704; 30/24/20/67, "Instructions to My Servants", December 1702. The 1702 campaign is discussed in P.R.O. 30/24/20/61, 30/24/20/63, 30/24/20/64; 30/24/45 I, ff.97–107; 30/24/45 IV, ff.49–50.

did not recover until 1705. That illness convinced him he would never have an active role in politics again. Indeed, it was at a distance from politics that he found his real vocation. During the next five years, he entered his maturity. He married and his wife gave birth to the next Lord Ashley. And, especially, he began to publish the essays that he then collected into *Characteristicks*.

During Anne's reign, he remained in constant contact with the London scene through his friend Sir John Cropley and took care to cultivate the Whig interest in the unpropitious ground of the West Country. Throughout he nursed a sense of menace and grievance with the ministries of Anne.[60] At the same time, he attained a more complacent view of the English political condition than he had had in the earlier period. We find him trying to convince a Dutch associate that, though there was a definite strain of anti-Dutch feeling and policy among the Tories, the Dutch needed not worry about their liberty for the simple reason that English liberty was firmly established.[61] While this letter was partly aimed at calming a worried Dutch spirit, it also attested a greater confidence in the cumulative worth of the Revolution Settlement and its subsequent amendments. Moreover, it construed the political scene entirely in terms of the polarity of Whig and Tory; liberty now existed under the auspices of the Whigs alone; the Country had dropped out of sight.[62]

Obviously, Shaftesbury's political stance and activity must be seen against the changing background of contemporary politics. Perhaps the most important conclusion to be drawn is that, while Shaftesbury began as a Whig in the Country mode, he could not in any simple way remain one. He certainly remained loyal to certain aspects of the Country program, those legal measures that would limit the power of the Court and Crown in their relations with Parliament. However, the Country ceased to be a useful rubric for him: after about 1702, he stopped using it to identify his affiliations. It seems clear that he increasingly saw the Country as embodying many propensities and policies (especially with

---

[60] For instance, P.R.O. 30/24/22/2, f.156, Shaftesbury to Awnsham Churchill (a London bookseller and sometime Dorset M.P.), January 20, 1705; ff.160–161, Shaftesbury to Rowland Gwin, February 24, 1705.

[61] P.R.O. 30/24/22/2, ff.170–172, Shaftesbury to John van't Wedde (a member of Benjamin Furley's circle in Rotterdam), January 17, 1705–06.

[62] This did not mean that his commitment to Country measures had disappeared. The most significant instance of Court-Country politics during Anne's reign concerned the place clause attached to the Regency bill of 1706. Shaftesbury has been called the *éminence grise* behind this Country Whig revolt. For some time after the Regency bill crisis, Shaftesbury seems to have been an object of attention by both the ministry and the Junto: Holmes, *British Politics in the Age of Anne*, pp.132–134, 222–223, and "The Attack on 'The Influence of the Crown' 1702–16," *Bulletin of the Institute of Historical Research*, 39 (1966), 55–59, 66–67; Hayton, "'Country' Interest and the Party System," pp.49–54.

respect to religion and foreign policy) with which he disagreed; increasingly Country was becoming synonymous with Tory.

In a parallel development, his sense of identification with the Whigs changed. The point is not that the allegiance became stronger, but rather that it became more tolerant of the compromises that governing entailed. Under the political conditions of the first decade of the eighteenth century, his commitments to toleration in religion and to anti-French and pro-Dutch policy in foreign affairs limited rather severely the degree to which he could entertain a political identity alternative to the mainstream of Whiggism.

What Shaftesbury inherited from the oppositionalist tradition in English politics was a discourse that focussed on virtue and liberty. As we will see in the next section, this discourse also sought to understand politics in terms of the wide net of moral and other traits summed up by the term "manners." To this Shaftesbury added a range of cultural interests still to be explored and, as well, his distinctive approach to morals, investigated in part I. The product was a cultural politics that aimed to undermine the Tory view of the world in the name of a distinctive Whig order.

The civic tradition and culture

The resources for developing a Whig cultural discourse were shaped by the Whig association with the Country. The Country, understood as a political perspective in early modern England, opened on a certain sociology and a certain set of values: from this perspective, England was peopled with autonomous landed gentlemen who were embodiments and guardians of English virtue and liberty. Grounding the perspective was the social actuality of the member of the landed elite, whose life combined the personalities of rentier, agriculturalist, businessman, politician, officeholder, member of local society, and leader in local religion. By the seventeenth century, this life had developed certain typical cultural expressions, such as law, history, antiquarian studies, and religion. Though such expressions might differ from those found among the elite at Court or among the mercantile elite of the City, they constituted a good deal more than rural vegetation.[63]

[63] On elite society in the country, Alan Everitt, *Change in the Provinces: the Seventeenth Century* (Leicester: Leicester University Press, 1969). Any number of studies reflect on the cultural concomitants of this life: for instance, J. T. Cliffe, *The Yorkshire Gentry from the Reformation to the Civil War* (London: The University of London Athlone Press, 1969), pp. 81–83; C. W. Chalklin, *Seventeenth-Century Kent: A Social and Economic History* (London: Longmans, 1965), p.206; David Douglas, *English Scholars* (London: Jonathan Cape, 1939), p.17. On rural vegetation, cf. Thomas Hobbes, "The Answer ... To Sir Will.

The Court and the City are relevant here because, in the seventeenth century, they were the obvious counterpoints in cultural characterization to the Country. As opposed to the City and the Court, the Country made claim to simplicity and raised images that seem only partly appropriate to the active life of the members of the county community. Simplicity suggested divergent qualities, corresponding to divergent classical models and divergent ways that the Country could be classicized.

In the first place, the Country became laden with the meanings of Augustan ruralism. In this model, the Country was a realm of retirement for aristocrats and courtiers in which leisure was decorated with the arts of life. The Country was a vacation resort for the display of courtly urbanity. The simplicity invoked in this model was a pattern of disciplined restraint in the context of a decorous life. The Jacobeans introduced this pastoral model, which had a long life afterwards. Since such a Country presupposed a Court from which adjournment was taken, this model simultaneously distinguished and coordinated Court and Country. The model sanctioned the continuation of courtly values in a different setting. While no political valence necessarily attached to the model, it did enable much poetry of a courtly, royalist and, later, Tory sort.[64]

More relevant to the Whigs, however, was the assimilation of England to the model of the civic humanist tradition. By this move, the Country, the corps of landed gentlemen in England, was recast as a citizenry on whose virtue the safety of the polity depended. Country virtue enabled the defense of liberty. The model tended to juxtapose Country to Court, which was seen as the primary source of political corruption. The model also invoked simplicity as a moral-cultural accompaniment of the virtuous Country, but the proper manners of a civically conceived Country ranged widely. Liberty and manners were connected in the civic tradition because the attempt to grasp the fragility and evanescence of liberty led writers to assess both the conditions for, and the rewards consequent on, its survival; and thereby stimulated discussion of the net of circumstance, material and moral, in which liberty and tyranny were enmeshed, both under present conditions and in a repertoire of foreign and historical illustrations.

Quentin Skinner's discussion of civic humanism in his survey of Renaissance political thought makes clear that, although a notion of public-oriented virtue consistently played a central role in civic thinking, the exact reflection of virtue in manners was susceptible to interpretive

---

D'Avenant's Preface before Gondibert," in David F. Gladish, ed., *Sir William Davenant's Gondibert* (Oxford: Clarendon Press, 1971), p.45.

[64] Malcolm Smuts, *Court Culture and the Origins of a Royalist Tradition in Early Stuart England* (Philadelphia: University of Pennsylvania Press, 1987), pp.84–98.

variations. Leonardo Bruni had argued that, because a free republic offered honor equally to all who strove, it unlocked the energies of the people, creating possibilities of greatness not only in the political but in all domains. Equality and openness allowed the emergence of all the forms of excellence that contributed to the power or reputation of the commonwealth. Such a view sanctioned diversity and also cultural elaboration.[65]

However, the civic tradition also encouraged a more centripetal approach to questions of virtue. The fear of privatism as detrimental to the republic issued in interpretations of virtue that required exclusivity and uniformity of public commitment. While Bruni and others praised wealth as a mode of virtue, other civic writers condemned the pursuit of wealth and its consumption as privatistic luxury. Such a view validated penury or frugality and insisted on equality not as a condition for diversity and excellence but as a condition for uniformity and exclusivity. Frugality, uniformity, and single-minded patriotism were often accompanied by the insistence that citizens serve in the armies that defended republics. Indeed, militarism and frugality came to the fore in the classic late Renaissance civic tracts, of which Machiavelli's was most influential in later centuries.[66] However, as the Bruni example shows, these emphases were not the only ones possible within a civic framework. This diversity is an important background to Shaftesbury's civic politics.

Nonetheless, the Machiavellian strain of republicanism was powerful in late seventeenth- and early eighteenth-century England, as Charles Davenant attested when he defined virtue as "Piety to our Country, Zeal for its Interest or Glory, Patience under Adverse Fortune, Temper in Prosperity, Obedience to Discipline and Laws, Foresight in Business, Secrecy and Firmness in Councils, Vigour in Action, Courage, Military Skill, Thirst of Honour, Magnanimity."[67] Influenced by the Machiavellian concern with the military basis of the free polity, Davenant invoked here not a moral concept but an entire way of life.

Thus, the concern with virtue and liberty modulated into a concern with manners. Though institutions could be seen as shaping manners, the relation between institutions and manners might be reversed. Indeed, many civic writers accepted as a truism that manners were the foun-

---

[65] Quentin Skinner, *The Foundations of Modern Political Thought* (Cambridge: Cambridge University Press, 1978), I, 80–81.
[66] Skinner, *Foundations of Modern Political Thought*, I, 41–45, 162–170.
[67] Charles Davenant, "An Essay upon Universal Monarchy," in *Essays upon the Ballance of Power, the Right of Making War, Peace, and Alliances, and Universal Monarchy* (1701), p.267. A concise statement about the relation of virtue and liberty is available in Bernard Bailyn, *The Ideological Origins of the American Revolution* (Cambridge: Harvard University Press, 1967), pp.61–66. The subject is treated extensively in Pocock's *Machiavellian Moment*.

dations of civic politics. In the Restoration period, Henry Neville assigned loss of liberty to "Debauchery of manners," and Algernon Sidney wrote that "Liberty cannot be preserved, if the manners of the People are corrupted."[68] During Anne's reign, then, it is not surprising to find Jonathan Swift asserting that "few States are ruined by any Defect in their Institution, but generally by the Corruption of Manners; against which, the best Institution is no long Security, and without which, a very ill one may subsist and flourish."[69]

The criteria of virtuous manners, listed by Davenant and widely endorsed among civic writers, have by now been frequently exposed. The manners conducive to liberty – independence, public-mindedness, martial strength, frugality, and simplicity – were those of the classical citizen as interpreted by Machiavelli. By contrast, the anti-world of the civic moralist was epitomized in luxury, a concept redolent of perversity: self-indulgent and private rather than public; soft and sensuous rather than martial; expensive rather than frugal; and excessive rather than simple – in all ways, a threat to economic and moral independence.[70] Such concerns with manners enabled writers of a neo-Harringtonian persuasion in the 1690s and early 1700s to enunciate a general view of politics in its historical relations. Their insistence on virtuous manners brought them into conflict not just with Court policies but with the direction of modern history, and so they admired cultures that, though culturally rudimentary, were free and virtuous: Sparta, early Rome, and Gothic Europe.[71]

The neo-Harringtonians accordingly offered a narrow defence of liberty. The particular interpretation of the civic tradition on which Andrew Fletcher and others based their case for liberty made impossible or difficult the assimilation of politeness and everything for which it stood in the way of moral and cultural development. However, the civic tradition did not validate only the narrow definition of civic virtue accepted by Fletcher.

As the example of Leonardo Bruni showed, liberty could have rich

[68] Henry Neville, *Plato Redivivus* (1681), pp.33–34, 64–65; Algernon Sidney, *Discourses Concerning Government* (1698), pp.111, 144–145, 201. See also Robert Molesworth, *An Account of Denmark, as it was in the year 1692*, 3rd edn (1694), sig. b1v; Andrew Fletcher, "A Discourse of Government with Relation to Militia's," in *The Political Works of Andrew Fletcher* (1732), p.13; Walter Moyle, "An Essay upon the Constitution of the Roman Government," in *The Works of Walter Moyle* (1726), pp.139–142.
[69] Jonathan Swift, "The sentiments of a Church-of-England Man with respect to religion and government," in *Prose Works*, II, 14. On the way that "manners" became a subject of political debate, see Peter Jones, "The Scottish Professoriate and the Polite Academy, 1720–46," in Hont and Ignatieff, eds., *Wealth and Virtue*, p.95.
[70] On luxury, see John Sekora, *Luxury: The Concept in Western Thought, Eden to Smollett* (Baltimore: The Johns Hopkins University Press, 1977).
[71] Lawrence Klein, "Liberty, Manners and Politeness in Early Eighteenth-Century England," *The Historical Journal*, 32 (1989), 583–605.

cultural associations. Liberty catalyzed the greatness of a people: in Sidney's words, "the Strength, Vertue, Glory, Wealth, Power, and Happiness of *Rome* proceeding from Liberty, did rise, grow, and perish with it."[72] Though greatness was in the first place a matter of power and heft, the ability to throw weight on the inter-state scene drew on such arts of peace as prosperity, social tranquillity, and, significantly, cultural achievement. In this light, it was less of a quandary how liberty might co-exist with sophisticated modes of human expression. The safety of liberty became the guarantee for the health of arts, letters, and learning.[73]

This relation was supported by the close ties that could be asserted between liberty and eloquence. Renaissance humanists, whose identity rested partly on their rhetorical interests, used the resources provided by ancient writings to support the association of liberty and eloquence. While the Isocratean view of eloquence as constitutent of all civilization played a role in this,[74] a larger part was played by the republican version of Roman cultural history, according to which the corruption concomitant on the fall of liberty included the decline of eloquence. Tacitus provided a great source for this perspective.[75]

This is the context for understanding the Old Whig side of Jonathan Swift's cultural outlook. Swift's early pamphlets provide capsule renditions of the theme of liberty, arts and letters, outlines of a classic cultural history of the ancient world from the civic perspective. In antiquity, he wrote, when "Arbitrary Government of single Persons" dominated most of the world, "*Arts* and *Sciences* took their Rise, and flourished only in

[72] Sidney, *Discourses*, p.116. In the introduction to the translation of Hotman's *Franco-Gallia* (1721), Molesworth traced the growth of wealth and population to the guarantees of liberty and property (p.xv).

[73] On the stock theme of the relation of liberty and arts and letters, see René Wellek, *The Rise of English Literary History* (Chapel Hill: The University of North Carolina Press, 1941), pp.32–34, 58–59. Michael Meehan's *Liberty and Poetics in Eighteenth Century England* (London: Croom Helm, 1986) is devoted to exploring this theme.

[74] Isocrates, *Nicocles or the Cyprians* 5–9. A variation on this account appeared in Cicero, *De inventione* I.i.2–3. This commonplace underlay Andrew Fletcher's approval of the view that "if a man were permitted to make all the ballads, he need not care who should make the laws of a nation. And we find that most of the antient legislators thought they could not well reform the manners of any city without the help of a lyrick, and sometimes of a dramatick poet": Andrew Fletcher, "An Account of a Conversation Concerning a Right Regulation of Governments for the Common Good of Mankind," in *Political Works*, p.372.

[75] Among Tacitean points of departure are *Dialogus de oratoribus* 36–40 and *Historiarum* I. For the Renaissance phase (Leonardo Bruni and, later, Poggio Bracciolini's expansion on Bruni in debate with the courtly Guarino da Verona), see Hans Baron, *The Crisis of the Early Italian Renaissance*, rev. edn (Princeton: Princeton University Press, 1966), pp.58–60, 66–67. For the eighteenth century, see Howard Weinbrot, *Augustus Caesar in 'Augustan' England* (Princeton: Princeton University Press, 1978), pp.68–79; Howard Erskine-Hill, *The Augustan Idea in English Literature* (London: Edward Arnold, 1983), pp.249–254.

those few small Territories where the People were *free*." The case of Augustan Rome showed only that "*Learning* may continue after *Liberty* is lost ... upon the Foundations laid under the Commonwealth." However, as a general rule, tyranny impeded cultural production, because "*Slavery*," as "the first natural Step from *Anarchy* or the *Savage Life*," was "the greatest Clog and Obstacle to *Speculation*."[76] Thus, freedom provided the basis for culture just as the decline of freedom dried up culture's resources.

Swift shared this sort of civic humanism with Shaftesbury, and much of the antique cultural history adumbrated in Swift's writings was given much fuller treatment in Shaftesbury. Indeed, part of Shaftesbury's accomplishment was simply the amplitude with which he elaborated the artistic and literary fecundity of free societies along with its corollary, the barrenness of tyranny. Like other civic writers, Shaftesbury found the classical and more recent past a fertile ground in which to develop his ideas. Cultural history in particular allowed Shaftesbury to present cultural change against the background of freedom. In the lineage and succession of wit, Shaftesbury detected the conjoined "Flourishing and Decay of *Liberty* and *Letters*."[77]

The association of liberty and letters could not be supported by the notion of citizenship to which Machiavelli and his English successors had subscribed. Athenian diversity rather than Spartan uniformity was the congenial setting for a cultural flowering.[78] The republican citizen had to have elements of personality which his identity as a member of a citizen-army need not deny him. Certainly, there were classical writings of a civic nature that lent themselves to use in this connection, most important, those of Cicero. Cicero spoke for and also embodied a notion of citizenship by means of which the association of liberty and letters could be authoritatively grounded.

In a number of ways, it is helpful to think of Cicero's idea of citizenship as senatorial. In the first place, that label links Cicero's ideas to their

---

[76] Swift, "Sentiments of a Church-of-England Man," p.18. For the linguistic dimension of this cultural history, see Jonathan Swift, "A Proposal for Correcting, Improving and Ascertaining the English Tongue," in *Prose Works*, IV, 8.

[77] "Soliloquy" II.i, I, 220 (Robertson, I, 144). Shaftesbury's account is discussed in chapter 10, pp.199–206 below.

[78] Cf. the remark by a discussant in Tacitus's *Dialogus* (40) that eloquence "is a plant that does not grow under a well-regulated constitution (*in bene constitutis civitatibus*). Does history contain a single instance of any orator at Sparta, or at Crete, two states whose political system and legislation were more stringent than any other on record? It is equally true to say that in Macedonia and Persia eloquence was unknown as indeed it was in all states that were content to live under a settled government. Rhodes has had some orators, Athens a great many: in both communities all power was in the hands of the populace": Tacitus, *Dialogus, Agricola, Germania* (Loeb Classical Library, Cambridge, Mass.: Harvard University Press, and London: William Heinemann, 1914), pp.122–125.

immediate context, the Roman republic. *Res publica* implied citizenship and participation and the absence of monarchy. Cicero's model was not the Roman republic in his own era (which he sometimes admitted was no longer anything but a name), but the republic as Cicero idealized it in its classic moment before the Gracchi. Then, according to Cicero, it was a mixed and balanced constitution of Few and Many, aristocracy and democracy, Senate and Assembly, in which the common good was pursued and the rights of all were respected.

While all were free, freedom was not the same for all. Cicero's senatorial perspective emphasized the commanding role of the Senate. He more or less distinguished between active and passive forms of citizenship: to the aristocracy, he assigned the effective direction of all affairs of state, while he compensated the rest of the citizens for their formal though empty role in politics with guarantees of their non-civic liberties and interests. As a *novus homo* himself, Cicero was not rigidly exclusive in his view of the aristocracy and allowed for meritocratic ascension.[79]

Though ordinary citizens were excluded from public affairs, senatorial citizenship was defined by active participation. The activities that defined senatorial citizenship were activities of the Senate, namely, debating and deciding the course of the republic. This was precisely the civic framework for the synthesis of wisdom and eloquence, discussed in chapter 1: eloquence and wisdom were both harnessed to a standard of civic behavior expected of senators. Since the ideal citizen was the orator, civic virtue was not expressed simply in the capacity to bear arms for the sake of the republic.[80]

Cicero could be seen as embodying his own ideal, a man of action and a defender of the republic at the same time that he was a man of culture and of learning.[81] Cicero stood for the attempt to integrate the political demands of an aristocratic republic with moral wisdom and eloquent expression. If Cicero's notions drew on realities of the great landowners of the senatorial aristocracy, this was no drawback for anyone attempting to conceptualize favorably the eighteenth-century regime in England. Moreover, Cicero provided some of the most extensive answers to the

---

[79] P. A. Brunt, *The Fall of the Roman Republic and Related Essays* (Oxford: Clarendon Press, 1988), pp.2, 13–14, 45; Z. S. Fink, *The Classical Republicans*, 2nd edn (Evanston: Northwestern University Press, 1962), pp.5–8; Elizabeth Rawson, *Cicero: A Portrait*, rev. edn (Ithaca: Cornell University Press, 1985), pp.147–156; Ronald Syme, *The Roman Revolution* (Oxford: Clarendon Press, 1939), pp.144–145.

[80] The civic significance of the union of eloquence and wisdom is evident throughout *De oratore*, I.viii.31–34, II.ix.35, II.xvi.68, III.xv.56–xvi.60, III.xix.72, III.xxxi.122–124, III.xxxiv.137, III.xxxv.140.

[81] For laudatory appraisals of Cicero in the eighteenth century, see Browning, *Court Whigs*, pp.217–228. For condemnations, Weinbrot, *Augustus Caesar in 'Augustan' England*, pp.15–17.

continuing question faced by eighteenth-century writers in the civic tradition: how was it possible to cultivate virtue.

There are important parallels between this Ciceronian notion of citizenship and the project of the third earl of Shaftesbury. Shaftesbury was addressing a context in which mixed constitution and oligarchical politics coincided. He also was addressing a political class that was aristocratic (in the broad sense), confining civic action to itself while presiding over a legal system that promised legal security to all. His goal, as Cicero's, was a program of education in which the moral and literary would be combined to produce virtuous public action.

Shaftesbury was designing a Whiggism that was civic and humanist though different from the "civic humanist paradigm" as J. G. A. Pocock has presented it. The civic tradition sought to coordinate liberty, virtue, autonomy, and citizenship. We have become accustomed to thinking of the civic tradition as readily useable for oppositionalist purposes in the post-1688 English polemical environment. However, the resources of the civic tradition were ample enough to allow Shaftesbury to use them to legitimize the post-1688 regime. Shaftesbury's demonstration that virtue and culture could coincide was a way of answering the Andrew Fletchers of the world, showing the harmony of Whiggism and culture.

It would be a mistake, however, to think that Shaftesbury was only repeating antique commonplaces. In Shaftesbury, the civic resources were decked out in terms of sociability and politeness and thereby enriched. Shaftesbury's discussion of liberty and politeness complicated the issue of autonomy which was a permanent element of the civic tradition. It also gave a more deeply psychological and cultural cast to the tradition.

The cultural politics of *Characteristicks*

Shaftesbury began "A Letter Concerning Enthusiasm" by observing that modern Britons lived in a culture of criticism, for which they were lucky and, indeed, uncommon. Usually, "the *Freedom of Censure*" was under restraint, and, according to Shaftesbury, restraint in part destroyed the effect of freedom in its entirety: "There can be no *impartial* and *free Censure* of Manners where any peculiar Custom or National Opinion is set apart, and not only exempted from Criticism, but even flatter'd with the highest Art."[82] In a clearly civic way, this comment related manners and liberty. However, in a way less obviously civic, the liberty at stake was a freedom to criticize or, more generally, a discursive liberty. Interestingly, in this statement, the alternative to discursive liberty was flattery,

---

[82] "Letter" ii, I, 9 (Robertson, I, 9).

which, as indicated in chapter 5, Shaftesbury thought a distorted and morally debilitating form of speech. Giving a discursive inflection to civic understandings of liberty betokened the general development of cultural politics in Shaftesbury's writing.

Shaftesbury proceeded in this section to specify the likely sources of threat to liberty: "'Tis only in a free Nation, such as ours, that imposture has no Privilege; and that neither the Credit of a Court, the Power of a Nobility, nor the Awefulness of a Church can give her Protection, or hinder her from being arraign'd in every Shape and Appearance."[83] Here was another civic resonance. The particular institutions that were most likely to menace liberty (though not in "free" modern Britain) were the Court, the nobility, and the Church, which corresponded to the elements of the English constitution to whose obsolescence James Harrington traced the collapse of the political order in the middle of the seventeenth century. Writing after the milestones of 1688, 1701 and 1707, Shaftesbury found himself in a topography in which Harrington's map provided orientation. It was possible for Shaftesbury to think that Harrington's projections had been realized in the half-century between the writing of *Oceana* and that of "A Letter Concerning Enthusiasm." This is not to say, of course, that Shaftesbury thought he lived in a republic or that he mistook the late Stuart constitution for that of Oceana. However, he did assume a post-Harringtonian polity: with Harrington, he shared a fundamental assumption that the gentlemen of England had risen to a prominence that they had not previously enjoyed. Furthermore, this prominence was defined in contrast to that of the monarch and his Court, the nobility, and the Church. So much attention has been given by historians to those who deployed Harringtonian insight in order to castigate the post-1688 order that it is significant to find a major writer using the Harringtonian framework to embrace modernity.

When Court, nobility, and Church successfully resisted liberty, the result was "imposture." Resonant with the vocabulary of sociability, "imposture" conveyed attributes of an unsociable character: the impostor was a figure of pretense, empty appearance, and affectation, who was prone to make false or untested claims and to impose them on others, by the vigor, impressiveness, or cloyingness of his presentation. The civic project of defending the closely associated values of liberty and manners was being cast here in terms of sociability and politeness. "Imposture" was the enemy of polite manners considered as a condition of discourse and culture. Thus, the question of civic virtue was being construed as a question of civic culture.

[83] "Letter" ii, I, 9–10 (Robertson, I, 9).

152   Polite Whiggism

This cultural politics was a thoroughly Whig project, nourished by civic impulses but lacking the ambivalence of those associated with Country or Old or oppositionalist Whiggism. The best proof of its Whiggism was that anti-Toryism was at the top of the agenda. At just about the time that *Characteristicks* was first making its appearance, Shaftesbury described its significance in a letter to John Somers. Though these words referred specifically to volume III, they were broadly applicable to the entire work, since volume III was a gloss on volumes I and II. Central to its purposes, Shaftesbury explained, was an attack on the Tories, that "most malignant party" and their "poysonous Principles, indeed, wch they dispence under a religious appearance." Such a passage set off a range of resonances: to mask poison behind righteousness was to impose in the specific manner of the religious hypocrite; implicated in imposture, the Tories were enemies to liberty and manners. Moreover, Shaftesbury pursued, in quite explicit terms, the interestingly cultural cast of this attack on Toryism:

Whilst their Soveraignty in Arts & Sciences, their Presidentship in Letters, their Alma-Mater's and Academical Virtues have been acknowledg'd & taken for granted, they who treated the Poor Rivall Presbitereans as unpolite, unform'd, without Literature, or Manners, will perhaps be somewhat mov'd to find themselves treated in the same way: not as Corrupters merely of Morals & Publick Principles; but as the very Reverse or Antipodes of Good Breeding, Schollership, Behaviour, Sense & Manners.[84]

This passage set the very clear and specific task of reversing the cultural associations of the two parties. Shaftesbury here acknowledged that Tory claims of a political nature had been bolstered by a widely supposed superiority in matters of social and literary culture. Meanwhile, the burden of *Characteristicks* was, among other things, to disclose the weakness of such claims, shifting the benefit of cultural accomplishment and renown in the Whig direction. This passage made clear that *Characteristicks* was not only political in a general sense but specifically partisan and polemical. Moreover, Shaftesbury presented himself in this passage as a cultural ideologist, whose *Characteristicks* engaged in cultural politics.

As Shaftesbury acknowledged in the passage, the fact that he felt he had to reverse the usual cultural associations of the political parties had its origins in cultural stereotypes of the seventeenth century. Though the passage referred only to the association of the Tories with the universities and of the Whigs with religious nonconformity, it took for granted languages of cultural characterization that distinguished Court and Country, Cavalier and Roundhead, orthodoxy and enthusiasm. The

---

[84] P.R.O. 30/24/22/4, ff.153–156, Shaftesbury to John Somers, March 30, 1711.

Tories' claim to proximity to the best in "manners" and "arts and letters" derived from their associations with the Court and the Church. It was these institutions, which combined political and cultural resources, that Shaftesbury had to attack in order to put forth a new vision of polite English culture under Whig auspices.

8 The critique of the Church

"Awefulness"

In a free nation, according to Shaftesbury, "the Awefulness of a Church" could not offer shelter to "Imposture" simply because the "*impartial* and *free Censure* of Manners," characteristic of free nations, deflated bogus religious and ecclesiastical claims.[1] It is indicative that Shaftesbury fixed on "Awefulness" as the ecclesiastical trait sheltering "Imposture." "Awefulness," and awesomeness, referred most immediately to a certain kind of impact on a beholder: the capacity to create feelings of dread or veneration. Thus, Church "Awefulness" implied specific relations between institution and individual: an "aweful" Church had an overwhelming majesty and an intimidating authority, to which the appropriate response was meekness, passivity, and silence. The institution's imposing qualities, which suppressed questioning and doubt, were intrinsically related to its capacity to nurture imposture. Because such a Church was not conductive to liberty and open discourse, it could not encourage the development of autonomous moral agents.

Indeed, the interactive structures sponsored by an "aweful" Church were fundamentally unsociable. As we have seen, Shaftesbury assigned a paradigmatic value to conversation among equal and autonomous agents just as he deprecated discursive situations marked by inequality and domination. In consequence, figures of discursivity and sociability informed his wider social and cultural understanding. In the Church, he saw an unfortunate model of human interaction generating a distorted style of discourse; in particular, he saw the condescending relationship of preacher to auditor generating a condescendingly magisterial and pedantic discourse. This chapter seeks to explore how Shaftesbury performed a critique of the Church in such discursive and cultural terms.

His views of the Church's role in polity and culture belonged to a Whig ideology motivated by a profound suspicion of clerics. He desired a polity

[1] "Letter" ii, I, 9–10 (Robertson, I, 9).

in which the Church would have no independent political power and would lack mechanisms to enforce uniformity in doctrine and discipline. Moreover, he sought to replace the role of the Church in the moral and social training of the elite with a regime of gentlemanly politeness in philosophy and culture. The role left for the Church was encouraging piety and morals, especially among ordinary people, through exemplary and didactic means.[2]

However, it would be a mistake to regard Shaftesbury's mature writings simply as an attack on the Church of England. In fact, the political conditions in which he operated demanded that he defend the Church as it was constituted in the post-1688 era. From the later 1690s, the Whigs faced aggressive claims on the part of High Church Tories in the name of a strong and independent Church at the head of a vibrant confessional culture. Thus, Shaftesbury was forced to defend the existing Church in arguing against any revival of ecclesiastical power and ecclesiastical "awefulness."

If his attitude toward the Church was not simple, neither was his attitude toward religion itself, For one thing, his own character was, in its way, highly religious: notwithstanding his desire to redistribute intellectual energy between religion and philosophy, a founding premise of all his moral thinking was an acknowledgement of divine reality and its inscription in the order of the universe.[3] In addition, he was capable of adopting a complacent stance toward the religious establishment. Though he dismissed the delusions of vulgar religion, he wrote that "Church misteryes, Rites etc:" were "Sacred" and so to be "reverenc'd." One conformed to what was widely accepted partly in order to confirm one's relatedness to "Men: Society: City: Laws" and partly out of respect for the prejudices of the weak-minded. The wise man consoled himself with the recognition that the fatuities of contemporary religion could be worse. In this respect, Shaftesbury saw himself as imitating antique sages who respected popular religion while recognizing it as a superstitious confection.[4]

Of course, Shaftesbury's real tie with Anglicanism was more substantial than this classical mugging suggests, since he was at home in intellectual traditions of the Church of England. When he declared his allegiance to principles of reason and moderation in religious matters, he related himself to the latitudinarian tradition. He specifically praised William

---

[2] For instance, he thought the contemporary clerical attack on the stage a misuse of "*sacred Oratory*" and urged clerics to aim their discourses "to refine our Taste and Judgment in sacred Matters": "Miscellany" V.i, III, 255 (Robertson, II, 314).
[3] See chapter 2, pp.53–55 above.
[4] P.R.O. 30/24/27/11, pp.13–14 [ff.8v–9r]; P.R.O. 30/24/27/14, p.132 [f.70v].

Chillingworth, Henry Hammond, Isaac Barrow, and John Tillotson, as well as some of the Cambridge Platonists. Obviously, his edition of Benjamin Whichcote's sermons attested to a respect for the moralizing religiosity that they contained. Among contemporaries he admired Benjamin Hoadly and especially Gilbert Burnet.[5] Moreover, his politics forced him to praise the Church. Repeatedly denying the High Church and Tory claim that the Church was in danger, he hailed the current bishops as distinguished examples of Christian piety and learning. He found in them a moderation "in the high Calvinistick Points" (presumably matters of soteriology) and in other matters, such as toleration (as demonstrated in their opposition to Occasional Conformity bills).[6] In one of his unpublished writings, he invented a persona who, after a close encounter with enthusiasts, thanked the "good Providence" which had provided the English with "such establish'd Rites of Worship as were so Decent, Chast, innocent, pure, and had plac'd us in a Religion and Church where, in respect of the Moderate Party, and far greater Part, ye Principle of Charity was really more extentive than in any Christian or Protestant Church besides in the world."[7] Thus, Shaftesbury was a conformist who found things to praise in the current establishment.

However, his praise was confined to the moderate element, whose control of the Church was tenuous. When his protégé Michael Ainsworth was about to take orders in 1711, Shaftesbury urged on him "Honesty, good Principles, Moderation, and true Christianity now set at nought and at defyance by the far greater Part and Numbers of that Body of Clergy call'd the Church of England." Ainsworth had to prepare to withstand "infamys and Calumnys such as are thrown upon the men call'd moderate, and in their stile *indifferent in Religion, Heterodox,* and *Hereticall.*"[8] In Shaftesbury's view, the Church of England was infested with a high-flying party distinguished by its extremism.

The entire thrust of *Characteristicks* was directed against this element in contemporary religious life, since it sought to draw the boundaries of gentlemanly behavior to the exclusion of strong and public religious commitment. At one point in the "Miscellaneous Reflections," he offered the instance of "a Gentleman of some Rank (one who was generally esteem'd to carry a sufficient Caution and Reserve in religious Subjects of Discourse, as well as an apparent Deference to Religion, and in particular to the national and establish'd Church)" who, "provok'd by an imper-

---

[5] P.R.O. 30/24/27/143, Shaftesbury to Michael Ainsworth, February, 25, 1707, December 30, 1709; also the letters of May 5, 1709 and July 10, 1710, in *Several Letters*, pp.34–35, 45ff.
[6] P.R.O. 30/24/20/143, Shaftesbury to Michael Ainsworth, February 25, 1707.
[7] P.R.O. 30/24/46A/81, a small bound notebook, pp.37–38 [f.22r–v].
[8] P.R.O. 30/24/22/7, f.510, Shaftesbury to Michael Ainsworth, May 11, 1711.

tinent Attack of a certain violent bigotted Party, was drawn into an open and *free* Vindication not only of Free-*Thinking*, but Free-Professing, and *Discoursing*, in Matters relating to Religion and Faith."[9] The persona was a Shaftesburian surrogate in his rank and in his posture toward established religion. The character accepted the religious establishment and addressed religious matters only indirectly and reluctantly. However, this character was stimulated into discursive action at the provocation of a partisan of religious violence and bigotry. Similarly, the context for Shaftesbury's writings on religion and the Church was the ideological confrontation between Whiggism and the revived High Churchmanship of Queen Anne's reign.

It is worth mentioning, however, that, while he defended free-thinking and discursive liberty in many contexts, Shaftesbury sought to distinguish himself from some free thinkers and deists. The wise man's treatment of popular religion had to show the same discursive sensitivity that, as we saw in part I, Shaftesbury thought should inform the entirety of philosophy. Thus, Shaftesbury made clear that the wise man was not to disturb the prejudices of the vulgar except in a careful way plotted to remove prejudice. He had no truck with gratuitous antagonism to the present religious order. In one passage, he self-consciously separated himself from what he saw as the atheistic challenge to Christianity promoted by "Epic[urians], Pyrr[honians], Hobbists, Witts, Libertines, Half-Believers . . . & those that bite the Chain, the contrary Enthousiasts, Sectarians, etc:"[10] He made clear in the stoic notebooks that moving a person from superstitious religious views to atheism constituted no spiritual progress. Thus, he condemned what "we call free-talking about matters of Religion & of Establishd Rites of Worship . . . especially if it be done after a certain manner: that is to say, if it be not still with a certain Economy & Reserve: if it be vehemently . . . acutely . . . as shewing Witt . . . ridiculingly & with Contempt."[11] He did not make clear exactly whom he was thinking of here, but, in one letter, he implied considerable unease at being confused with writers such as John Toland, Matthew Tindal, Anthony Collins, John Asgill, and Jonathan Swift (of *A Tale of a Tub*).[12] The "Economy & Reserve" that Shaftesbury commended in critical writings on religion was one instance of the veiled irony that, as we saw in chapters 5 and 6, Shaftesbury said should characterize the social stance of

---

[9] "Miscellany" V.iii, III, 317–318 (Robertson, II, 353).
[10] P.R.O. 30/24/27/11, p.13 [f.8v].
[11] P.R.O. 30/24/27/10, pp.120–121 [ff.61v–62r].
[12] P.R.O. 30/24/22/4, ff.67–70, Shaftesbury to John Somers, March 1708. The main subject of this letter was Shaftesbury's apprehension that the manuscript version of *A Letter Concerning Enthusiasm*, sent to Somers, had made its way into other hands and was about to be published (as a product of Jonathan Swift's hand).

the philosophical gentleman and the discursive stance of the philosophical writer.

What is remarkable in Shaftesbury is the degree to which his discussion of discursive and ecclesiastical matters was penetrated by the idioms of sociability and politeness. Insofar as *Characteristicks* constituted a "Plea for *Complacency, Sociableness*, and GOOD HUMOUR *in Religion*," it sought to submit religion to the disciplines of politeness.[13] What exactly did this mean? Shaftesbury's insistence on the sociability of religion opened several broad vistas on the religious landscape.

Religious sociability was partly of doctrinal significance. Like morals themselves, human religiosity had its foundations in natural affection. While the capacity to feel relation to whatever was outside the self exercised itself first in one's closest human relationships, it extended ultimately to the cosmic and divine framework of all existence. Affective sociability made it possible for humans to grasp and appreciate the cosmological framework in which they were located. Thus, religion was a manifestation of intrinsic human sociability.[14]

Clearly, this sort of religiosity left little room for revealed religion, except perhaps as a supplement to what was available naturally in human affections and rationality. Indeed, there was little in Shaftesbury's religion of a specifically Christian sort. He talked little of Jesus and assigned him no role except that of moral exemplar. He talked of providence but in a way that, owing little to Christianity, was hard to distinguish from Epictetus's discussion. In one of his less complacent moods, he condemned the "vulgar Religion" of the age, in which he had been bred, and "what impressions [were] yet remaining of that sordid shamefull Nauseouse Idea of Deity."[15] He was thinking of an anthropomorphic deity who made humans frail and then proceeded to punish and reward them for what they could not help. As chapter 2 indicated, *An Inquiry Concerning Virtue* had been an attempt to undercut this sort of portrait of godhead, first by endowing humans with the natural capacity for goodness, and second by insisting that virtue could not be the result of prudential calculation about post-mortal rewards and punishments. Thus, sociability in religion meant not only religion that arose within the human affections but, particularly, religion that honored sociability as a source of human morality and worth.

However, sociable religion implied more than a series of doctrinal choices. It pointed toward the social configuration of religion. It meant,

---

[13] "Miscellany" II.iii, III, 111 (Robertson, II, 224).
[14] This point is made in several places: e.g., "Moralists" I.iii, II, 210–217 (Robertson, II, 20–23); "Miscellany" II.iii, III, 114–115 (Robertson, II, 226).
[15] P.R.O. 30/24/27/10, p.100 [f.51v]; also, p.118 [f.60v].

The critique of the Church 159

for Shaftesbury, a religion that operated within society, according to principles of sociability and politeness. Religion had to be sociable not only in its substance but also in its means. Such a demand raised questions about religion as a social pattern, about the style of religious discourse, and about the nature and role of the Church.

Some of these issues were broached, though not rigorously pursued, in the section of the second miscellany commenting on the defense of raillery in "Sensus Communis." Adopting a formal pose, Shaftesbury announced:

Our purpose, therefore, being to defend an Author who has been charg'd as too presumptuous for introducing the way of WIT and HUMOUR into *religious* Searches; we shall endevour to make appear:

1st, THAT WIT and HUMOUR are corroborative of *Religion*, and promotive of *true Faith*.

2ly, THAT they are us'd as proper *Means* of this kind by the holy founders of Religion.

3ly, THAT notwithstanding the dark Complexion and sour Humour of some religious Teachers, we may be justly said to have in the main, A *witty* and *good-humour'd Religion*.

The show of form quickly dissolved into a loose argument, interspersed with anecdote and stylistic digression, before being abandoned entirely.[16] The third point was the most substantive, but, unfortunately, Shaftesbury gave up his experiment in "formalism" before reaching it. Still, it is clear that the proposition was intended to praise beneficent views of divinity, morally exemplary interpretations of Jesus, and the benevolent ethic taught by Christianity. Shaftesbury did devote considerable attention to the second point, contending that the chief "voices" in the Judaeo-Christian tradition spoke in a good-humoured way. Shaftesbury cast as polite writers the Old Testament authors, Jesus, the Apostles, and God himself.[17] However, this second point was illustrative of the first, which sought to establish the relation between religion and wit and humour.

Here Shaftesbury sought to situate religion in the context of discourse, opening perspectives on the psychology and sociology of religion. He asserted that human belief was usually shaped by varying combinations of custom, authority, and force. This observation called attention to the frailty of human cognitive claims not only in religion but in all domains. If custom and authority determined belief, then anything whatsoever might be established. ("'Tis certain that MAHOMETISM, PAGANISM, JUDAISM, or any *other* BELIEF may stand, as well as *the truest*, upon this Foundation.")

[16] "Miscellany" II.iii, III, 98–99 (Robertson, II, 217). Shaftesbury here toyed with the relation between seriousness and formal method. When he failed to follow through on this procedure, he begged the "methodical Reader" to forgive "Writing which is govern'd less by Form than Humour": "Miscellany" II.iii, III, 129 (Robertson, II, 236).
[17] "Miscellany" II.iii, III, 115–123 (Robertson, II, 227–231).

A cognitive scepticism thus seems inherent in the cultural perspective on human knowledge that Shaftesbury was here sketching.

However, for Shaftesbury, there were forces to be set in motion that would aid in the discrimination of truth: "there can be no rational Belief but where *Comparison* is allow'd, *Examination* permitted, and a sincere *Toleration* establish'd." Such processes drew on the resources of sociability. Like other aspects of human social and cultural life, religion and especially religious discourse had to operate according to the criteria of polite society. Thus, while religious experience arose originally from human sociable instincts, It had to be regulated by the highest standards of sociability, namely, politeness. True religion had to withstand the test of free, polite discourse: comparison and toleration were the only foundations for rational belief.

By contrast, "if there be on earth a proper way to render the most sacred Truth suspected, 'tis by supporting it with *Threats*, and pretending to *terrify* People into the Belief of it."[18] This point was capable of both a psychological and a sociological application. On one level, this observation applied to the enthusiast, who used threats and terror in social interaction for purposes of intimidation. Discussing "enthusiasm" allowed Shaftesbury to pursue the relations between religion and social personality. However, on another level, when threat and terror became the instruments of institutions, one was talking about organized phenomena that could be treated under the head of "priestcraft." "Priestcraft" allowed Shaftesbury to discuss the relation between religion and the fabric of culture. In the next section, the languages of "enthusiasm" and "priestcraft" as they were available in the later seventeenth century are sketched as a background for Shaftesbury's use of them.

Priestcraft and enthusiasm

Shaftesbury's Whiggism was expressed in his support for toleration and in his attacks on Tory High Church loyalties. However, the materials that Shaftesbury used against the ecclesiastical propensities of Toryism had arisen in the seventeenth century to combat rather different objects. The argument against "priestcraft" had its origin in the Protestant attack on the powers of the Catholic Church while the argument against "enthusiasm" arose in the Protestant attempt to subdue its own more extreme expressions.[19]

---

[18] "Miscellany" II.iii, III, 104–107 (Robertson, II, 220–222).

[19] On "priestcraft" and "enthusiasm" in eighteenth-century religious discourse, see Frank Manuel, *The Changing of the Gods* (For Brown University Press, Hanover and London: University Press of New England, 1983), pp.34–51.

Protestantism was, among other things, a rebellion against the institutional form of the Catholic Church, since the Reformation arose in the belief that priests had destructively inserted themselves between believers and God, making true religious understanding impossible. The panoply of Catholic "superstitions" was a conspicuous outcome of the power arrogated by priests. Therefore, Protestants insisted on the sovereignty of civil authority, a sovereignty to which priestly functions were subordinate, and the idea of a "civil religion" became a theme in early modern Protestant countries. While "Popery" was the very embodiment of unfortunate extensions of clerical power, it was clear that Protestant churches could sponsor their own forms of clericalism. The introduction into discussion of the term "priestcraft" by James Harrington was a means to generalize about exaggerated clerical claims, whether Catholic or episcopal or presbyterian. Harrington's own insights about religious organization and belief were related to his political analysis, discussed in chapter 7. In Harrington, "priestcraft" underpinned the critique of religious opinions with a material analysis. He pointed to the landed endowment of the medieval church as the foundation for its hold over the medieval mind and believed that the revolution in Church lands consequent on the Reformation brought an instability, of which the collapse of monarchy in his own time was the clearest expression. As the movement of history favored the establishment of a republic of gentlemen, so it favored the establishment of a truly civil religion.[20] Elements of Harrington's discussion were carried forward by Henry Neville and Robert Molesworth and, as we will see, by the third earl of Shaftesbury.

While "priestcraft" provided a political economy of distorted belief, another seventeenth-century idiom provided a psychological and social account of perverted religiosity. "Enthusiasm" arose within Protestant discourse as a way to characterize and asperse excesses of Protestant fervor. The term first appeared in the early seventeenth century, meaning "divine possession." While early applications were classical (sybilline or bacchanalian possession), the term was easily adaptable to Christian subjects, such as antinomians in the early history of the Church. "Enthusiasts" first appeared in an English dictionary of 1656, referring to Reformation Anabaptists as "a sect of people that thought themselves inspired with a Divine spirit, and to have a clear sight of all things which

---

[20] Mark Goldie, "The Civil Religion of James Harrington," in Anthony Pagden, ed., *The Languages of Political Theory in Early Modern Europe* (Cambridge: Cambridge University Press, 1987), pp.197–222; J. G. A. Pocock, introduction, *The Political Works of James Harrington* (Cambridge: Cambridge University Press, 1977), pp.77–99.

they believed."[21] Religious radicals in the mid seventeenth century also claimed extraordinary access to the divine and so were perceived as dangerous from a range of less radical standpoints, both Arminian and Calvinist. Though antinomianism was as much a threat to Puritanism as it was to Arminianism, "enthusiasm" became an epithet particularly associated with Puritanism or, after the Restoration, with Nonconformity.[22]

"Enthusiasm" could be transformed from a specific attack on those who claimed "Light" or "Spirit" to a general slur on Nonconformists because it attacked religious positions in terms of the believer's psychology. It transferred religious argument from issues of doctrine to estimations of social personality. Thus, though Henry More's *Enthusiasmus Triumphatus* (1656) had specific targets (radical sectarians, such as the Quakers, and philosophical radicals in the hermetic tradition), the work offered a vocabulary of wider relevance. "Enthusiasm," More wrote, was founded in "Temper," or rather in a "Distemper" that "disposes a man to listen to the Magisterial Dictates of an over-bearing *Phansy*, more then to the calm and cautious insinuation of free *Reason*." The hypertrophy of "Phansy" or "Imagination" was affected by "sundry *material* things": it was tied to "Blood and Spirits," which in turn were affected by various meteorological and physiological criteria. However, at the root of the matter was melancholy and its effects.[23] Thus, the "enthusiast" was a character type: a creature of passions, verging on madness, capable of contrary extremities (of heat/zeal/fervor/fire and cold/sobriety/gravity), extravagant and unsociable. What More offered was not an argument against claims to inspiration as such, but an analysis of the personality-type that made false claims. In the form of such a vocabulary, "enthusiasm" was deployed during the Restoration as a general weapon against the Nonconformists and formed a tropological underpinning to many Anglican discourses.

The prominence of "enthusiasm" was part of a larger infiltration of religious discussion by psychological and social language. This development can be traced, in large part, to two related emphases of the Cambridge Platonists and latitudinarians. First, to counter the Puritan emphasis on faith over reason, they privileged the terms "reason" and

---

[21] These instances are drawn from the Oxford English Dictionary entry, s.v. enthusiasm, and from Susie I. Tucker, *Enthusiasm: A Study of Semantic Change* (Cambridge: Cambridge University Press, 1972), p.15.

[22] For instance, Joseph Glanvill wrote that the "dangerous Follies, and Extravagancies" of Nonconformists had "opened the door to Atheism, and Enthusiasm," in "Mr. Glanvill His Letter to Mr. Sherlock," in *An Account of Mr. Ferguson His Common-Place-Book* (1675).

[23] Henry More, *Enthusiasmus Triumphatus* (1662; Augustan Reprint Society Pub. No. 118, Los Angeles: William Andrews Clark Memorial Library, 1966), pp.2, 4, 5–7, 8, 10, 23f., 28–29.

"rational," thus eliding the rational and the spiritual. Second, reacting against the Puritan emphasis on faith over works, they tended to collapse ethics and theology. "Reason," rehabilitated as against faith, helped to validate a paramount concern with conduct in the life of the Christian. Restoration "reason" was multivalent. While the interest in "reason" led to such undertakings as Cudworth's *True Intellectual System of the Universe*, an uncompleted colossus of investigation into the rational structure of creation, "reason" also referred to "reasonableness" – not a cosmos-structuring principle, but a value in social life.[24] The prestige of "reason" did conduce to the development of science and the elaboration of rational theology, but it also urged an ethics and ideal of sociability. "Enthusiasm" evoked "sociability" as its contrary, but so too the current of "reason" flowed into "sociability" in the form of "reasonableness."

Just as "enthusiasm" was used to assault personality types, so the positive side of the argument took on a psychosocial dimension, in which "sociability," "manners," and "civility" were deployed in defense of Anglican religion. Benjamin Whichcote, whom Shaftesbury edited, epitomized the irenic approach. For Whichcote, reason was authoritative, as a divine principle in the world and as a human faculty for apprehending divinity. This natural and rational divinity bore on human social and moral personality since, according to Whichcote, religion in a human's life was a matter not of notions or speculations, but of temper and disposition. A sweet and civil personality was the gift of religion to the adherent, and the pursuit of religion by the religious was "Pleasantness."[25] While religion enhanced human good nature, atheism corroded human sociability. So did enthusiasm: "The more False anyone is in his Religion; the more Fierce and Furious in Maintaining it: the more Mistaken, the more Imposing." The abandonment of reason created "a Monster, a Prodigy." The alternative to religious complaisance was a

---

[24] C. A. Patrides, *The Cambridge Platonists* (London: Edward Arnold, 1969), pp.8, 13–14; Norman Sykes, *From Sheldon to Secker* (Cambridge: Cambridge University Press, 1959), pp.68–90, 145–148; G. R. Cragg, *From Puritanism to the Age of Reason* (Cambridge: Cambridge University Press, 1966), pp.42–44, 60f.; J. A. Passmore, *Ralph Cudworth* (Cambridge: Cambridge University Press, 1951), pp.19–28; Meyrick Carré, "Ralph Cudworth," *Philosophical Quarterly*, 3 (1953), 342–351.

[25] Benjamin Whichcote, *Moral and Religious Aphorisms* (Norwich, 1703); p.3; *Select Sermons*, ed. Anthony Ashley Cooper (1698), p.181. Indeed, the forms of inner appropriation recommended here were not distant from enthusiasm itself. This helps to explain how the third earl of Shaftesbury, who assimilated the Platonism of Whichcote and his colleagues, could transform "enthusiasm" into a term of approbation. On Whichcote, see: Frederick J. Powicke, *The Cambridge Platonists* (London and Toronto: J. M. Dent & Sons, 1926), pp.51–73; Wilbur K. Jordan, *The Development of Religious Toleration in England*, 4 vols. (Cambridge: Harvard University Press, 1932–1940), IV, 99–116; and James Deotis Roberts, Sr., *From Puritanism to Platonism in Seventeenth-Century England* (The Hague: Martinus Nijhoff, 1968), a full-length study.

passionate and lustful state, restless and unquiet, a "tumult of Imagination."[26] Thus, Whichcote, deployed reformed manners, refined spirits, good nature, and sociability as a testament to the value of religion.

While Whichcote was Shaftesbury's ideal of a cleric, Whichcote's contemporary, Samuel Parker embodied Shaftesbury's nightmare of a furious prelate.[27] Nonetheless, Parker's most famous work shows how the language of social personality infiltrated the defense of Anglicanism. *A Discourse of Ecclesiastical Politie* (1670) aimed to undermine the basis of a permanent Nonconformist community by arguing the supremacy of the civil power in ecclesiastical matters and demolishing the notion of liberty of conscience. Like latitudinarians, Parker attacked the Nonconformist emphasis on faith, with which "they have brought into fashion a Godliness without Religion, Zeal without Humanity, and Grace without good Nature, or good Manners."[28] Parker here summoned to mind an empty hull of a religion, contrasting with a true religion whose natural kernel included "Humanity," "good Nature," and "good Manners."

Parker attacked the psychological and social dispositions of Nonconformists, building up a composite image of unsociability. They were "morose and churlish Zealots," a "Wild and Fanatique Rabble" whose pride sparked a "sullen and unsociable Niceness" and whose "morose and surly Principles" made them "the rudest and most barbarous people in the World." This language was not an attack on doctrine, but on social personality. At the same time, Parker staked out the territory of sociability and civility for the established Church. Opposed to Dissenting "sullenness" stood Anglican "sobriety" and "wisdom." The Anglican's was "a loving and Divine Temper of mind" and so Parker's own vehemence was "a Zeal of Meekness and Charity and a prosecution of the grand and diffusive duty of humanity, and proceeds only from an earnest desire to maintain the common Love and Amity of Mankind."[29] Though his own tone subverted his claim to be on the side of "good manners," he must be seen as registering an important aspect of the ideological project of the Restoration Church.

[26] Whichcote, *Aphorisms*, p.19; *Select Sermons*, pp.31, 180.
[27] Reading Parker tends to confirm the opinion of the Nonconformist Robert Ferguson, that Parker's language and tone "ill become the extraction and civility of a Gentleman, the Education of a Christian, and the Profession of a Divine." In raising "civility," Ferguson was merely throwing back at Parker a matter he himself raised frequently: Robert Ferguson, *A Sober Enquiry into the Nature, Measure and Principle of Moral Virtue* (1693), preface. As for Andrew Marvell, *The Rehearsal Transpros'd* repeatedly threw doubt on Parker's "Honour" and gentlemanliness with ironic references to his "Civility": Andrew Marvell, *The Rehearsal Transpros'd and The Rehearsal Transpros'd The Second Part*, ed. D. I. B. Smith (Oxford: Clarendon Press, 1971), pp.3, 6, 9, 10.
[28] Samuel Parker, *A Discourse of Ecclesiastical Politie* (1670), pp.65ff., 74.
[29] Parker, *Ecclesiastical Politie*, pp.ii–iii, iv–viii, xx, xxviii–xxix.

Later, the language of "enthusiasm" would be added to other elements of Restoration discourse in the concoction of Roger l'Estrange's *Observator*, a classic expression of the 1680s reaction. L'Estrange was another unlikely proponent of "manners." Like Parker, he attacked a complex enemy, a protean composite of Dissenter and atheist opportunist who had caused the Civil War and again disrupted the kingdom in the later 1670s, shaking "the very Foundations of *Religion*, and *good Manners*." The "*Scandalls*" propagated by the exclusionists "are an *Offence* to *Good Manners*, in the very *Lewdness* of them; to *Religion*, in the *Falseness*, and *Malice* of Them; to *Government*, in the *Example* and *Contagion* of them."[30] Good manners, religion, and government sound like a trinity here, a characteristic, though not so frequently noticed, amplification of the more common Restoration binary formulation, given in the title of a Samuel Parker's 1684 tract, *Religion and Loyalty*.

Through polemicists such as L'Estrange and Parker, "enthusiasm" was associated with the Whigs and their Dissenting backers.[31] Loyalty to a Tory version of the Anglican Church could be affirmed by reference to its civility and sociability. It was the weight of this discourse that Shaftesbury was trying to overcome in *Characteristicks*.

Shaftesbury and enthusiasm

In the Restoration period, the valence of "enthusiasm" was entirely negative; but, by the 1690s, the term was under transvaluative pressure. John Dryden, for instance, used it in a purely literary context in the preface to his translation of Juvenal in 1693. However, the change was particularly evident in writings of John Dennis, whose project of rooting literary excellence in religion involved a favorable estimate of the uses of passion and of enthusiasm in particular.[32]

Shaftesbury made a twofold contribution to the transformation of "enthusiasm." First, he joined in the transvaluation, establishing more firmly than Dennis a positive meaning for it. Second, he continued the polemical and aspersive uses of "enthusiasm" but found new objects for them.

Shaftesbury's rehabilitation of the affections as foundations of moral

---

[30] Roger L'Estrange, *Seneca's Morals By Way of Abstract* (1678), p.v; *Observator*, II, 21 (February 25, 1683).
[31] On the associations of Whiggism with religious extremism, see T. N. Corns, W. A. Speck, and J. A. Downie, "Archetypal Mystification: Polemic and Reality in English Political Literature, 1640–1750," *Eighteenth-Century Life*, VII N.S., 3 (May 1982), 7–11.
[32] For Dryden, see Oxford English Dictionary, s.v. enthusiasm. For Dennis, see Edward Niles Hooker, ed., *The Critical Works of John Dennis* (Baltimore: The Johns Hopkins University Press, 1939), I, 6, 201, 215–216, 227–228.

agency sanctioned a re-estimation of such a passionate phenomenon as enthusiasm. Shaftesbury embraced it as an important expression of natural affection, saying of himself: "So far is he from degrading *Enthusiasm*, or disclaiming it in himself; that he looks on this Passion, simply consider'd, as the most *natural*, and its Object as the *justest* in the *World*."[33]

He seems to have evolved toward this position. In 1698, reflecting on the moral cowardice of most people, he called to mind the resoluteness of enthusiasts. While he did not yet praise enthusiasm, he recognized something worse, namely, a kind of coldness in the face of the divine, an insufficiency of being "affected." However, by early 1700, he had progressed towards his individual conception of "enthusiasm." Sketching a Platonic love that lifted the individual towards higher and ultimately divine things, he asked: "Is this *Enthousiasme*? Be it: and so may I be ever an Enthousiast. Happy me, if I can grow in this Enthousiasme, so as to loose all those Enthusiasms of every other kind, and be whole towards *this*."[34] Here "enthusiasm" became the Platonist's love of the ultimate beauty. The last sentence set this "enthusiasm" in a continuum with other "enthusiasms," all those forms of passionate devotion which had as their object something less than the ultimate and divine beauty. This same continuum appeared in *Characteristicks*. While enthusiasm at its best was a Platonic divine love that inspired in the individual an understanding of the world order and a respect for ultimate beauty, it existed in all manner of lesser states. At all levels, however, enthusiasm lifted the individual to a recognition of wider matters beyond the self.[35] Thus, it was an essential feature of humanity, closely related to the sociability first described in the *Inquiry Concerning Virtue*.

Offering a positive view of enthusiasm in *Characteristicks*, Shaftesbury rebelled against the major tendency of fifty years of Anglican polemic. His positive view was controversial since it mitigated the worst dangers to be expected from enthusiasts, who became objects of fun rather than fear. However, the universalization of enthusiasm also allowed an important shift in the term's polemical uses. "A Letter Concerning Enthusiasm" was

[33] "Miscellany" II.i, III, 33 (Robertson, II, 176); see also P.R.O. 30/24/22/7, ff.499–500, Shaftesbury to Pierre Coste, February 19, 1709.
[34] P.R.O. 30/24/27/10, pp.103, 153 [ff.53r, 78r].
[35] See especially section VI of "A Letter Concerning Enthusiasm." The enthusiastic sources of all human achievements were further explored in Shaftesbury's gloss on the "Letter" in "Miscellany" II.i, III, 30–33 (Robertson, II, 174–175). See Grean, *Shaftesbury's Philosophy of Religion and Ethics*, pp.19–36; A. O. Aldridge, "Shaftesbury and the Deist Manifesto," *Transactions of the American Philosophical Society*, 41 N.S. (1951), 314–322. Martin Price sets Shaftesburian "enthusiasm" in its Platonic setting in *To the Palace of Wisdom* (Carbondale and Edwardsville: Southern Illinois University Press, 1964), pp.79–105, esp. 92–93.

provocative because Shaftesbury used the appearance in London of the French "prophets" not just to trivialize the enthusiastic band, but also, and more significantly, to offer a broad critique of public discourse.[36] Reducing the "prophets" to peripherality, he proceeded to attack the Church in terms of enthusiasm. Since enthusiasm was the common currency of human life, enthusiastic prophets were all too likely to induce enthusiasm in the reigning clerics and magistrates. Zealots were to be found inside the established Church as well as at its borders. Thus, Shaftesbury took a stock element of Anglican polemic and turned it against the Anglican Church, or at least its High Church element. The "high-flyers" were, in Shaftesbury's vocabulary, "enthusiasts," "zealots," and "fanatics."

In keeping with the tradition he inherited, Shaftesbury defined religious enthusiasm as uncontrolled passion. He wrote that "every Worshipper of the *Zealot*-kind" was affectively unhinged, "no longer self-govern'd, but set adrift to the wide Sea of Passion." He made clear that enthusiasm was a condition in which basically sound affections grew to extremity, liberating themselves from any control by mind. It was a classic instance of the self's loss of autonomy, as described in the *Inquiry*, since reason no longer shaped affection. Moreover, as the *Inquiry* would lead one to predict, enthusiasm was highly conducive to vice. Aside from inherently vicious affections, affections were liable to become vicious only when they were not harmoniously balanced or rationally moderated. This was the case with enthusiasm. Thus, "above all other enslaving Vices, and Restrainers of *Reason* and *just Thought*, the most evidently ruinous and fatal to the Understanding is that of SUPERSTITION, BIGOTRY, and *vulgar* ENTHUSIASM."[37]

Shaftesbury's caricature of the zealot was laced with the figure of unsociability. In "The Moralists," the "serene, soft, and harmonious" enthusiasm of Theocles was contrasted with "the fierce unsociable way of modern *Zealots*; those starch'd, gruff Gentlemen, who guard Religion as Bullys do a Mistress."[38] This epitome of unsociable characterization implied that enthusiasm was a social mode verging on barbarity. It was marked by rigidity ("starched") and gravity ("gruff"). Moreover, its aggressivity ("fierce," the image of the bully) implied a claim to unquestioned authority (dogmatism, in short) and a horror of openness and freedom in inquiry. The enthusiast was anxious to impose on others and to force them to submit; he was the opposite of the person who, in social interaction, did all to bring out others and foster their sense of autonomy.

[36] On the context for this essay, see Introduction, pp.18–19.
[37] "Miscellany" II.i, III, 40 (Robertson, II, 180) and V.iii, III, 305 (Robertson, II, 345).
[38] "Moralists" I.iii, II, 218 (Robertson, II, 24–25).

thus, the enthusiast, who was the High Church defender, was a highly undesirable character from the standpoint of sociable standards.

As against this social character, Shaftesbury mounted his defense of raillery as a servant of reason. A "Freedom of Raillery" was a "a Liberty in decent Language to question every thing, and an Allowance of unravelling or refuting any Argument, without offence to the Arguer."[39] The assertion that certain subjects were too grave to be ridiculed had to be dismissed since "*Gravity* is of the very essence of imposture." The substance and tone of public discourse had to be as free as possible of unwarranted claims to authority. Of course, it was necessary to distinguish true gravity from false. Only the former could withstand ridicule, but even it had to be tested. Indeed, a public discourse that was not grave but "light" was quite probably the most serious discourse of all.

The great reservoir of authoritative solemnity was the Church, though raillery had already diminished much of the force of religious enthusiasm. However, "if something of this militant Religion, something of this Soul-rescuing Spirit, and Saint-Errantry prevails still, we need not wonder, when we consider in how solemn a manner we treat this Distemper, and how preposterously we go about to cure enthusiasm." Religion still had too much enthusiasm in it: "the melancholy way of treating Religion is that which, according to my Apprehension, renders it so tragical, and is the occasion of its acting in reality such dismal Tragedys in the World."[40]

Shaftesbury detected an intimate relation between the psychological impact of the Church and its institutional character. He warned Michael Ainsworth on the eve of his ordination against the conceit inherent in the priestly calling: "And since we think fitt to call it Preisthood, & have brought *Preists* into Christianity (a thing wch in my Reading & Capacity I cou'd never discover or apprehend) see, that this Preisthood be of a kind not to make Thee say or think of Thyself in the presence of another *that thou art holyer than he*."[41] Aside from his willingness to call into question the entire legitimacy of a "Priesthood" as a feature of organized Christianity, Shaftesbury cast doubt on the capacity of any priest to engage in a morally sound relationship with those he served, since the priest functioned in an inherently unequal and hence perverse structure of social relations. The inequality had a psychological character: the priest was in a position to dominate psychologically because of the spiritual conceit that inhered in his position.

Warning against the intimidating power of priestly authority, Shaftes-

---

[39] "Sensus Communis" II.iv, I, 69 (Robertson, I, 49).
[40] "Letter" ii, I, 20 (Robertson, I, 16) and iv, I, 32 (Robertson, I, 24).
[41] P.R.O. 30/24/20/143, Shaftesbury to Michael Ainsworth, December 30, 1709.

bury, thus far, rehearsed objections he developed in his critique of authoritarian styles of discursive expression.[42] However, in his letter to Ainsworth, he quickly associated spiritual and psychological domination with the hunger for domination in more tangible forms:

> He thou ownst to be thy Master & Legislator made no Laws relating to civil power or interfering with it. So that all the pre-eminence Wealth or Pension wch thou receiv'st or expects't to receive by help of this assum'd Character, is from the Publick, from whence both the Authority & Profit is deriv'd, & on wch it legally depends: all other Pretension of *Preists* being Jewish & Heathenish, & in our State Seditious, disloyal & Factiouse, such as is that Spirit wch now reigns in our Universitys, & where the high Church (as they are call'd) are prevalent.[43]

The psychologically domineering character of the Church was matched by its hunger for wealth and for real and independent political power. However, all such pretensions of the Church were to be dismissed since the Church had a specifically secular foundation, as the silence of Jesus on such topics and the legal framework of the English Church confirmed. At Shaftesbury indicated, he was responding to ideas of ecclesiastical independence recirculated during the High Church revival of the late 1690s and early 1700s.

Egypt and Rome

Shaftesbury's references to the "Jewish & Heathenish" provenance of priestly pretensions are of interest, since, in "Miscellaneous Reflections," he elaborated on ecclesiological matters in a historical discussion of the material and institutional as well psychological and cultural parameters of religious life. Here he operated in the idiom of "priestcraft."

Egypt served as the *locus classicus* of a priest-ridden polity, the first and best case of the hierocratic state. Not surprisingly, it was "where first religion grew unsociable."[44] The main feature of Shaftesbury's account of Egypt was the mutually supporting relationship between priesthood and superstition. The number of priests tended to increase because the priesthood was a hereditary caste with no limit to its numbers or its wealth. At the same time, Egypt was particularly susceptible to the multiplication of deities, beliefs, and rites for a number of reasons, though a particularly interesting one, in light of the question of sociability, was the Egyptians' "solitary idle life whilst shut up in their Houses by the regular Inundations of the NILE."

However, the main reason that beliefs multiplied was that priests

---

[42] See chapter 5, pp.99–100.
[43] P.R.O. 30/24/20/143, Shaftesbury to Michael Ainsworth, December 30, 1709.
[44] "Moralists" III.i, II, 387 (Robertson, II, 122).

multiplied. "'Twill ... as I conceive, be found unquestionably true, according to political Arithmetick, in every Nation whatsoever; 'That *the Quantity* of SUPERSTITION (if I may so speak) will, in proportion, nearly answer *the Number* of Priests, Diviners, Soothsayers, Prophets, or such who gain their Livelihood, or receive Advantages by officiating in religious Affairs.'" The explanation for this was economic. In ancient Egypt, Shaftesbury said, the priests maintained themselves with whatever contributions they received from believers, gifts of land and other items that remained the property of the clergy in perpetuity. It was, therefore, incumbent on the ever increasing body of priests to convince believers in an ever increasing body of doctrine. The priests, thus, became heirs not only to great wealth but to great psychological and intellectual power. They became arch manipulators whose manipulations were the knub of the mutual dependence of priestly numbers and superstitious beliefs.

The Egyptian case illustrated the general point that the hypertrophy of the priesthood disfigured an entire culture, enveloping its members in an ever thickening fog of false belief. Indeed, sooner or later a powerful priesthood on the Egyptian model subverted the independence of the state. The Egyptian state condoned the earlier stages of this priestly development, acquiescing in the hereditary priesthood and failing to set limits on clerical wealth and influence. "Nor," at a later point, "is it strange that we shou'd find the *Property* and Power of the *Egyptian* Priesthood, in antient days, arriv'd to such a height, as in a manner to have swallow'd up the State and Monarchy." Deploying a Harringtonian maxim ("'That *Dominion* must naturally follow *Property*'"), Shaftesbury said that no state could withstand the encroachments of a powerful enough clergy.[45]

Egypt served as more than a cautionary example, since it was the font of superstition. As the Egyptian priesthood sought spiritual domination over the Egyptians, so Egypt sought spiritual conquest outside its borders. Indeed, in the course of time, this "*Zealot*-People ... came by degrees to spread their variety of Rites and Ceremonys, their distinguishing Marks of *separate* worships and *secrete* Communitys, thro the distant World; but chiefly thro their neighbouring and dependent Countrys." The Egyptian pattern was found in Ethiopia, Persia, Mesopotomia, and, notably, among the ancient Hebrews, whose dependence on the Egyptians for institutions and ideas Shaftesbury spent considerable effort trying to establish.[46]

As a function of its priestliness, ancient Egyptian religion was unsociable. The relation of priests to believers was unequal, manipulative, and

---
[45] "Miscellany" II.i, III, 42–50 (Robertson, II, 181–187).
[46] "Miscellany" II.i, III, 50–58 (Robertson, II, 187–193).

authoritative, denying the autonomy of the believer. However, Egyptian religion was unsociable in a more elementary way too. As the Egyptian pattern of religion spread, so did beliefs and rites, religions and ceremonies. "Thus Provinces and Nations were divided by the most *contrary* Rites and Customs which cou'd be devis'd, in order to create the strongest *Aversion* possible between Creatures of a like Species ... From hence the Opposition rose of Temple against Temple, Proselyte against Proselyte." Religious antagonism was fertilized by the introduction of philosophical discussion into religious dispute. Thus, the fruit of religious zealotry, orchestrated by a priesthood, was religious warfare, the ultimate expression of religious unsociability.[47]

For reasons that will be evident later, Shaftesbury bracketed the religious organization of classical Athens and republican Rome.[48] However, later Rome could be seen as replicating important aspects of the Egyptian pattern.[49] The growth of imperial tyranny, according to Shaftesbury, brought with it a corresponding increase in superstition. As in Egypt, the number of heathen priests as well as their wealth increased. Moreover, this increase in priestly wealth was underpinned by a flood of gifts in land and other forms from private persons. Late Roman religion then had traits seen in Egypt: a priesthood, ever wealthier and ever more numerous; a weakening state; a multiplication of preposterous beliefs that encouraged the gifts that supported the priesthood. The conversion of the Emperor made Christianity the heir of the material and psychological equipment of the later Roman heathen religion. Christianity was unified on the structural and spiritual perversities of Roman religion. When imperial rule disappeared from the West, the situation of the Rome-based Christian church was very similar to that of the ancient Egyptian hierocracy.

If this were not enough to assure that the history of Christianity in Western Europe would be an unsociable one, Shaftesbury pointed out one more development, again parallel to a development in the ancient world. "When ... the *Schools* of the antient Philosophers, which had been long in their Decline, came now to be dissolv'd, and their sophistick Teachers became Ecclesiastical Instructors; the unnatural Union of *Religion* and *Philosophy* was compleated, and the monstrous Product of this Match appear'd soon in the World." Antique Christianity became a battle-ground among parties who warred under philosophical banners. In place of the hieroglyphic emblems of the quarrelsome Egyptian sects, "*sophistical Chimera's, crabbed Notions, bombastic Phrases, Solecisms,*

---

[47] "Miscellany" II.i, III, 60–62 (Robertson, II, 194–195).
[48] See chapter 10, pp.199–206.
[49] "Miscellany" II.ii, III, 77–79 (Robertson, II, 204–205).

Absurditys, and a thousand Monsters of a *scholastick* Brood, were set on foot, and made the Subject of vulgar Animosity and Dispute."[50]

Since religious warfare was now propelled with new philosophical fuel, the history of religious unsociability entered a new phase with the Christianization of Rome. Indeed, philosophical enthusiasm destroyed classical culture:

> *Mysterys* which were heretofore treated, with profound respect, and lay unexpos'd to vulgar Eyes, became publick and prostitute; being enforc'd with Terrours, and urg'd with Compulsion and Violence, on the unfitted Capacitys and Apprehensions of Mankind ... That which was naturally the Subject of profound Speculation and Inquiry, was made the necessary Subject of a strict and absolute Assent. The *allegorical, mythological* Account of Sacred Things, was wholly inverted. Liberty of Judgment and Exposition taken away. No Ground left for Inquiry, Search, or Meditation. No Refuge from the *Dogmatical* Spirit let loose ... All was reduced to Article and Proposition.[51]

Shaftesbury was depicting here a world of spiritual bullying, which had supplanted the classical antique culture of inquiry, scepticism, and toleration. This was a world of competing dogmatisms, each seeking the extirpation of the others. The mental atmosphere of the era was embodied in the creed or catechism, which bespoke indifference to the internal condition of belief, reducing spirituality to an external exercise.

The consummation of these developments was the rise of the medieval Catholic Church, an elaborate mechanism for the nurturing of a hierarchy. The achievement was founded on psychological observation of "the various *Superstitions* and *Enthusiasms* of Mankind, and ... the different Kinds and Force of each": "All these seeming Contrarietys of human Passion they knew how to comprehend in their political Model and subservient System of Divinity." Thus, the Roman Church began with the very insights that underlay Shaftesbury's own *Inquiry*: the foundational importance of the affections, their multiplicity and dynamism, the malleability of the consciousness founded on them. However, where the *Inquiry* used the psychology of affection and consciousness to foster moral responsibility, the Church used it to establish a system for manipulating believers. Dismissing "*that* ENTHUSIASM which ran upon *Spirituals*, according to the simpler Views of the divine Existence" (that is, the enthusiasm of Theocles in "The Moralists"), the Catholic Church dedicated itself to the alternative enthusiasm, "which ran upon external Proportions, Magnificance of Structures, Ceremonys, Processions, Quires, and those other Harmonys which captivate *the Eye* and *Ear*. On this account they even added to his *latter* kind, and display'd Religion in a

---

[50] "Miscellany" II.ii, III, 79–80 (Robertson, II, 206).
[51] "Miscellany" II.ii, III, 81 (Robertson, II, 206–207).

yet more gorgeous Habit of Temples, Statues, Paintings, Vestments, Copes, Miters, Purple, and the Cathedral Pomp." In short, the Roman Church cultivated a visual and ritual "Awefulness" which allowed it to conquer Europe and erect an "almost Universal Monarchy" and which has proved enduringly imposing over the centuries.[52] Catholic magnificence had offered shelter to imposture for centuries because it subdued those acts of intelligence that might have exposed the preposterousness of Catholic belief and practice.

The end of Shaftesbury's discussion of the rise of the Roman Church made explicit the relevance of these historical observations to the role and mission of the Church of England. Shaftesbury pointed out that, even on Protestants, the accumulated magnificence of the capital of Catholicism, "the Hierarchal Residence, the *City* and *Court* of ROME," had an extraordinary impact. He then suggested that the spiritual domination of the Roman Church "seems less intolerable" on account of its age and duration than "under the petty Tyrannys and mimical Politys of some new Pretenders."

The former may even *persecute* with a tolerable Grace: the latter, who wou'd willingly derive their Authority from the former, and graft on their *successive Right*, must necessarily make a very aukard Figure. And whilst they strive to give themselves the same air of Independency on the Civil Magistrate; whilst they affect the same Authority in Government, the same Grandure, Magnificence, and Pomp in Worship, they raise the highest Ridicule, in the Eyes of those who have real Discernment, and can distinguish *Originals* from *Copies*.[53]

The object of ridicule here was the High Church position, which sought independent authority for the Church from the civil authority, made much of apostolic succession, and elaborated the mystery of ritual. The High Church position was dangerous, and ridicule was required to deflate its pretensions.

Shaftesbury's ideal of sociable religion allowed him to mount a Whiggish critique of religion and its role in society. Though clearly he did believe in the importance of true religiosity, he saw countless moral, political and cultural dangers in the traditional forms taken by religion in Britain and indeed in European nations generally. While clearly he wanted to disenfranchise the Church, he was perhaps even more anxious to delegitimize its normative claims over the moral and cultural life of society. Underpinning Shaftesbury's discussion of religion was a rich sense of sociability and its implications. His account of religion and its past was informed by both a psychological and a sociological imagin-

[52] "Miscellany" II.ii, III, 90–91, 93 (Robertson, II, 212–214).
[53] "Miscellany" II.ii, III, 93–94 (Robertson, II, 215).

ation. A fundamental structuring device was the relationship of priests to believers, an inherently unequal relationship open to psychological, spiritual, and intellectual manipulation. The clerical component of institutionalized religion almost necessarily created conditions unfavorable to well-motivated discourse and so to moral and cultural well-being. Thus, this history of religion explored fundamental themes, casting problems of sociability and discourse in a historical mold. It was an excursus on the fate of discourse and of culture under a priesthood, utilizing the exemplary disasters of Egypt and Rome to make its point. In the end, the discussion helped delineate the ground on which a truly polite society would be founded. The demonstration was continued in Shaftesbury's critique of the Court.

9 The critique of the Court

"Dazzle"

In November 1706, Shaftesbury wrote a letter to Pierre Coste, examining the psychological impact of the Court:

> Where a Court absolutely governs, it is too dazzling a thing to suffer its Vices and Corruption to be understood or thought as it deserves. To tell a royall bred Gentleman, the Pupill of a Court, or any one who ... has look'd with admiration on the great doings there – to tell such a one (I say), an adorer of Court-greatness and Politeness; that there is a Politeness far beyond, that there is hardly any thing there, that can possibly be of a true Relish and simplicity in Things or Manners, this would be astonishing, and have little Effect more than to raise Disdain perhaps or Contempt.[1]

The "dazzle" of the Court – its brilliance, grandeur, and magnificence – was an instrument by which admiration was encouraged. But since "dazzle" impeded vision and grandeur flattened perspective, the Court distorted perception and misdirected cognition in moral matters. Like the "Awefulness" of the Church, the "dazzle" of the Court pacified, enervated, and rendered the subject uncritical. The Court, thus, had the effect of making its beholders complacent and passive. By this psychological means, it diminished liberty.

In addition, these reflections on the Court brought to the fore the status of politeness, conceived broadly as a moral and cultural condition. The "politeness" of courts was summed up in "dazzle" itself. However, Shaftesbury insisted there was an alternative politeness, a true politeness, here identified with "a true Relish and simplicity in Things or Manners." The institutional framework of the Court, with its particular configuration of human relations, shaped not just the moral character of subjects but their formal perceptions and their expressive natures. Thus, the Court bore not only on the psychosocial health of subjects but also on the

---

[1] P.R.O. 30/24/20/118, Shaftesbury to Pierre Coste, November 15, 1706.

expressive possibilities of their culture. The Court was a force that warped the fields of ethics and insight, discourse and expression.

Shaftesbury's juxtaposition of courtly and true politeness occurred in a letter offering an interpretation of Horace's career to Pierre Coste, the Huguenot émigré. Shaftesbury recognized that, since Coste was French, writing him about Horace posed a particular challenge. Horace spent time at the imperial Roman Court, which Shaftesbury insisted on discussing with reference to its modern equivalents. No matter what might be said about the English Court, the most proximate modern equivalent of the Court of the Caesars was the French Court: what could be more "dazzling" than a court that revolved around a Sun King? This recognition framed the task of delivering an interpretation of Horace to Shaftesbury's sympathetic albeit Gallic friend. Getting Horace right would require Coste's "honest heart & English Sence," for "were you the wisest and politest man of that Nation where you were born, you could never have a tast of this without some of those Principles and that Sence, which is only acquired in a free Nation like one of those where you have been bred."[2] The best wisdom and politeness to which the French could aspire were hopelessly faulty, partial, and blind: their courtly culture necessarily failed to develop those perceptions and sensibilities to which the inhabitants of a free nation were, by contrast, heir.[3]

In the interpretation of Horace's life and work, Horace's association with the Court of Augustus was the sticking-point. Seeking to dissociate Horace from the Court, Shaftesbury analyzed Horace's life into three periods: an "*Original, Free, Republican State*," in which his patron was Brutus and his philosophy was "Civil, Social, Theistic" and "Socratic"; a "*Debauched, Slavish Courtly State*," in which his patron was Maecenas and his philosophy was the "Contrary" of his former philosophy, that is, a Shaftesburian caricature of privatism and self-indulgence; finally, a "*Returning, Recovering* State," in which Horace rebelled against Maecenas and returned to "his First Philosophy, & Principles." Horace was an "old Whig;" his original philosophy, that of such ancient "Common-Wealth's Men" as Brutus, Cato, Laelius, and Scipio. Yet, Horace's susceptibility to courtly temptation was understandable, for a court "even

---

[2] P.R.O. 30/24/20/118, Shaftesbury to Pierre Coste, November 15, 1706. Coste was born in France in 1668, but, after the Revocation of the Edict of Nantes, was forced to pursue his clerical and literary career in Holland. Through Jean LeClerc, he made English connections and found employment as a tutor in a number of households, including that of Francis Masham where, with Locke's aid, Coste translated *An Essay Concerning Human Understanding* into French (E.S. DeBeer, ed., *The Correspondence of John Locke*, Oxford: Clarendon Press, 1979, V, 395n.).

[3] For another description of the limited capacities of the French to understand liberty, see P.R.O. 30/24/20/91, Shaftesbury to Arent Furley (son of Benjamin Furley), February 18, 1705.

in our days, & in our Nation proves, we see, but too fatall to all good Patriots, especially old-whigs, such as was Horace."[4]

This was the language of the commonwealthman. Written in 1706, it bespoke the continuing appeal of Country language to Shaftesbury and his continuing suspicion of the Court. For Shaftesbury, Court and Monarchy were terms joined in opposition to moral and political liberty. Elsewhere he noted that a court always had a "Despotick Air" and commiserated with polities "where *single* WILL prevails, and Court-Power, instead of Laws or Constitutions, guides the State."[5]

The analysis of Horace's career also witnessed the relevance Shaftesbury found in classical experience to contemporary life: "Now wee Englishmen that are used to Revolutions between Court and Country, wee understand this Character very well. We know what makeing Terms is, with the Court. We know what getting a Place is, and how a Republican or a man of the contrary party gets into favour after disgrace and outlawry."[6] This was a protest of the Country independent against the accommodation required of anyone who would make peace with the Court.

However, as chapter 7 pointed out, Shaftesbury was no republican, and his relation to the commonwealthmen of his own era grew attentuated over the years as his Country bent was mitigated by stronger Whig impulses. We have already seen the hostility to cultural development that informed much civic political thinking. By contrast, Shaftesbury lovingly evoked a wealth of historical and cultural reference, parading cultural history in order to quash courtly pretension. While his historical reference points were both classical and modern, his cultural ones ranged over both the domains of "manners" and "arts and letters." In addition to literary and artistic matters, he was interested in the conditions of wit and sense, of taste and sensibility, of manners and ethics. Penetrating much of this was the consistent concern with discourse, sociability, and politeness. Thus, Shaftesbury's suspicion of the Court was articulated in terms that were foreign to the idioms of the Country tradition, constituting a novel cultural-political defense of Whiggism.

As we will see, much of his criticism of courts was fuelled by hostility to France, but his polemical target was the Tories, who, in his view, opposed liberty by supporting not only an oppressive Church but also an oppressive Monarchy. Shaftesbury saw them as elaborators of Court ideology and fifth columnists for France. The Tory claim to be guardians of culture

---

[4] P.R.O. 30/24/22/7, ff.522–529, Shaftesbury to Pierre Coste, October 1, 1706.
[5] P.R.O. 30/24/22/4, f.7, Shaftesbury to Rowland Gwin, April 19, 1704; "Miscellany" I.iii, III, 23n (Robertson, II, 169–170n).
[6] P.R.O. 30/24/20/118, Shaftesbury to Pierre Coste, November 15, 1706.

was based in part on their friendliness to the Court. Since Shaftesbury was anxious to reverse this claim, this relation must be examined here first.

The Court and the Tory interpretation of cultural history

By Shaftesbury's era there was already a Tory version of English cultural history, applying the dynamics of political royalism to the zone of culture. According to this history, the seventeenth-century monarchs and their courts had had a particularly important role in encouraging English culture in the forms of both "manners" and "arts and letters." The civilizing monarch confronted forces of political and religious disruption that also subverted culture. Since, as Shaftesbury recognized, the parties of his own era stood in specific relations to seventeenth-century royalism and its opponents, the parties inherited parallel but opposite cultural associations: while the Tory "Soveraignty in Arts & Sciences" and all the rest was "acknowledg'd & taken for granted," the Whigs were treated as "unpolite, unform'd, without Literature, or Manners." Historically minded cultural royalism accorded well with the attack on "enthusiasm," since enthusiasts were well equipped to foil culture as well as religion.

Dryden wrote, not long after 1660, that the King and his people were "a pair of matchless Lovers,"[7] but there were many ways to articulate this liaison. Though the notion of a mixed polity in which king and subjects both had their place was a model of growing influence in the later seventeenth century, it did not exhaust the institutions of governance, let alone all the bonds of symbolism and sentiment between monarch and people. Divinity, patriarchy, heroics, and refinement invoked expectations for the seventeenth-century king.[8] The Court was central both to the King's execution of his functions and to his enactment of his various roles. It was a site for dispensing power, legitimacy, and all manner of material rewards, but it was also a symbolic platform on which the importance and dignity of kingship could be displayed.

---

[7] John Dryden, dedicatory epistle, "Annus Mirabilis," *The Works of John Dryden* (Berkeley: University of California Press, 1956-), I, 48.

[8] Mixed constitution and ancient constitution were discussed in chapter 7, pp.125–131; on patriarchal theory, James Daly, *Sir Robert Filmer and English Political Thought* (Toronto: University of Toronto Press, 1979) and Gordon Schochet, *Patriarchalism and Political Thought* (New York: Basic Books, 1975); on the King's divinity, J. N. Figgis, *The Theory of the Divine Right of Kings* (Cambridge: Cambridge University Press, 1896); on absolutism, James Daly, "The Idea of Absolute Monarchy in Seventeenth-Century England," *Historical Journal*, 21 (1978), 227–250; on sacred tropes of kingship, Steven Zwicker, *Dryden's Political Poetry: The Typology of King and Nation* (Providence: Brown University Press, 1972); on the continuity of royalist sentiment into the eighteenth century, J. C. D. Clark, *English Society, 1688–1832* (Cambridge: Cambridge University Press, 1985).

Charles II had a complex relationship to his inheritance. His father had remodeled the culture of the English Court, making it up-to-date and much more like Continental courts. He inspired it with a cohesive program, encouraging a more diverse and, at the same time, more focussed cultural production. Of course, this pattern, particularly as it contrasted with Tudor practice, did not play well with the entire nation. The Court's cosmopolitan tastes made it seem to emulate the courtly programs of Continental monarchs who were both Catholic and more effectively "absolute" than the English king.[9] Charles I's Court was a liability in a number of ways, and its culture figured among them.

Charles II came to the throne twenty years after his parents had last performed a masque. In the meantime, monarchy had undergone the most extreme possible attack, aristocracy had been eclipsed in many respects, and severity in manners, morals, and artistic expression had been imposed. Charles II was able to take advantage of the subsequent reaction, in which royalism flourished. Royalism meant guarding the flame of Charles I's memory, celebrating the majesty and piety of that monarch, and condemning the iniquity of his deposition. It also meant hailing the present monarch, to which a revived court culture contributed, even if it lacked the seriousness and consistency of Charles I's. After the twenty-year hiatus, celebrating kingship was welcomed.[10]

Thus, Charles II's reign was one to which Augustan imagery could be reapplied.[11] Aurelian Cook's *Titus Britannicus* contained characteristic emphases, ascribing to the King a doubly Augustan character, as restorer of the kingdom and nurturer of the arts, letters, and sciences. Cook contrasted the asperities of civil war with the cultural efflorescence associated with restored order. The king's "Knowledg" of useful learning, his "insight" into "softer Arts," and his "Wit" stood in analogous and genetic relationship to the general prosperity of sciences, arts, and courtly manners during his reign.[12]

Under the pressures of panegyric, Cook converted Charles II's earlier

---

[9] These are major points in the analysis by Malcolm Smuts, *Court Culture and the Origins of a Royalist Tradition in Early Stuart England* (Philadelphia: University of Pennsylvania Press, 1987). Smuts's comprehensive survey provides a more nuanced account of issues suggested in P. W. Thomas, "Two Cultures: Court and Country under Charles I," in Conrad Russell, ed., *The Origins of the English Civil War* (London: Macmillan, 1973), pp.168–193. See also Kevin Sharpe's reappraisal of this discussion in *Criticism and Compliment : The Politics of Literature in the England of Charles I* (Cambridge: Cambridge University Press, 1987).

[10] David Underdown, *Revel, Riot and Rebellion: Popular Politics and Culture in England, 1603–1660* (Oxford: Clarendon Press, 1985), pp.271–275.

[11] Howard Erskine-Hill has made clear the continuing usefulness of Augustan imagery in early modern England: *The Augustan Idea in English Literature* (London: Edward Arnold, 1983); on Augustan resonances of Charles II's reign, see pp.213–233.

[12] Aurelian Cook, *Titus Britannicus* (1685), sigs. b3v–b4v.

exile into a *Bildungszeit*. In Cook's account, Charles used his visits to the great courts of Europe to observe the excellencies and defects of foreign governments, accumulating a knowledge that he later deployed in wise governance.[13] While Cook traced Charles's political wisdom to his stay in Europe, the count de Grammont found in it the origins of Charles's aspiration to "Reputation," "Politeness," and "Vertue." The aspiration was fulfilled at home, according to Grammont who wrote that, notwithstanding expectations raised on "the Grandeur of the Court of *France*," he was "yet surpriz'd with the Politeness and Pomp of that *England*." The King himself was polite and radiated "politeness" so that it illuminated all who surrounded him in one fashion or another.[14] Grammont measured the English Court against the French standard and did not find it wanting. It is interesting that "Politeness" is associated in this passage with "Grandeur" and "Pomp." This was a French courtly *politesse* translated to England, a "Politeness" against which Shaftesbury would juxtapose a deliberately unimposing sort of politeness, a politeness befitting a post-courtly society.

In John Dryden's writing, one finds a version of Charles II's reign that, while manifestly royalist, also points toward Shaftesburian politeness in its focus on conversation. Dryden's contention that his own era surpassed preceding ones in refinement had an institutional dimension, since he traced literary refinement to refined conversation, which he domiciled in the Court. In the commonplace way, Dryden attributed this phenomenon to the King's exile, which offered him the opportunity of becoming "conversant in the most polish'd Courts of *Europe*." When Charles returned to England, sunk not only in "Rebellion" but also in "Barbarism," he forgave the former and "reform'd" the latter through "the excellency of his manners."[15] As the religious aspirations of the Restoration Church defined themselves against mid-century "enthusiasm" so the cultural aspirations of the Restoration Court could be propped against a notion of mid-century "barbarism." Thus a perspective opened on the Civil War, linking Christian zeal and cultural regression, a common classicist device from Vasari through Gibbon. It was a perspec-

---

[13] Cook, *Titus Britannicus*, p.499.

[14] Anthony Hamilton, count de Grammont, *Memoirs of the Life of Count de Grammont*, trans. Abel Boyer (1714), pp.92–93. Grammont came to England for the second time in 1662, having made a visit during the Protectorate.

[15] John Dryden, "Defence of the EPILOGUE [to *The Conquest of Granada*, Part II]. Or, *An Essay on the Dramatique Poetry of the Last Age*," *The Works of John Dryden*, XI, 216. Charles appears similarly in "To my Dear Friend Mr Congreve" (1694), of which Erskine-Hill's analysis is illuminating (*Augustan Idea in English Literature*, pp.228–229). Francis Atterbury, reflecting on Edmund Waller, also wondered "whether in *Charles* the Second's Reign, *English* did not come to its full perfection" (preface, *The Second Part of Mr. Waller's Poems*, 1690, sig. A4r).

tive that suggested how the hopes of both the Restoration Church and the Restoration Court (which are usually and understandably taken as disparate) might converge on a notion of civility.[16]

A recognition of the polite quality of Charles's Court was shared in a passage of John Evelyn's diary, written just at the time of the King's death in February 1685. Charles was "a Prince of many virtues, and many great imperfections." Among other things, he "brought in a politer way of living, which pass'd to luxury and intolerable expence."[17] Charles was associated with an increase in "politeness," but here only with a qualification that tells us something about both politeness and the handicaps of the Tory version of cultural history. Not only was "politeness" perceived as unstable and susceptible to decay, but also the prospective hero of the Tory cultural history was liable to embody precisely this sort of deterioration. Therefore, the stereotypes bred by Charles's Court included many unflattering elements. Indeed, as writings of the earl of Clarendon and Samuel Butler show, royal luxury was a characterization used by the King's supporters as well as by his political enemies.[18]

The negative traits of the reign of Charles II were not so easy to incorporate into the Tory version of cultural history, as Jonathan Swift's writings make clear. Like Dryden, Swift pointed to the exemplary role of the monarchy in the development of English culture, but the details of Swift's account were very different from those in Dryden. Swift's immediate point of reference was his own era, in which immorality, irreligion, and unpoliteness flourished together under Whig auspices.[19] Whig immorality and impiety set the tone of the age, but the damage did not end there. Swift disparaged the cultural character of his own day, referring to "the great Depravity of our Taste; and the continual Corruption of our Style," "Ignorance, and Want of Taste." The age's anxious quest for refinement had led only to "the Affectation of Politeness," but not the real thing.[20]

It is true that Swift did not simply ascribe this cultural debauchery to the Whigs. One intention of Swift's proposal for an English academy on

[16] Dryden described this process as a growth in English sociability under French influence: "The Dramatic Poetry of the Last Age," pp.216–217. See also D. A., *The Whole Art of Converse* (1683), pp.116, 122, which echoes Dryden's points.
[17] William Bray, ed., *Memoirs, Illustrative of the Life and Writings of John Evelyn* (London, 1818), entry for February 4, 1685.
[18] Edward Hyde, earl of Clarendon, *The History of the Reign of King Charles II* (1757?), pp.47, 51, 53–54; Samuel Butler, "The Court Burlesqu'd," in *Posthumous Works* (London, 1715), and "Satire upon the Licentious Age of Charles II," in *The Works ... With a Preface ... by Samuel Johnson* (London, 1803).
[19] Jonathan Swift, "A Project for the Advancement of Religion and the Reformation of Manners," in *Prose Works*, II, 62.
[20] *Tatler*, No. 230 (September 28, 1710), Bond, III, 191–195.

the French model was to remedy cultural limitations of a longstanding historical nature: "we are naturally not very polite."[21] However, some of his cultural commentary was politically pointed. His nostalgia directed him not to the reign of Charles II but to the cultural achievements of the earlier seventeenth century, particularly the earlier reign of Charles I, which, as he said once, was "the highest Period of Politeness in England." At that time, royal patronage and a salon culture added genuine refinement to English conversation and cultural production.[22] Flattering the cultural accomplishments of a Stuart, particularly the Caroline, Court was a propensity of a Tory sort as was the willingness to emphasize the cultural damage done in the subsequent "Fanatick Times," in which "Enthusiastick Jargon" intruded itself into English. In the wake of that debacle, the Court never restored itself in the cultural domain and instead became the hotbed of "Licentiousness." The lapse of the Court was a source of England's current cultural predicament.

Moreover, to fill the cultural vacuum, coffeehouses and gaming rooms had taken over.[23] Wit, a refugee from the blasted Court, sought dubious protection in the Town, where pretensions to "politeness" thrived. Later in life, Swift reflected on the coffeehouse where wits dispensed "Trash, under the Name of Politeness, Criticism and Belles Lettres."[24] This was Will's, the famous Whig gathering place and a fitting site for Swift to imagine a reunion among the massed enemies of virtue, religion, and culture. Whiggish susceptibilities were associated not only with irreligion but also with a sham cultural ideal.[25]

Thus, although Swift employed "politeness" as a cultural ideal, he maintained that the ideal was unobtainable under current conditions. Those conditions were partly institutional (the decline of the Court and of the cultural leadership of the nobility, the rise of the Town and its characteristic locales) and partly discursive (the language of "politeness" had been seized to legitimize those very institutions that Swift thought worked against true politeness). The implicit villain was Whiggery which dominated the Townscape and had captured "politeness." Thus invoking "politeness," Swift fashioned a tool for bludgeoning the Whigs.[26]

---

[21] Jonathan Swift, "A Proposal for Correcting, Improving and Ascertaining the English Tongue," in *Prose Works*, IV, 12.
[22] Jonathan Swift, "Hints toward an Essay on Conversation," in *Prose Works*, IV, 94–95.
[23] Swift, "Proposal for Correcting ... the English Tongue," p.12.
[24] Swift, "Hints toward an Essay on Conversation," p.90.
[25] This same polite, free-thinking Whiggish population reappeared as the satirized objects of Swift's "Argument to Prove That the Abolishing of Christianity in England, May as Things Now Stand, Be Attended with Some Inconveniences," in *Prose Works*, II, 30, 33, 35.
[26] Though Swift was a formulator of the Tory version of English cultural history, his cultural vision was complex. He never called himself a Tory, but insisted always that he

It was precisely this sort of polemic that Shaftesbury dedicated himself to reversing.

Courtliness

For Shaftesbury, the Court was in its very nature inimical to sociability and thus to both moral and cultural refinement. We can begin by looking again at the "dazzling" quality of the Court. Courtly "dazzle" blinded judgment, producing an uncritical respect toward the Court and an uncritical desire to come close to the "dazzle." The psychological impact of court "dazzle" had an important function by engaging gentlemen in the Court's operations.

Shaftesbury supposed the case of "some *noble Youth* ... of *honourable Descent*; with a *generous free* MIND, as well as *ample Fortune*." These very endowments made him susceptible to courtly enchantment since he was likely to have a vibrant and responsive imagination. Materializing elegance, grandeur, and magnificence, the Court captured the imagination of this noble youth who, thereby, lost his freedom: "A *Princely* Fancy has begot all this, and a *Princely* Slavery, and *Court*-Dependence must maintain it."[27]

This servility was, in the first place, material since participating in court life was costly. Meeting the expenses of life in the courtly circle pulled the gentleman beyond the limits of his income and encouraged him to become a court dependent. However, courtly servility also had a social and discursive dimension since it involved submitting to the Court's social demands: "*Favourites* must be now observ'd, *little Engines* of Power attended on, and loathsomly caress'd: an honest Man dreaded, and every free Tongue or Pen abhor'd as dangerous and reproachful."[28] Interaction and conversation at court were hopelessly distorted by the vectors of patronage, the need to please those in power or with access to it. The courtly game required the abandonment of directness, openness, and honesty in favor of pandering and flattering, the dominant forms of courtly interaction. Such complaisance was, of course, a mode of politeness, but of that courtly politeness against which Shaftesbury warned.[29]

---

was an Old Whig: see J. A. Downie, *Jonathan Swift, Political Writer* (London: Routledge and Kegan Paul, 1984), pp.ix–x, 26–27, 81–83. On the conditions at Court that were diminishing its cultural importance, see R. O. Bucholz, "'Nothing but Ceremony': Queen Anne and the Limitations of Royal Ritual," *Journal of British Studies*, 30 (1991), 288–323, esp. 309–314.

[27] "Miscellany" III.ii, III, 172–173 (Robertson, II, 262–263).
[28] "Miscellany" III.ii, III, 174 (Robertson, II, 263).
[29] This section of "Miscellaneous Reflections" made frequent reference to flattery as the basic form of discourse at Court: "Miscellany" III.ii, III, 171–172 (Robertson, II, 261–262). Shaftesbury often referred to the inherent dishonesty and unreality of courts:

Shaftesbury's insistence on the inauthenticity of court life is reminiscent of the tensions, bared in his notebooks, between sociability and moral autonomy. In fact, the notebooks made explicit that courtly experience was paradigmatic of social inauthenticity. Courts were the prime habitat of that feverish sociability grounded in a shallow but persistent egoism. Having asserted that the self that failed to know itself often sought distraction in social commerce, Shaftesbury wrote:

See with whome this is in common. See the Nation & People yt are the most insatiable in this Way & hunt after Conversations, Partyes, Engagements, Secrecyes, Confidencyes, & Friendships of this kind, with the greatest Eagerness, Admiration, Fondness. And see in what Place this reigns the most. The Court, & Places near the Court: the Polite World: the Great-Ones.[30]

Dominated by an absolutist court, France was infected by this hypertrophy of sociability, which was especially virulent at court. This false sociability derived from the moral incompleteness of courtiers – in the terms developed by Shaftesbury in his notebooks, from their failure to achieve sufficient interiority through the practice of soliloquy.

However, if one symptom of underdeveloped interiority was this feverish sociability, another was egoism. Though the Court was organized to encourage a certain perverse sort of sociability, its structures also authorized rampant egoism of a pre-eminently unsociable sort. Shaftesbury used a discussion of Juvenal's eighth satire, concerning pride of birth, to depict the Court as a perfectly Hobbesian world. Monarchs and courtiers were complete egoists with "no other *Sense* than that of *private Good.*" In this, they were nothing but the anticipated products of "*Court-Education,*" which (in Shaftesbury's reading of Juvenal) failed to nourish a single element of public spirit. Rather, the Court indulged young men in their passions and encouraged a total self-centeredness and, even, a tyrannical outlook. Moreover, courtly conditions reinforced the principles of their education, preserving them from the very experiences that activated and nurtured natural affection: "A PUBLICK Spirit can come only from a social Feeling or *Sense of Partnership* with Human Kind. Now there are none so far from being *Partners* in this *Sense,* or Sharers in this *common Affection,* as they who scarcely know *an Equal,* nor consider

honesty was "a real mystery in most Courts," which were inhabited by chameleon-like courtiers (Shaftesbury to Robert Molesworth, January 6, 1709, in *Letters to Molesworth,* p.20); independence from courts was the only way to be entirely what one pretended to be (Shaftesbury to Robert Molesworth, February 21, 1709, in *Letters to Molesworth,* pp.28–31); courts were "Super-natural things" where "all is miraculouse ... and out of the order of Common human policy" (P.R.O. 30/24/22/4, ff.1–2, Shaftesbury to Rowland Gwin, January 23, 1704); friendship at Court bore no relation to real friendship since the former was entirely a matter of currying or doling out favor ("Moralists" II.ii, II, 246 [Robertson, II, 41]).

[30] P.R.O. 30/24/27/10, p.176 [f.89v].

themselves as subject to any Law of *Fellowship* or *Community*." Juvenal's satire made clear the impossibility of locating "what *Community* subsisted among Courtiers; or what *Publick* between an Absolute Prince and his Slave-Subjects."[31]

In this way, Shaftesbury diagnosed the perversions of sociability inherent in the courtly situation, showing how the structures of court life constituted discursive conditions which limited and deformed those who participated. However, as Shaftesbury's treatment of Horace implied, the unhappy consequences of "Court-Politeness" were not just moral ones. Because the moral and the formal domains were so closely related, courtly perversion bore on created forms. In other words, courts, creating a culture that accorded with their peculiar modes of sociability, were responsible for disastrous effects in the arts and literature.

Rome and France

Shaftesbury's view of cultural history was in part an elaboration of the commonplace relating liberty to the arts and letters.[32] According to the commonplace, tyrannical monarchy, of which a court was a classic feature, disfigured and ultimately destroyed moral character and cultural expressiveness. Following a range of civic writers and their classical sources, Shaftesbury located a paradigmatic example of this courtly debasement of manners and culture in ancient Rome, where no sooner had the arts begun their rise than liberty fell and so too the arts. Shaftesbury exclaimed: "how fast the World declin'd in Wit and Sense, in Manhood, Reason, Science, and in every Art, when once the ROMAN Empire had prevail'd, and spread an universal Tyranny and Oppression over Mankind." It was not just political virtue that was eclipsed by tyranny, but the life of the mind and imagination. Culture itself, inextricably associated by Shaftesbury with liberty, was effaced by political catastrophe. "*Barbarity*" and "*Gothicism*" invaded the arts long before barbarians and Goths invaded the empire.[33]

---

[31] "Sensus Communis" III.i, I, 103–107 (Robertson, I, 69–72). The expression *sensus communis* (which Shaftesbury takes to mean 'a sense of common good') appears in Juvenal's satire. Shaftesbury traced his personal struggles to his having been heir to status and power in a Court-based polity: his own inner life was actuated by the concoction of unrestrained passions, febrile sociability, and self-seeking egoism that marked the soul of the courtier (P.R.O. 30/24/22/4 [back of volume], Shaftesbury to "Tiresias," February 5, 1704). Since the womb of Shaftesbury's personal *angst* was an identifiable political and cultural matrix, it is not surprising that his philosophical resolution had direct implications for a critique of culture and politics.

[32] See chapter 7, pp.144–148.

[33] "Soliloquy" II.i., I, 219, 221–222 (Robertson, I, 143, 144–145); "Miscellany" II.ii, III, 77 (Robertson, II, 204).

Shaftesbury construed this process in specifically discursive terms. As we will see in the next chapter, Shaftesbury associated eloquence with political liberty on account of rhetoric's civic functions in the political world of antiquity. Using rhetorically informed models, Shaftesbury sketched the decline of culture in imperial Rome as a decline in eloquence. Roman eloquence deteriorated "after such a Relaxation and Dissolution of Manners, consequent to the Change of Government, and to the horrid Luxury and Effeminacy of the *Roman* Court, even before the time of a CLAUDIUS, or a NERO." Under such decadent conditions, there was "no more possibility of making a Stand for Language, than for Liberty." Devoted to glorifying the monarch, courtly culture expressed the basic discursive mode of the Court, namely, flattery. Since culture, in the Shaftesburian view, was a continuation of moral and political education by other means, a courtly culture, forcing culture into the service of tyranny, had to betray the fundamental burdens of culture.

It should be noted that Shaftesbury made these generalizations in connection with Seneca who, though a man of "noble Sentiments, and worthy Actions" and a "*Patriot*, and *good minister*," was a discursive spoiler: he gave credit to a "*false* Stile and Manner" and deserved to be known as "*The Corrupter of* ROMAN *Eloquence*." Though Shaftesbury's criticism of Senecan writing had a number of features, one point of criticism was the dishonesty of offering to the public pseudo-epistles: these were not part of a real correspondence and had no real historical context in an epistolary exchange but rather "were never writ in any other view than that of being made publick, or to serve as Exercises or Specimens of the Wit of their Composer."[34] Thus, the writing became a tool for authorial display, a discursive equivalent to the theatrical self-projections that characterized court life in general. This point was typical of the homologies between the condition of sociability in society and the condition of sociability in a text that Shaftesbury identified.

The Roman political and cultural debacle pre-dated Seneca, of course, occurring at the time of Augustus. The Augustan moment had served for several centuries as a positive reference point for the cultural claims of European monarchs and their courts. Shaftesbury joined others in de-Augustanizing this cultural imagery, when he described Augustus's court as "a wretched, vile thing, a place unworthy of any Man bred in great or generous Principles, or to a right Taste of Life."[35]

While Shaftesbury was at pains to undermine the dignity of Augustus's

---

[34] "Miscellany" I.iii, III, 22–23 (Robertson, II, 169).
[35] P.R.O. 30/24/20/118, Shaftesbury to Pierre Coste, November 15, 1706. See Howard Weinbrot, *Augustus Caesar in "Augustan" England* (Princeton: Princeton University Press, 1978).

court and culture, he did want to salvage as much as possible the reputation and achievement of the Augustan poets, especially Horace. The following passage contained both these impulses:

> With their Liberty [the Romans] lost not only their Force of Eloquence, but even their Stile and Language it-self. The *Poets* who afterwards arose amongst them, were mere unnatural and forc'd Plants. Their *Two* most accomplish'd, who came last, and clos'd the Scene [Horace and Virgil], were plainly such as had seen the Days of Liberty, and felt the sad Effects of its Departure. Nor had these been ever brought in play, otherwise than thro the Friendship of the fam'd MAECENAS, who turn'd a Prince naturally cruel and barbarous to the Love and Courtship of the MUSES. These *Tutoresses* form'd in their Royal Pupil a new Nature. They taught him how to charm Mankind. They were more to him than his Arms or military Virtue; and, more than Fortune her-self, assisted him in his Greatness, and made his usurp'd Dominion so inchanting to the World, that it cou'd see without regret its Chains of Bondage firmly riveted. The corrupting Sweets of such a poisonous Government were not indeed long-liv'd. The Bitter soon succeeded. And, in the issue, the World was forc'd to bear with patience those natural and genuine Tyrants who succeeded to this specious Machine of Arbitrary and Universal Power.[36]

Literary declension followed in the steps of political tyranny, but the presence of the great Augustan poets at the ebb of liberty had to be explained. They were crepuscular figures, those who knew the light of liberty and now carried that knowledge sadly into the tyrannic night. Moreover, they only were noticed at all because of the intervention of that unusual figure Maecenas, who gave Augustus the gift of cultural politics. The Muses did actually serve Augustus, but the imagery here was at best ambiguous. These Muses were more like sirens, serving the purposes of enchantment and dissociation from reality. They allowed Augustus to proffer "corrupting Sweets" of "poisonous Government." These indeed were evanescent, preparing the path from the age of false gold to that of true lead.

Among the indicators of the plight of literature in the courtly context was the fate of tragedy. In Shaftesbury's reading, Horace's epistle to Augustus (Epistle II.i) was a satire and a subtle critique of the emperor's taste. On the basis of lines from the poem, Shaftesbury interpreted Horace as pointing to the frustration of efforts to refine and render polite the literature of Rome: instead of becoming more refined, it "grew rather wors by running into *the marvellouse*, the *outrageouse, the extream* of things." Tragedy was a case of the limited development of Roman literature. Part of the explanation for this was strictly political since tragedy was an artistic vehicle for republican sentiments. According to

---
[36] "Soliloquy" II.i, I, 219–220 (Robertson, I, 143–144).

Shaftesbury, the taste for tragedy grew out of the ethos of a republic – popular dignity, moral severity, equality, and legality. Tragedy warned against the dangers of tyranny by allowing a sort of political voyeurism. The populace was made privy to the interior life of the palace where its unphilosophical creatures (asphyxiating from insufficient interiority) were strangled in their own egoism and unbridled passion. Thus, virtues of the republic were confirmed.[37] Of course, as the polity went, so went the arts. The Roman flowering of tragedy quickly shrivelled.

If the drift toward flattery was one defect of courtly culture, another was the drive to bedazzle the courtly beholder. Courtly culture had a standing tendency to inflate its means for the sake of making an impression – an elephantiasis of the expressive capability. Following Pliny on painting in imperial Rome, Shaftesbury asserted that the fundamental value of painting was "severity," which defined the art's materials, the lives of its master practitioners, its formal properties, and its effects. Roman painting declined on account of the rise of the opposing principle, namely, luxury. With the decline of the republic, "*Taste* and *Manners*" also changed, and Pliny (an "excellent, learned, and polite Critick") "represents to us the *false Taste* springing from the Court it-self, and from that Opulence, Splendour, and Affection of Magnificence and Expence proper to the place." This escalation of the means of expression, of which Shaftesbury provided numerous details, sprang from conspicuous consumption, through which the Court put on a rivetting show for all its beholders.[38]

This discussion conveyed a politics of artistic classicism. The formal criteria of simplicity, truth, elegance, and decorum were praised and set against a range of characteristics summed up under the category of "luxury." ("Luxury" was not a purely moral characterization but an aesthetic one as well, since it covered both the elements of artistic expression and the appetites.) Moreover, this formal opposition found expression in a political arena. Since courts were, naturally, luxurious, a critique of courts could be mounted in terms of the classical traits, which thereby assumed a tangibly political character.

France, of course, was the modern analogue of imperial Rome, so Shaftesbury set into play against it the same sort of politics of discursive and artistic expression. As the latest in the series of actual or attempted universal monarchies, France threatened to replicate the nastiness of the

---

[37] P.R.O. 30/24/22/7, ff.499–500, Shaftesbury to Pierre Coste, February 19, 1709.
[38] "Soliloquy" III.iii, I, 340–342n. (Robertson, I, 219–220n). Notes toward this passage can be found in the small notebook, P.R.O. 30/24/27/13, under the head "Pictura" (pp.112–113), with references to Shaftesbury's Latin edition of Pliny. Pliny's discussion of painting appeared in Book 35 of his *Natural History*.

worst of them, unless Britain and the Netherlands could successfully resist. France was that "Power which, e're Mankind had well recover'd the Misery of those barbarous Ages consequent to the *Roman* Yoke, has again threaten'd the World with a Universal Monarchy, and a new Abyss of Ignorance and Superstition."[39] As in the case of Rome, the French political threat enclosed a threat to manners, culture, and the human spirit.

Shaftesbury's attempt to dissociate politeness from the Court was a discursive move against the cultural hegemony of France. During the seventeenth century, as is well known, France moved into a position not only of political preponderance, but of cultural dominance with respect to the elites of the various European countries. In its classic form, that culture was an emanation of Versailles. The elite of seventeenth-century Britain confronted this cultural situation in a range of ways. Imitation was one possibility, and, indeed, Francophilia was a strand in early modern English cultural history.[40] Literary and artistic imitation was part of this phenomenon, especially in the Stuart courts where the force of the French cultural model was reinforced by ties of blood. The tendency of the English Court to assume Gallic dress was an irritant and source of exasperation to many Englishmen.[41]

Shaftesbury's cultural criticism of France paralleled his criticism of ancient Rome. French culture was defined by the Court, which he construed as having a distinctive psychosocial structure and impact. In a number of ways, this structure shaped and informed expressivity in the arts. Again, Shaftesbury praised the virtues of classicism and identified the Court as hostile to classical values.

Some of Shaftesbury's more revealing remarks about France concerned painting. On the basis of Pliny and other writers, Shaftesbury conjured a vision of the painting of the ancient world embodying classical values. He conceded, albeit in a qualified way, that Italian painting of the Renaissance had revived classical values. Raphael, he admitted, was one genius among moderns who unequivocally embodied the classical in painting. However, the rise of France had thrown great impediments in the way of modern painting. He was aware of the unconventional character of his judgment: "France that seems to have done so much has held back &

---

[39] "Soliloquy" II.i, I, 216–217 (Robertson, I, 141); P.R.O. 30/24/22/4, ff.358–359, Shaftesbury to "Tiresias," November 29, 1706. On the language of "universal monarchy," see Steven C. A. Pincus, "Popery, Trade and Universal Monarchy: The Ideological Context of the Outbreak of the Second Anglo-Dutch War," *English Historical Review*, 107 (1992), 1–29, esp. 18–22.

[40] Katherine Lambley, *The Teaching and Cultivation of the French Language in England during Tudor and Stuart Times* (Manchester: Manchester University Press, 1920).

[41] Thomas, "Two Cultures?," pp.168–193.

debauch'd Taste." His was a "France wch discourag'd and cou'd not bear her Poussin (not he her) [and] spoilt even le Brun's [taste]." In fact, Shaftesbury regarded most French painting as beneath consideration. Poussin was the one great post-Raphaelite painter: his "Genius" was "chaste, sever, just & accurate." However, his very "Fidelity to Art" forced him into estrangement from France, where he was "caballed" against by a courtly conspiracy against taste. Poussin's value was inextricably linked to his alienation from France and his resort to Italy.[42]

While chastity, severity, and correctness were the moral–aesthetic terms with which Shaftesbury identified the artistic achievement of Poussin, affectation and artificiality characterized the presiding spirit of most modern French painting. Since the artist in France could only survive through a pandering to a precious audience, he was forced into artificiality. The example of LeBrun served to point up the frailties of an art nursed in the French Court. In LeBrun's ceiling for the Hall of Mirrors at Versailles, Shaftesbury observed "his long Peruk'd bare neck'd *Gallo-Grecian* Heroes, these Monstrositys & the *Manière lechée* & florid Colouring with affected Gesture & Theatrical Action of the Womanish Court" and called that style "a Bane to Painting & infectiouse through Italy & Europe."[43] The courtliness of LeBrun's painting and its concomitant stylistic infelicity were typical of all modern French painting. Only the rarest of moderns rose "above the modern turn & species of Grace. above the Dancing-Master. above the Actor & the Stage. above the other Masters of Exercise." Despite the efforts of moderns to avoid "the Tragick or *Theatrical* Action," it remained: "Yet the Sneer retain'd; the Twist, the affected Contraste."[44] Theatricality and affectation were inscribed into French seventeenth-century painting because they were engendered in the essentially theatrical environment of the French Court.

Shaftesbury made similar points about certain aspects of French literature, although he also allowed here for a greater degree of complexity. We find Shaftesbury admitting to the French a certain sort of literary politeness. The English "natural genius" was superior to that of the French, "that airy neighbouring nation." (Its "airs" were a matter both of preten-

---

[42] P.R.O. 30/24/27/15, pp.51v, 52v, 62v, 64r, 83r [ff.59v, 60r, 70v, 72r, 91r].
[43] P.R.O. 30/24/27/15, p.83r [f.91r]. The cycle of painting represented a compromise between classical and contemporary iconography: it consisted of scenes of the life of Louis XIV, shown as a Roman emperor in the company of ancient deities. The incidents chosen to illuminate the monarch's career, such as "La Resolution Prise de Faire la Guerre aux Hollandais, 1671" (which Shaftesbury mentioned in particular) and "Prise de la Ville et Citadelle de Gand en 6 Jours, 1678," were painful subjects for Shaftesbury to contemplate. See: *Charles LeBrun, 1619–1690*, Exposition, Chateau de Versailles, July-October 1963, pp.108–119; Anthony Blunt, *Art and Architecture in France 1500 to 1700* (Baltimore: Penguin Books, 1954), pp.237–238.
[44] P.R.O. 30/24/27/15, p.91r [f.99r].

tious and artificial manners, of the sort Shaftesbury found in French painting, and of discursive flatulence.) Yet, "it must be confessed that with truer pains and industry they have sought politeness, and studied to give the Muses their due body and proportion, as well as the natural ornaments of correctness, chastity, and grace of style." Such "pains and industry" were exactly what Shaftesbury wanted to see in Britain.

Though Shaftesbury had some positive words for Boileau and for the modern French epic poets, he thought that French dramatists were impeded by difficulties of the sort that the Romans had faced. In "Soliloquy," Shaftesbury repeated the same observations about the nature of tragedy he had made in correspondence with Pierre Coste.[45] However, here the subject was French and not Roman letters. In this passage, he explicated why a form of drama that spoke to the egalitarian condition of free and independent citizens had to be hobbled under French conditions, for he postulated "how little [the tragic] Model is proportion'd to the Capacity or Taste of those, who in a long Series of Degrees, from the lowest Peasant to the high Slave of Royal Blood, are taught to idolize the next in Power above 'em, and think nothing so adorable as that unlimited Greatness, and Tyrannic Power, which is rais'd at *their own* Expence and exercis'd over *themselves*."[46] The adoration of greatness and the slavishness before power inhibited receptivity to the tragic meanings, which warned against the great and their ambitions and which affirmed the role of individuals in their appropriate estate in a regulated and lawful state.

In another place, Shaftesbury admitted that the French had "some legitimate Authors of a just Relish, correct, and without any mixture of the affected or spurious kinds."[47] However, this was a clause in a complaint against the general run of French books that comprised the ordinary reading of supposedly polite youths. Only exceptional French authors were "form'd upon the natural Model of the Antients"; the rest were victims precisely of affectation and spurious aspirations.

This characterization of the dominant tendency in French letters was expanded in a passage complaining of the dialogic barrenness of modern literature. Shaftesbury contrasted the genre of dialogue particularly with "that more complaisant modish way, in which an Author, instead of presenting us with other natural Characters, sets off his own with the utmost Art, and purchases his Reader's Favour by all imaginable Compliances and Condescensions." Whereas dialogue instituted a distance

---

[45] See note 37 above. The letter to Coste was written in February 1709. *Soliloquy* was first published in 1710. The wording of the two formulations was quite similar.
[46] "Soliloquy" II.i, I, 218–219 (Robertson, I, 142–143).
[47] "Soliloquy" III.iii, I, 335n. (Robertson, I, 216n).

between author and his spokespeople, the way in fashion was a literature of the first-person, in which the author had the opportunity to improve and present himself in the most self-flattering of ways and at the same time to flatter and play to the reader. The metaphors that Shaftesbury used to explain the relationship were exactly those of a questionable, if not perverse, sociability:

> And as in an Amour, or Commerce of Love-Letters; so here the Author has the Privilege of talking eternally of himself, dressing and sprucing up himself; whilst he is making diligent court, and working upon the Humour of the Party to whom he addresses. This is the *Coquetry* of the modern Author; whose Epistles Dedicatory, Prefaces, and Addresses to the Reader, are so many affected Graces, design'd to draw the Attention from the Subject, towards *Himself*; and make it be generally observ'd, not so much *what he says*, as *what he appears*, or *is*, and what figure he already makes, or hopes to make, in the fashionable World.[48]

The figures here evoked the world of social glitter, the surface of social pleasing, the shallowest rendition of politeness. The social mode of the Court infected texts (it was not accidental that Shaftesbury used the expression "making diligent court"), and this mode was, of course, profoundly self-concerned, simultaneously narcissistic and cravenly subject to the perceptions of others.

According to Shaftesbury, the French were particularly liable to inscribe their texts with such theatrical sociability (with its affectations, narcissism, and flattery).[49] This unfortunate discursive mode was embodied in the memoir, a genre particularly suited for the exploitation of the self's promiscuous, yet egoistic, resources. The memoir allowed the author to wallow in the liquidity of the first-person: he assumed the shapes he would, for purposes of presenting the self and pleasing the other. Moreover, in France, whole ranges of textual possibilities had been absorbed to the form of the memoir and so shaped in its worst possibilities. Thus, French literary and intellectual creations received the stamp of French courtly politeness. The texts themselves re-enacted the theater of Versailles.

Thus, the fortunes of true "politeness" in France were necessarily hindered. Instead of liberty, France was characterized by both slavish hierarchalism and insidious courtliness. Such a political culture gave a distorted shape to its expressive culture. In making these points, Shaftesbury contradicted expectations, according to which France and politeness were naturally associated. The aim of course was partly to expand into the

---

[48] "Soliloquy" I.iii, I, 199–200 (Robertson, I, 131).
[49] "Soliloquy" I.iii, I, 200 (Robertson, I, 132).

cultural realm the means for vilifying France and partly to set terms for a program of British cultural improvement.[50]

While Shaftesbury tended to articulate his discursive and cultural complaint against courtliness with reference to ancient or foreign courts, the argument had a native dimension. The Tories were the object of the cultural politics of *Characteristicks*. It was they whom Shaftesbury saw as fellow-travellers of the French, "preferring rather that abominable Blasphemouse Representative of Church Power attended with the worst of Temporal Governments as we see it in perfection of each kind in France."[51] It was they too who subscribed to a royalist tradition of exalting the dignity and power of monarchs.

While, as the next chapter points out, Shaftesbury devoted some words in *Characteristicks* to the English cultural past, his references to the Stuarts, from James I to James II, were muted. Yet, he did make a few brief remarks about the Stuarts and culture in "A Letter Concerning the Art, or Science of Design." There he blamed English failures in musical taste on "the long Reign of Luxury and Pleasure" of Charles II, though he noted that the more recent turn from French to Italian musical idioms was transforming English musical taste for the better.[52] Similarly, the unfortunate condition of English architecture was entirely the fault of "one single Court-Architect" who dominated the architectural field "through several Reigns." Shaftesbury characterized Christopher Wren's architectural idiom in the same terms that he characterized the mistaken stylistic propensities of the Roman and French Courts: expensive, false, magnificent, and deformed. Meanwhile, Wren's London churches were accurately but, by Shaftesbury, pejoratively described as "retaining much of what Artists call the *Gothick* Kind."[53] In other words, English culture had suffered, as a culture must, from courtliness. In Shaftesbury's vision, the culture England had inherited from the seventeenth century was a product of the Stuart Court, which, tending to overstate and overspend, betrayed the elegancy of classical values. The Court's inherently pernicious tendencies were amplified by reliance on French models, which, as we have already seen, were the modern quintessence of courtliness.

The cultural program Shaftesbury did endorse was a program for a post-courtly European culture. He depicted a culture in which a court was not the central agency of patronage. While admitting that any artistic and

---

[50] Here cultural nationalism was a tool of aristocratic Whiggism. Later, it would become an anti-aristocratic and radical project: see Gerald Newman, *The Rise of English Nationalism* (New York: St. Martin's Press, 1987).
[51] P.R.O. 30/24/20/143, Shaftesbury to Michael Ainsworth, February 25, 1707.
[52] "Letter Concerning Design," pp.399–400 (Rand, p.20). Shaftesbury also found a rise in the taste for Italian painting, as against French, encouraging for the condition of taste.
[53] "Letter Concerning Design," pp.400–402 (Rand, pp.21–22).

literary patronage was an exchange of benefits, he was wary of court involvement. If the Court that patronized was not "truly virtuous and wise," it would only harm "since 'tis not the Nature of a Court (such as Courts generally are) to improve, but rather corrupt *a Taste*. And what is in the Beginning set wrong by their example, is hardly ever afterwards recoverable in the Genius of a Nation."[54] In "Soliloquy," he rejected, rather more absolutely, the role of the Court in cultural patronage:

'Tis with us at present as with the *Roman* People in those early Days, when they wanted only repose from Arms to apply themselves to the Improvement of Arts and Studys. We shou'd, in this case, need no ambitious Monarch to be allur'd, by hope of Fame or secret views of Power, to give Pensions abroad, as well as at home, and purchase Flattery from every Profession and Science. We shou'd find better Fund within ourselves, and might, without such Assistance, be able to excel, by our own Virtue and Emulation.[55]

The passage situated Britain at a moment of cultural opportunity: when Britain defeated France, the accumulation of cultural fertility would bring forth fruit. However, the mode of that incipient age of cultural productivity would not mimic the courtly pattern. No monarch would be manipulating people for cultural gain nor would culture proceed as a form of flattery. Rather, culture would resume its healthy identity as an expression of autonomous and free individuals, whose very autonomy and freedom guaranteed their virtue. It was in the realm of such beings that Shaftesbury wanted to locate the promise of a healthy culture, a realm in which liberty underpinned politeness.

[54] "Letter Concerning Design," p.405 (Rand, p.23).
[55] "Soliloquy" II.i, I, 223 (Robertson, I, 145–146).

10 The culture of liberty

"Politeness"

Shaftesbury may have had qualms about the links between Whiggism and the Court after 1688, but polemics in Queen Anne's reign demanded simplicity. Thus, in his published writings, the Whigs were, simply, the party of liberty, the party that made the 1688 Revolution and opposed the French, the Stuart tyrants, and the High Churchmen. While Shaftesbury identified political liberty with post-1688 political arrangements, he was largely concerned with what we can identify, variously, as cultural, intellectual and, especially, discursive liberty. Thus, for Shaftesbury, liberty was the condition for full human development: "Tis Liberty indeed that can only polish & refine the Spirit & Soul as well as Witt of Man." Such liberty operated in the related fields of discourse and politics, "Freedome of Reason in the learnd world, & Good Government & Liberty in the civil world."[1] Since the Church and the Court dominated discourse in unhealthy ways, assuming magisterial or awing postures that promoted their political authority at the expense of individual autonomy, Shaftesbury urgently and repetitively asserted the importance of discursive liberty. Having examined how Shaftesbury mounted a critique of the Church and the Court in psychosocial and discursive terms, we can turn to the positive side of the argument, the promise of Whig political hegemony to initiate a distinctive and flourishing age in British culture.

Shaftesbury sketched his program in a letter of 1706, anticipating that the ultimate victory of Britain over France would lead to a great advance in "Letters and Knowledge." He acknowledged that, like "all good Things," "Liberty of Thought and Writing" had their "Inconveniences," specifically, "a sort of Libertinisme in Philosophy." Nonetheless, the price was worth paying since liberty had the tendency to correct its own excesses. He noted, for example, that, though the early Protestant reformers had been guilty of excess, "Blasphemouse Enthousiasts and

---
[1] P.R.O. 30/24/20/91, Shaftesbury to Arent Furley, February 18, 1705; 30/24/20/143, Shaftesbury to Michael Ainsworth, May 10, 1707.

195

reall Phanaticks" no longer posed a danger because excess had diminished naturally. Indeed, he wrote: "I am farr from thinking that the Cause of Theisme will lose any thing by fair Dispute. I can never ... wish better for it than when I wish the Establishment of an intire Philosophical Liberty."[2] Here, in summary, were Shaftesbury's basic themes: the circumstances were propitious for a great leap forward in British culture; those circumstances centered on liberty, the only felicitous context for cultural and intellectual development; while liberty referred, conventionally, to political arrangements, it also meant specifically discursive liberty, freedom of expression and criticism.

Shaftesbury developed these themes in later essays, especially "A Letter Concerning Enthusiasm" and "Sensus Communis," first published in 1708 and 1709 respectively.[3] In the "Letter," Shaftesbury offered the dynamics of discursive liberty as a solution to the topical problem of handling enthusiasm. As a natural and inevitable component of human character and social relations, enthusiasm had to have its vent. Since suppression bred what it sought to eliminate, freedom for enthusiasts was preferable to attempts at magisterial control. Shaftesbury believed society could afford such toleration because discursive liberty meant not only freedom to express but also freedom to examine and criticize. A liberty of reason was the best means to puncture false claims, to reduce imposture, and to drain enthusiasms of their tumescence. Indeed, one form of critical liberty was the liberty to mock and make fun, the freedom of raillery that Shaftesbury investigated further in "Sensus Communis," subtitled "An Essay on the Freedom of Wit and humour."

"Sensus Communis" used the defence of raillery to frame a discussion of the moral principles stated in Shaftesbury's earlier *Inquiry Concerning Virtue*. As a discussion of discursive liberty, "Sensus Communis" elaborated points made in the "Letter" and broadened the range of the discussion beyond the "Letter"'s topical concerns. In particular, "Sensus Communis" proposed rational and sociable conversation as a model for intellectual activity and cultural habits. The critical enterprise, he argued, was essential for moral and cultural health.

Shaftesbury's concern in these two essays with discursive freedom led to explicit and classic formulations of the cultural dimensions of liberty. According to the "Letter":

---

[2] P.R.O. 30/24/22/2, ff.175–176, Shaftesbury to Jean LeClerc, March 6, 1706. The next sentence set the limits of freedom and the conditions for calling in the magistrate: "prophane, mocking, and scurrilouse Language that gives the just offence, makes fatall Impressions on the Vulgar, and corrupts Men in another manner than by their Reason."
[3] Another extensive "defence of that freedom of thought" appeared, fittingly, as a conclusion to the "Miscellaneous Reflections" and so to *Characteristicks* itself: "Miscellany" V.iii, III, 297ff. (Robertson, II, 341ff.).

Justness of Thought and Stile, Refinement in Manners, good Breeding, and Politeness of every kind, can come only from the Trial and Experience of what is best. Let but the Search go freely on, and the right Measure of every thing will soon be found. Whatever Humour has got the start, if it be unnatural, it cannot hold; and *the Ridicule*, if ill plac'd at first, will certainly fall at last where it deserves.[4]

Intellectual and discursive freedom had the negative capacity to dissolve unnatural humors (including all pernicious enthusiasms) and, beyond that, to curtail all manner of excess. Hence, truth, civility, and all expressive refinement depended on the freedom of the intellectual and discursive search, what we might call the 'essayistic' ventures of a community of inquiring intellects.

In "Sensus Communis," the same idea was expressed with greater attention to the specific processes of liberty:

Wit will mend upon our hands, and *Humour* will refine it-self; if we take care not to tamper with it, and bring it under Constraint, by severe Usage and rigorous Prescriptions. All Politeness is owing to Liberty. We polish one another, and rub off our Corners and rough Sides by a sort of *amicable Collision*. To restrain this, is inevitably to bring a Rust upon Mens Understandings. 'Tis a destroying of Civility, Good Breeding, and even Charity itself, under pretence of maintaining it.[5]

The passage brought into direct conjunction the two key terms, politeness and liberty: politeness summed up the proper state of wit, humor, understanding, and manners, in individuals and in society at large, while liberty referred to the condition of unlimited interaction and unlimited criticism. Since the essence of freedom was friendly interaction, the passage lays before us, as the setting for moral and cultural development, a scene of polite conversation, the decorous freedom of discussion among gentlemen. Liberty was thus figured in terms of a healthy interactive situation. At the same time, refined sociability was being constituted as an open-ended and unconstrained ideal, free from authoritarian interference. As we saw in chapter 5, this conversational scene was the paradigmatically apt discursive situation, most likely to eliminate the psychosocial postures that inhibited reason and autonomy. Just as the Church and the Court were associated with interactive models, so too was liberty.

All politeness was owing to liberty because free discussion and interaction tended to eliminate the excessive and the false. However, the relation between liberty and politeness was also based on the fact that the interactions that comprised politeness did themselves constitute a form of

---
[4] "Letter" ii, I, 10 (Robertson, I, 10).
[5] "Sensus Communis" I.ii, I, 64–65 (Robertson, I, 46).

liberty. In a sense, conversation itself here became a paradigmatic mode of liberty, and, thus, liberty was assimilated into the notion of culture itself.

In such passages, Shaftesbury gave a significant twist to the notion of liberty. Although he clearly saw his discussion in a Whiggish political light, "liberty" did not refer in these passages to a patently political condition, neither to the establishment of rights nor to independence nor to self-government. Rather, it referred to a social and cultural condition, a condition of unlimited interpersonal interaction. Liberty in the modern world was thus associated with a lively public culture, a public engaged in a culture of examination, criticism, and exchange. This was a significant expansion on the cultural politics of the civic tradition since here the eloquence of senators was transformed into an all-embracing medium for society. The conventional civic point was that cultural achievements had a specifically political foundation: Letters or Arts were based on Liberty, which was a condition of civic existence. Here, however, Shaftesbury was emphasizing liberty's character as a condition of social and cultural life, a condition of discourse and cultural production in society. This was a less civic standpoint. Certainly, the second sense of liberty can be seen as an extension of the first: that is, one can assert – and this no doubt was Shaftesbury's intention – that an aspect of *civic* liberty is *discursive* and *cultural* liberty. At the same time, however, one cannot help but regard Shaftesbury's concern with discursive and cultural liberty as a significant shift of emphasis, one that distanced liberty from its specifically civic setting.

Shaftesbury's advocacy of such a public culture was intended to have a Whiggish force: he was defining what we take as a characteristic feature of eighteenth-century culture as a partisan achievement. However, Shaftesbury's cultural politics also mitigated the stressful relations between virtue and culture in writers of the civic tradition. A truly polite people was no longer in danger of losing its liberty since that liberty was secured in the very fact of the people's being polite. Politeness was so thoroughly enmeshed in discursive and cultural liberty that politeness was not conceivable without such liberty. Shaftesbury had reached a point at which he could dispense with the fear that cultural development in itself threatened liberty or with the conviction that liberty required the utmost cultural simplicity. Thus, he rejected explicitly the nostalgic propensity of the civic tradition, not only in its specifically political respects but in its longing for manners of a by-gone day. Moreover, as we will see, this transvaluation of the cultural put the improvement of taste and the elaboration of criticism at the center of the moral and political endeavor.[6]

---

[6] For criticism's centrality, see "Miscellany" V.i, III, 251–252 (Robertson, II, 312–313).

Greece

Abandoning nostalgia did not necessarily mean giving up the search for one's bearings through an examination of the past; and, as Shaftesbury deployed cultural history in his critiques of Church and Court, so he deployed it to elucidate the character and impact of liberty. "A Letter Concerning Enthusiasm" offered a taste of this in its brief evocation of "ancient policy" toward religious and philosophical opinion:

> Not only the Visionarys and Enthusiasts of all kinds were tolerated, your Lordship knows, by the Antients; but on the other side, Philosophy had as free a course, and was permitted as a Ballance against Superstition. And whilst some Sects, such as the *Pythagorean* and latter *Platonick*, join'd in with the Superstition and Enthusiasm of the Times; the *Epicurean*, the *Academick*, and others, were allow'd to use all the Force of Wit and Raillery against it. And thus matters were happily balanc'd; Reason had fair Play; Learning and Science flourish'd. Wonderful was the Harmony and Temper which arose from all these Contrarietys. Thus Superstition and Enthusiasm were mildly treated; and being let alone, they never rag'd to that degree as to occasion Bloodshed, Wars, Persecutions, and Devastations in the World.[7]

This passage provided a pedigree to Shaftesbury's faith in the refining power of liberty as a discursive condition. Ancient discursive freedom was contrasted to the policy of modern governments, which interfered forcefully in matters of religious and other belief in order to guard uniformity of opinion.

Elsewhere in his writings, Shaftesbury elaborated the historical picture adumbrated here, fixing on ancient Greece as the classical locus of politeness. That Shaftesbury regarded the ancient Greeks as supremely polite was patent. Jean LeClerc remembered Shaftesbury asserting that "the Grecians were more civilized and more polite than we ourselves, notwithstanding we boasted so much of our improved wit and more refind Manners."[8] In Shaftesbury's own words, ancient Greece was the fountain of all divinity, philosophy, and "polite learning"; it was the "politest of all Nations," the "sole polite, most civiliz'd, and accomplish'd Nation."[9] The politeness of the Greeks was then a cultural condition, signifying both their achievements in society, intellect, expression, and art and also the congruence of all these with (what Shaftesbury designated) natural standards and a just taste. Shaftesbury's Hellenism was aggressive and reductive. His dismissal of alternative claims eliminated complicated and

---
[7] "Letter" ii, I, 18 (Robertson, I, 14–15).
[8] P.R.O. 30/24/22/7, ff.487–488, a MS. translation of Jean LeClerc's dedication of his edition of Menander and Philemon (Amsterdam, 1709) to Shaftesbury.
[9] P.R.O. 30/24/20/143, Shaftesbury to Michael Ainsworth, December 3, 1709; "Miscellany" III.i and V.i, III, 138, 152, 231 (Robertson, II, 241, 250, 298).

multiple explanations. "The GREEK *Nation*, as it is *Original* to us, in respect to these polite Arts and *Sciences*, so it was in reality *original to it-self*." Greek accomplishment towered over all innovations of its predecessors. Politeness was an absolutely pure and unitary stream, of which Greece was the spring.[10]

The thrust of Shaftesbury's cultural-historical investigation was significantly non-Roman. Indeed, cultural Hellenism was the complement to Shaftesbury's anti-Augustanism. One reason for this shift of emphasis was the fact that the history of ancient Greece was not yet as predetermined by paradigmatic formulations as the history of ancient Rome. We have already seen how, according to the classical republican version of Roman history, republic and liberty passed into empire and tyranny. Since civic decline was accompanied by the refinement in manners and arts in ancient Rome, republican formulations insisted that liberty was unpolished while politeness was slavish. The model was too thoroughly vested with the presumptions of the Country critique of the Court, leaving no room for Shaftesbury's particular needs to honor both Country and courtly traditions, both civic virtue and politeness.

Of course, the civic humanists had not ignored Greece, but their interest and affection had always fallen on Sparta. For all its cultural achievements, Athens had an unstable political history, which rarely commended itself to civic writers. However, when Shaftesbury wrote of Greek politeness, he was thinking of Athens. The manner in which polite Athens could serve as a model of liberty and virtue is revealed in the sorts of liberty that Shaftesbury thought were actualized there. Shaftesbury used the Athenian experience to elaborate on the relations of liberty and cultural development. In his discussion, discourse was the exemplary arena in which politics and culture interacted. Moreover, Greek instances put Shaftesbury in a position to specify further the parameters of polite and impolite forms of expression. At the same time, Shaftesbury's discussion helps us to understand the extent to which he had developed a sophisticated cultural discourse, in which both liberty and culture submitted to the discipline of sociability.

Shaftesbury began with a very general genealogy of human culture. The

---

[10] "Miscellany" III.i, III, 137 (Robertson, II, 241). Shaftesbury's assertiveness fits with Martin Bernal's account of how the European scholarly tradition denied ancient Near Eastern, especially Egyptian, influences on ancient Greece: see Martin Bernal, *Black Athena: The Afroasiatic Roots of Classical Civilization* (New Brunswick: Rutgers University Press, 1987), I, 1–2, 23–27, 165–167, 174–175. This assertiveness also illustrates the distance between Shaftesbury and John Toland, whose hermetic interests led him to see a positive model of civic religion in ancient Egypt. Viewing Egypt as the model of a priest-ridden society, Shaftesbury was in no position to accept its claims as a source of *prisca sapientia*. For Shaftesbury, *sapientia* was Greek. See Margaret Jacob, *The Radical Enlightenment* (London: George Allen & Unwin, 1981), pp.36, 153.

primitive state of humans was acultural: social life was rudimentary, and language was just sufficient for conferring about wants and necessities. Man's linguistic condition was at zero degree, without self-consciousness, speculation or art. As society became less rudimentary and more secure, discursive opportunities expanded. Discussion of important matters evolved into debate, and speechmaking became common, with a double result. The orators themselves, in order to enhance their powers of persuasion, developed the arts of expression. Meanwhile, the auditors developed a sensitivity to distinctions in the realm of expression, learning what they found agreeable and what not.[11] In short, the exigencies of persuasion and the comparison of oratory were the foundations of linguistic self-consciousness and expressive refinement.

From the start, Shaftesbury's natural history adumbrated a politics of eloquence, since the polishing of expression arose in the public arena, in the competition for the assent of something like a primeval public. The existence of this public implied a popular or consensual politics of some sort. Shaftesbury was quick to make this implication explicit. In those of these early societies that gravitated towards the rule of one or of a few and where the power of force, awe or terror replaced that of assent, rhetorical arts atrophied. The very opposite occurred where government remained popular, for there persuasion remained important in the public realm and the rhetorical arts had to be elaborated as a basic element in governance.[12] The progress of oratory depended on liberty, and the liberty in which oratory flourished was the civic liberty of "*Free Nations*."

However, another kind of liberty is evident in Shaftesbury's version of the polishing process. The career of eloquence was launched and propelled by a dialectic between rhetorical practice and rhetorical receptivity. While a sophisticated audience put pressure on the orator to be his best, the orator himself had an interest in training the audience, promoting "that *Taste* and *Relish* to which they ow'd their personal Distinction and Pre-eminence."[13] The growth of eloquence occurred, in Shaftesbury's account, because of the mutual interactions of orator and audience, the orators seeking to please and the audience learning its desires. (It was into this orator–audience relation that Shaftesbury inserted the critics, who "taught the public to discover what was just and excellent in each performance" of oratory.) Thus, the progress of oratory depended on latitude of interaction as well as civic liberty. Even in this most generalized of accounts, Shaftesbury specified two related but non-identical

[11] "Soliloquy" II.ii, I, 236–237 (Robertson, I, 153–154).
[12] "Soliloquy" II.ii, I, 238–239 (Robertson, I, 155).
[13] "Soliloquy" II.ii, I, 239 (Robertson, I, 155).

conditions for the refinement of expression: a politics of popular assent and also a condition of free interaction.

Since this genealogy of culture was itself of directly Hellenic inspiration, Shaftesbury had put himself in a position to develop these ideas further with specific regard to the ancient Greeks, who were, as we have seen, the fundamental datum in the history of politeness. He summarized the polishing of the Greeks in "Miscellaneous Reflections," asserting that it was they who first "brought their beautiful and comprehensive Language to a just *Standard*." Politeness, having established itself in the domain of their oratory, spread to every aspect of Greek culture. The refinement of the tongue became paradigmatic for all manner of expression in society, "from *Musick, Poetry, Rhetorick*, down to the simple Prose of History, thro all the plastick Arts of *Sculpture, Statuary, Painting, Architecture*, and the rest."[14] Politeness operated as a standard for all formal expression. Moreover, the refinement of all the arts was implied in the refinement of the central linguistic one.

In "Miscellaneous Reflections," Shaftesbury traced this development not to specifically political but to more general associative factors. Despite geographical dispersal and political disunity, the Greeks shared a common "Extract" and a common language. More important, "animated by that social, publick and *free* Spirit, which notwithstanding the Animosity of their several warring States, induc'd them to erect such Heroick Congresses and Powers as those which constituted the AMPHICTONIAN Councils, the OLYMPICK, ISTHMIAN, and other Games; they cou'd not but naturally polish and refine each other." Politeness here was traced not to political liberty nor to a political condition but rather to sociability, a drive to associate in public, that answered the needs both of cooperation and competition. Greek cultural evolution depended on associating in a public arena devoted to ritual cooperation (the amphictyonies) and to physical agonistics (the games), an arena from which civic politics was absent. On the other hand, a concern with the civic was never far from Shaftesbury's mind, and he appears to have been willing to slide from one sort of liberty to the other. So, shortly after this discussion, he mentioned that the polished Greeks, having attained "SIMPLICITY and NATURE," were able to preserve it "till the Ruin of all things, under a Universal Monarchy," Alexander's.[15]

Shaftesbury's discussion in "Soliloquy" did much to indicate the further specifications of politeness. Generally, the refining process involved moving from showy aspirations, affectation, and falseness to easiness, naturalness, and honesty. The discipline to which cultural arti-

---

[14] "Miscellany" III.i, III, 138–139 (Robertson, II, 242).
[15] "Miscellany" III.i, III, 138, 141 (Robertson, II, 241–242, 243).

facts were to submit was a discipline of sociability: modes of cultural expression had to avoid the sorts of postures that were condemned in social life itself.

The labor of the early critics was to banish discursive affectation, by identifying "what was specious and pretending," allowing "no false Wit, or jingling Eloquence," and exposing "the weak Sides, false Ornaments, and affected Graces of mere Pretenders." The aspirations to effect, to which these features corresponded, were found notably in "the *Miraculous*, the *Pompous*, or what we generally call the SUBLIME." That the sublime characterized the earliest writing is fitting, according to Shaftesbury.

Astonishment is of all other Passions the easiest rais'd in raw and unexperienc'd Mankind. Children in their earliest Infancy are entertain'd in this manner: And the known way of pleasing such as these, is to make 'em wonder, and lead the way for 'em in this Passion, by a feign'd Surprise at the miraculous Objects we set before 'em. The best Musick of *Barbarians* is hideous and astonishing Sounds. And the fine Sights of *Indians* are enormous Figures, various odd and glaring Colours, and whatever of that sort is amazingly beheld, with a kind of Horrour and Consternation.[16]

Shaftesbury here set going several devices to signal the complex unpoliteness of the sublime. Developmentally, it was infantile. Culturally, it was primitive. The passage put together a vocabulary of wonderment and wonderfulness ("astonishment," "wonder," "miraculous," "hideous and astonishing," "enormous," "odd and glaring," "amazingly," "horror and consternation") that demarcated the terrain of enthusiasm and superstition. Moreover, sublime writing partook formally of the traits of "Awefulness" and "dazzle," with which our discussion attempted to summarize Shaftesbury's formal sense of the Church and Court. Thus, Shaftesbury could see the sublime as eliciting a sort of responsiveness which was not that of thoroughly morally realized individuals, but rather that of passive and irresponsible subjects. That the sublime constituted, in its way, an unsociable style, Shaftesbury made explicit when he wrote: "In Poetry, and study'd Prose, the *astonishing* Part, or what commonly passes for *Sublime*, is form'd by the variety of Figures, the multiplicity of Metaphors, and by quitting as much as possible the natural and easy way of Expression, for that which is most unlike to Humanity, or ordinary Use."[17]

Shaftesbury assembled this account out of loose and imaginative use of Aristotle. From there, too, he derived the notion that Homer arrived on the scene as a reformer of style who removed the infelicities of the

[16] "Soliloquy" II.ii, I, 241–242 (Robertson, I, 156–157).
[17] "Soliloquy" II.ii, I, 242–243 (Robertson, I, 157–158).

sublime. Homer was described in the vocabulary of discursive preference: the decent, the natural, the simple, beauty of composition, unity of design, truth of characters, imitation of nature.[18] In turn, the Homeric move became paradigmatic for Greek literature generally.

In the rise of politeness, nature was the signature of the polite artifact. When Shaftesbury wrote that "the real *Lineage* and SUCCESSION of *Wit*, is indeed plainly founded in *Nature*," he referred back to one of his founding premises, that of a designed cosmos in which principles of form and sociability both inhered.[19] Nature was not opposed to the human world, since the normative principles of the human world were already, in Shaftesbury's view, pre-inscribed in the cosmos. Because nature provided the criterion of taste and, one might say, politeness, the lineage of wit – cultural history, we might say – was founded in nature. The vicissitudes of politeness could only be traced using the standard of nature.

In the case of Greece, nothing underlay the formation of culture but nature itself. The first rise of politeness was the Greek self-formation, "wrought out of Nature, and drawn from the necessary Operation and Course of things, working, as it were, of their own accord, and proper inclination."[20] What precisely did this mean for the polite artifact? "In the Days of ATTICK Elegance," Shaftesbury wrote,

Workmen ... were glad to insinuate how laboriously, and with what expence of Time, they had brought the smallest Work of theirs (as perhaps a single Ode or *Satir*, an *Oration* or Panegyrick) to its perfection. When they had so polish'd their Piece, and render'd it so natural and easy, that it *seem'd* only a lucky Flight, a Hit of Thought, or flowing Vein of Humour; they were then chiefly concern'd lest it shou'd *in reality* pass for such, and their Artifice remain undiscover'd.[21]

Attic elegance was the art of the natural: at the limit of its perfection, it risked being mistaken for the natural itself; its artifice was at risk of oblivion. We see here how polished cultural artifacts had the qualities of polished social action. Polite expression in the arts submitted to the same standards as polite behavior in society. The standard was striving through real effort to create effects of ease and naturalness. The standard aimed to create pleasure through benign unaffectedness.

This passage suggests the general applicability to cultural artifacts of Shaftesbury's aspirations to sociability and politeness in the creation of the philosophical text (observed in part I). The passage generalized

---

[18] "Soliloquy" II.ii, I, 243 (Robertson, I, 158). Another version of the transition from sublime to natural appears in "Miscellany" III.i, III, 140–141 (Robertson, II, 243).
[19] "Miscellany" III.i, III, 137 (Robertson, II, 241). On cosmic design, see chapter 2, pp. 54–55.
[20] "Miscellany" III.i, III, 140 (Robertson, II, 242).
[21] "Soliloquy" II.ii, I, 233 (Robertson, I, 151–152).

Shaftesbury's laudatory description of the simple style of Xenophon, which "being the strictest Imitation of Nature, shou'd of right be the compleatest [style], in the Distribution of its Parts, and Symmetry of its Whole, [and] is yet so far from making any ostentation of Method, that it conceals the Artifice as much as possible: endeavouring only to express the effect of Art, under the appearance of the greatest Ease and Negligence."[22] The simple was the ultimately polite style, for it brought into precise focus both nature and art, ease and order, negligence and control. In such a passage, one sees the natural affinity between the classical vocabulary and the vocabulary of politeness. The classical aesthetic criteria approximated those of good fellowship in polite society. The politeness of polite artifacts was a matter of having been polished but also a matter of having been made pleasing in a social way. And as the supposition of the polishing process was a certain sort of liberty, so the result of the process was an artifact understood in terms of the regime of polite sociability in which liberty had a place.

Of the various movements toward refinement in the history of Greek culture, the evolution of comedy, as described by Shaftesbury, was particularly illustrative not only of the dynamics of refinement but of the specific connections between politics and politeness.[23]

To begin with, the Greek Old Comedy, arising out of earlier farce and phallic festivals and assuming some formal coherence at the time of Aristophanes, was the enemy of all affectation and pomposity. Its dialectical operations, directed at "every thing which might be imposing, by a false Gravity or Solemnity," were precisely, according to Shaftesbury, acts of unmasking. The Old Comedy was thus a step toward politeness insofar as politeness eschewed the sorts of pretensions that could not stand up to the Old Comedy's laughter. The Old Comedy exercised the refining power of raillery, and, therefore, like the operations of raillery in modern conversation, depended on freedom of expression.[24]

However, the freedom of the Old Comedy writers was liable to degenerate into license, and their progress toward politeness was limited. Even Aristophanes' achievement was stunted. The progress of politeness could only proceed through a further dialectical move with the appearance of the New Comedy. All that was lacking in the Old Comedy was made up in the New, for Menander represented the perfection of comedy.

Relying on Horace's *Ars poetica*, Shaftesbury proposed that the tran-

---

[22] "Soliloquy" II.ii, I, 258 (Robertson, I, 168–169).
[23] Shaftesbury's discussion of the evolution of Greek tragedy was brief, culminating with Euripides, who recapitulated the Homeric movement from sublimity to nature and simplicity: "Soliloquy" II.ii, I, 244–245 (Robertson, I, 158–159).
[24] "Soliloquy" II.ii, I, 245–247 (Robertson, I, 160–161).

sition from Old to New Comedy was the product of a legal intervention, new laws that effected the cultural change.[25] However, his understanding of this development was highly significant, since it assumed the coherence of political and cultural sophistication. The new laws arose from a "real Reform of *Taste* and *Humour* in the Commonwealth or Government it-self": "Instead of any Abridgment, 'twas in reality an Increase of *Liberty*, an Enlargement of the Security of *Property*, and an Advancement of private Ease and personal *Safety*, to provide against what was injurious to the good Name and Reputation of every Citizen." Thus, the curtailment of the excesses of the Old Comedy expressed not the limiting of freedom but, rather, a new and more sophisticated appreciation of it. A more secure grasp on the nature of liberty, a grasp that itself derived from the experience of political liberty, led to cultural change. Moreover, the laws reforming comedy were reflections of the desires of the Athenian public. Refinement in political sensibility was conjoined to refinement in other areas, so that the legislative reform of drama was merely one expression of the polishing process.

As this Intelligence in Life and Manners grew greater in that experienc'd People, so the Relish of Wit and Humour wou'd naturally in proportion be more refin'd. Thus GREECE in general grew more and more polite; and as it advanc'd in this respect, was more averse to the obscene buffooning manner. The ATHENIANS still went before the rest, and led the way in Elegance of every kind.[26]

This polishing of the expressive modes was merely the outward manifestation of a profound and inner transformation, the refinement of sensibility.

Shaftesbury's admiration for the ancients did not constitute a rejection of modernity since the ancient had a clarifying, not a disparaging, relation to the modern. Though he ascribed the greatest achievements in art and literature to the Greeks, Shaftesbury was progressive in his views of history. The point of looking back to the Greeks was not to mourn a loss but to celebrate a possibility. While politeness had been realized among the ancients, it also was the end of modern life. To embrace antiquity was to foster a particular sort of modernity.

Britain

Shaftesbury's account of culture and politics in ancient Greece was, obviously, a way of pursuing more immediate and, even, programmatic

---

[25] The relevant lines from Horace are 282–284. There is no evidence that such edicts had any effect. See the comment, s.v. "Comedy (Greek), Old," in *The Oxford Classical Dictionary*, 2nd edn (Oxford: Clarendon Press, 1970), pp.269–270.

[26] "Soliloquy" II.ii, I, 250 (Robertson, I, 163).

ends. The Greek past suggested patterns for British cultural history and possibilities for the British cultural future. The Greek model implied an alternative to the Tory interpretation of British cultural history, since it insisted on the relation between politeness and liberty, dissociating politeness from the courtly environment. Shaftesbury's hopes for the present also put him at a distance from the propensities associated with the Country. In the same way that he rejected Country nostalgia for a virtuous polity in the British past, so he had little use for the British cultural past. As British political history was a history of the growth of liberty, so British cultural history was a history of the growth of politeness.

The opportunities for a new British culture were set against the background of the international political conflict between Britain and France in the post-Revolution period. If barbarism was the accompaniment of universal monarchy, the progress of France threatened to replicate that of Rome. Britain was thus allowed to champion liberty against universal monarchy and politeness against ignorance and superstition. Elsewhere, Shaftesbury found it convenient to cast France not as Rome but as another historical incarnation of empire, namely, Persia. This, of course, allowed Britain to retrace the steps of ancient Greece, and most particularly those of Athens, as the champion of liberty. That Britain was also in a position to repeat the Hellenic cultural performance was evident in Shaftesbury's anxiety to exploit, in his own words, "some kind of Comparison between this antient *Growth* of TASTE, and that which we have experienc'd in modern days, and within our own Nation."[27]

In Shaftesbury's view, his own era was an auspicious moment for British cultural improvement, and the opportunity was offered not only by the international situation, but also by the recent rebirth of freedom in Britain itself. The affirmation of British liberty in 1688 had brought new opportunities for British culture: "For in our Nation, upon the foot Things stand, and as they are likely to continue; 'tis not difficult to foresee that Improvements will be made in every Art and Science." The Revolution had set the seal on liberty and law, assuring the progress of politeness. The only impediment remaining, said Shaftesbury, was the preoccupation with the Continental wars.[28]

There were tensions within the view that Shaftesbury was sketching. On

---

[27] "Soliloquy" II.i, I, 216–217, 222–223 (Robertson, I, 141, 145); "Miscellany" III.i, III, 141 (Robertson, II, 243). Shaftesbury reckoned neither with the imperial career of Athens nor with the Augustan aspect of Periclean Athens, though he once indicated that Pericles' virtue had been compromised, which might attest to some diffidence on the issue: P.R.O. 30/24/27/10, p.192 [f.97v]. On the language of "universal monarchy," see chapter 9, note 39.
[28] "Soliloquy" III.i, I, 215–216, 223 (Robertson, I, 141, 145).

the one hand, he was arguing for British cultural superiority on the basis of British genius and British politics. At the same time, however, he recognized the deficiencies of British culture. The British culture that would serve as a counterweight to the force of Continental culture had yet to be created. While "our natural Genius shines above that airy neighbouring Nation," it had to be admitted "that with truer Pains and Industry, they have sought *Politeness*." Nonetheless, he maintained that French politics stunted French culture whereas it was easy to see "what effect [Britain's] establish'd Liberty will produce in every thing which relates to *Art*; when *Peace* returns to us on these happy Conditions."[29] Still, the argument for British cultural superiority was proleptic. Shaftesbury was dissatisfied with much that he found of British culture. His writings, thus, involved a simultaneous effort to remove the locus of politeness from France to Britain and to create a British culture worthy of the ascription "polite."

British impoliteness was patent, and Shaftesbury pointed to several impediments to British cultural growth: Britain was insular, xenophobic, and resistant to positive influences from outside; it was also remote from the breeding grounds both of ancient and modern culture and always came by its culture late.[30] All of this stood in contrast to the associative character of the Greeks who not only interacted among themselves in various athletic and ritual occasions but also (and notwithstanding their originality) traveled widely and tasted cosmopolitanly in their Levantine world. Of course, we have already examined the greatest impediments to British politeness, namely, the domination of politics and culture by courtly and ecclesiastical institutions.

On the other hand, Britain evinced the potential for refinement. Complaint about "the Genius of our People" was commonplace among writers, he said, but "we are not altogether so *Barbarous* or *Gothick* as they pretend." Indeed, "we are naturally no ill Soil; and have musical Parts which might be cultivated with great Advantage, if these Gentlemen wou'd use the Art of Masters in their Composition." Thus, the British were disposed to become more polite: they were ready for cultivation.[31]

---

[29] "Soliloquy" II.i, I, 218–219 (Robertson, I, 142–143).
[30] "Miscellany" III.i, III, 151–152, 153–154 (Robertson, II, 249–250, 250–251).
[31] "Soliloquy" II.iii, I, 274–275 (Robertson, I, 179). A related passage is found among Shaftesbury's jottings in a 1712 Italian almanac (P.R.O. 30/24/24/14, f.5), in which he noted his belief in design's primacy over color in painting: "Pleasure of Colours, the Debauch-Pleasant Painting! – The Shop. ... Must be quitted for a true Taste & consequent Enjoymt. English Temper. Hope from It. Affecion of Hardship. Severity in Style, Sense, etc. This may run too far. ... But easily temper'd. This the right Side. Mark of a good Genius." The passage related the tension between design and color to that between stoicism and Epicureanism and identified the English with the stoic/design pole of the

The culture of liberty 209

In fact, Shaftesbury found reason to believe that the British had already begun to imitate ancient Hellenic experience. The history of the English language parallelled the evolution of the Greek examined earlier. While, to judge by "the *Speeches* of our Ancestors in Parliament," the discourse of the Middle Ages was "very short and plain, but coarse, and what we properly call *home-spun*," the Renaissance brought in a new sophistication, which Shaftesbury characterized, suspiciously, as "scholastic" and "pedantic": "the Fashion of speaking, and the Turn of Wit, was after the *figurative* and *florid* Manner. Nothing was so acceptable as the high-sounding Phrase, the far-fetch'd Comparison, the capricious *Point*, and Play of Words; and nothing so despicable as what was merely of the plain or natural kind." As in the sublime phase of Greek writing, the writers of English in the sixteenth and seventeenth centuries affected artfulness, seeking astonishing effects and dramatizing their creations and themselves. They called attention to themselves, seeking to be admired. By contrast, the improvements that Shaftesbury observed in recent years bespoke a different principle, that "the *natural* and *simple* Manner which *conceals* and *covers* ART, is the most truly *artful*, and of the genteelest, truest, and best study'd Taste."[32] Here again was the ideal of self-effacing self-expression, which we have observed shaping Shaftesbury's estimate of cultural products generally and also his notion of philosophic behavior and writing.

The model of evolution from sublimity and other distortions of form towards politeness informed many of Shaftesbury's judgments about literature. He summed up his view of British literature in these very terms when writing of the infantile state of the British muses:

They have hitherto scarce arriv'd to any-thing of Shapeliness or Person. They lisp as in their Cradles: and their stammering Tongues, which nothing besides their Youth and Rawness can excuse, have hitherto spoken in wretched Pun and Quibble. Our *Dramatick* SHAKESPEARE, our FLETCHER, JONSON, and our *Epick* MILTON preserve this Stile. And even a latter Race, scarce free of this Infirmity, and aiming at a false *Sublime*, with crouded *Simile* and *mix'd Metaphor*, (the Hobby-Horse, and Rattle of the MUSES), entertain our raw Fancy, and unpractis'd Ear; which has not as yet had leisure to form it-self and, become truly *musical*.[33]

This passage offered a complex characterization of literary impoliteness. To begin with, it was a picture of impoliteness because the literature under discussion did not, in Shaftesbury's view, correspond to certain formal criteria. However, impoliteness in the passage was an indication of

tension. Thus, the English were disposed to actuate Shaftesbury's moral and aesthetic programs.
[32] "Miscellany" III.i, III, 141–142 (Robertson, II, 243–244).
[33] "Soliloquy" II.i, I, 217 (Robertson, I, 141–142).

the unsociability of this literary discourse, an unsociability that was cast on two levels of characterization. In the first place, the writers were cast as infants and children, obviously not thoroughly socialized and not capable of mature expression. However, in addition, the stylistic devices with which Shaftesbury associated them are parts of an unsociable literary equipment. "Pun and Quibble," "crouded Simile and mix'd Metaphor," were devices of literary artifice striving self-consciously for effect, seeking either in the most blatant way for our attention, in the manner of children, or "aiming at a false *Sublime*," more in the manner of adolescents.

The growth of politeness in Britain meant the maturation of the various modes of expression, what, in keeping with the themes of this study, we can think of as their full socialization. The concept of politeness referred not just to refinement, but to the specific cast of this refinement. Politeness was refinement that had submitted to the disciplines of sociability: the combination of self-confidence and unpretentiousness, the naturalness and ease, the honesty and elegance, of the fully autonomous being.

In sum

At the end of his life, retired in Naples, Shaftesbury wrote *A Letter Concerning the Art, or Science of Design to My Lord*****. Completed by March 1712, it was included in some copies of the second edition of *Characteristicks* in 1714 but only became a standard feature of the eighteenth-century printings of *Characteristicks* in the fifth edition of 1732.[34] The *Letter Concerning Design* was originally a cover letter to John Somers, the "Lord" of the title, accompanying Shaftesbury's *Notion of the Historical Draught or Tablature of the Judgment of Hercules*, which Shaftesbury also wrote in Naples. The *Letter Concerning Design* described the contents of the other essay, but what gave the *Letter Concerning Design* enduring value were the many connections it made between culture and politics: indeed, it was, practically, a broadside encapsulation of the cultural-political themes of *Characteristicks*.

The central point of the *Letter Concerning Design* was that Britain was approaching a new cultural age. Though reiterating several times the excellence of British genius, Shaftesbury focussed on the new circumstances that would allow British genius to flower. Those circumstances were construed in a political and specifically Whiggish way. Shaftesbury congratulated the Whig policy of war with France, assuring the reader, "in a kind of spirit of Prophecy," that victory in war would mean the

---

[34] On the peculiar printing history of *A Letter Concerning Design*, see Kerry Downes, "The Publication of Shaftesbury's 'Letter Concerning Design,'" *Architectural History*, 27 (1984), 519–523.

victory of liberty and the constitution. In turn, this political outcome would have cultural consequences: the development of the national personality in the form of increased knowledge, industry, sense, and, indeed, politeness.[35] Shaftesbury also based his hopes for cultural efflorescence on Britain's domestic political nature: "As her *Constitution* has grown, and been establish'd, she has in proportion fitted her-self for other Improvements."[36] The opposite side of this coin was the criticism of the dire cultural consequences of Stuart rule in passages of the *Letter Concerning Design* examined in chapter 9.

Yet, more important than the bald assertion of the connection between liberty and culture was the process by which these two domains were related. In a dense but significant statement, Shaftesbury wrote:

When the *free* spirit of a Nation turns it-self this way [that is, toward the arts]; Judgments are form'd; Criticks arise; the publick Eye and Ear improves; a right Taste prevails, and in a manner forces its way. Nothing is so improving, nothing so natural, so *con-genial* to the liberal Arts, as that reigning Liberty and high spirit of a People, which from the Habit of judging in the highest Matters for themselves, makes 'em freely judge of other subjects, and enter thorowly into the Characters as well of *Men* and *Manners*, as of the *Products* or *Works* of Men, in Art and Science. So much, my Lord, are we owing to the Excellence of our national Constitution, and legal Monarchy; happily fitted for Us; and which alone cou'd hold together so mighty a People; all sharers (tho' at so far a distance from each other) in the Government of *themselves*.[37]

Explaining why the reign of liberty improved the arts, this passage draws together themes we have been examining throughout this book. Liberty was, in its essence, autonomy, judging for oneself "the Characters ... of *Men* and *Manners*." As moral autonomy consisted in having a character, moral judgment consisted in understanding others' characters. However, if moral liberty was ultimately individual in its frame of reference, political liberty was the collective version – each person sharing, though at a distance from others, in the government of himself. Thus, the passage returns us to the problem of part I: how it was possible for humans to attain some autonomy given their status as sociable beings. A free polity was the political form most likely to encourage the autonomy of human beings. Given the extent to which humans were discursive beings, it was the discursive freedom of a free polity that could best nurture the possibility of human autonomy. Unfree polities (and, of course, Shaftesbury was thinking of polities in which Church and Court were domineering

---

[35] "Letter Concerning Design", p.398 (Rand, pp.19–20).
[36] "Letter Concerning Design", p.405 (Rand, p.23).
[37] "Letter Concerning Design", p.404 (Rand, pp.22–23).

entities) created discursive conditions tending to quash the autonomy on which humanity entirely depended.

The next step in the argument was that only the sort of autonomy which was present only in a free polity conduced to autonomous judgment in other matters. Judgment in moral and political characters correlated with judgment in cultural matters. If autonomy was required to grasp character in moral and political forms, then it was required to grasp expressive forms as well. In short, liberty was required for taste.

The beginning of the passage offered another way of putting this. There Shaftesbury suggested that a true public was found only under conditions of liberty. It was impossible for those who were not free to form judgments of any legitimacy since, if they were not free, their judgment had to be a reflection of some authority outside themselves. Moreover, under conditions of unfreedom, it was impossible for judgments to interact in a way that allowed the winnowing of true from false, good from bad, polite from impolite.

Concomitantly, under conditions of freedom, the progress of taste and politeness was irresistible. Once there was a public, people felt a vested interest not only in political matters but in artistic ones. As he said in another passage: "In reality *the People* are no small Partys in this *Cause*. Nothing moves successfully without 'em. There can be no PUBLICK, but where they are included."[38] Thus, the notion of a public only made sense in the context of liberty, and only free polities would have a public. The public was that entity that occupied the cultural zone. The training of the public in morals and taste became a central task. *Characteristicks* and Shaftesbury's other writings were attempts first to define that task and second to carry it out.

[38] "Letter Concerning Design", p.403 (Rand, p.22).

Index

absolutism, 133, 139, 177, 184, 185, 187
Addison, Joseph, 2, 9, 12, 36–37, 40–41, 42, 129–131
affectation, *see* theatricality
affection, 53–54, 55–59, 67, 70, 72n, 74, 76, 123, 158, 165–167
ancient constitution, 125, 127, 134
Ancients and Moderns, 46
anti-clericalism, 1, 16, 154–155, 168
Antisthenes, 43
Archimedes, 82
Aristotle, 43, 60–61, 203
Arrian, *see* Epictetus
arts and letters, 5, 21, 69, 147, 177, 178, 179, 185, 198
Asgill, John, 157
atheism, 31, 52, 157
Athens, 148, 171, 200
atomism, 61, 62, 64, 71
Atterbury, Francis, 32n, 180n
Augustinianism, 56, 64
Augustus Caesar, 176, 179, 186–187
authority in discourse, 112–114, 159–160, 167–169
autonomy, 54–59, 70, 73–74, 80, 81, 83, 86, 91, 93–96, 98–99, 112–114, 167, 184, 211

Bakhtin, Mikhail, 89n
balloting reform, 135
Barish, Jonas, 75
Barrow, Isaac, 156
Bayle, Pierre, 17, 52n
Becker, Marvin, 3
Berkeley, George, 2
Bloom, Edward and Lillian Bloom, 129
Boileau, Nicolas, 191
Bolingbroke, Henry St. John, Viscount, 124, 129
Browning, Reed, 130
Bruni, Leonardo, 145, 146
Burke, Edmund, 125–126
Burnet, Gilbert, 63, 136, 156

Butler, Samuel, 181

Calvinism, *see* Nonconformity
Cambridge Platonism, 33, 61, 66, 156, 162
Cassirer, Ernst, 29n
Catholicism, 161: in Middle Ages, 172–173; on contemporary Continent, 133, 139
character, 80, 91–93, 96; *see also* self
Charles I, 179, 182
Charles II, 127, 179–182, 193
Chillingworth, William, 156
Christianity, 31, 53, 54, 159, 171–172: doctrine of rewards and punishments, 32, 53, 158
Church, Shaftesbury's critique of the, 8–9, 21–22, 31–33, 37–38, 52, 100, 106–107
Cicero, 42, 44–46, 63, 79, 115, 130, 148–150
City, the, 143–144
civic humanism, 126–129, 131, 144–150, 198, 200
civic life and citizenship, 45, 60, 62, 108, 130, 144
civic virtue, 124, 126, 128, 132, 135, 139, 143–147, 150
civil religion, 161
Clarendon, Edward Hyde, earl of, 181
classicism, *see* humanism
coffeehouse, 8, 11, 12, 182
Collins, Anthony, 157
commonwealthmen, 1, 16, 125, 137–138, 176–177
conversation, 4–5, 6, 9, 41, 52, 107, 118–119, 160: at Court, 180, 183–185; dangers of, 76–78; inner, 88–90, 104–106, 111–112, 117; paradigm of, 8, 9–10, 96–100, 196–197; *see also* Shaftesbury: Politeness and philosophy: politeness in philosophy; Shaftesbury: Textual practices: discursivity
Cook, Aurelian, 179–180
cosmic design, 52, 53, 54–56, 60, 70–71, 155, 158, 204

213

Index

Coste, Pierre, 175–176
Country: as cultural ideal, 144; tradition in politics, 126–128, 134–137, 143, 177; Whigs, 125; *see also* civic humanism; commonwealthmen
Court, the, 10, 36, 128, 135, 143–144, 175–194: French, 176, 177, 184, 189; Roman, 176–177, 185–186; Shaftesbury on Court culture, 8–9, 151–153, 175–178, 183–194; Stuart, 178–182, 193–194
courtesy literature, 94, 102
criticism, 1, 20, 97, 99, 150, 201
Cropley, John, 15, 142
Cudworth, Ralph, 33, 55, 163
cultural politics, 8, 16, 22, 124–125, 132, 143, 150–153
culture, as influence on affections, 54, 58–59
Cumberland, Richard, 33, 55
custom, *see* opinion

Darby, John, 123
Davenant, Charles, 110n, 137, 138, 145–146
Defoe, Daniel, 129–130
deism, 1, 16, 33, 137, 157
deity, 61, 64, 65, 66, 70–71, 76, 158, 159; *see also* cosmic design
Democritus, 60–61
Dennis, John, 5, 165
deportment, 92
Descartes, René, 27, 40, 53, 61n, 66
Desmaizeaux, Pierre, 48
Dilthey, Wilhelm, 29n
Diogenes, 43
Disbanding Act, 135–137
diversity, 12, 145
dogmatism, 99, 167
Dryden, John, 6, 15, 110n, 165, 178, 180

egoism, 4, 53, 55–58, 61–69, 74–76, 85, 184–185
Egypt, 169–171, 200n
Elias, Norbert, 3, 14
enthusiasm, 22, 58, 156, 160–168, 172, 178, 182, 196, 197
Epictetus, 43, 60, 71, 74, 77, 81, 83n, 84, 86, 89n, 91, 93, 107n, 158
Epicureanism: ancient, 60–63; modern, 28, 42, 53, 61–69
Epicurus, 61–62, 71
Evelyn, John, 181

Felton, Henry, 6
flattery, 78, 100, 150, 186

Fletcher, Andrew, 16, 126, 137, 138, 146, 147n
France, 133, 208: Court, 176–177, 184, 189; as universal monarchy, 188–189, 207; cultural influence, 181–182, 189; painting, 189–190; literature, 190–192
free thinking, 65, 157
"French prophets," 18, 167
Furley, Benjamin, 17

Gadamer, Hans-Georg, 29
genre: dialogue, 116–118, 191; essay, 114; letter, 115; memoir, 192; sermon, 32–34, 100
gentlemanly: culture, 1, 3–6, 9–10, 21–22, 41, 100, 156; style, 6–8, 43–44, 51
gentlemen: as political and cultural elite, 20, 119, 143, 144, 151; as readers, 79, 105–107, 108–110
Grammont, Anthony Hamilton, count de, 180
gravity, 48–51, 95, 97, 99, 104, 168
Grean, Stanley, 84
Greece, ancient, 100: compared to Rome, 130, 200; cultural evolution, 200–206; literature, 202, 204–206; model for Britain, 207, 209; politeness, 7, 199–200, 202, 204–206; sociability, 202, 208
Grotius, Hugo, 67
Gwin, Rowland, 135

Habermas, Jürgen, 13–14, 29n, 30n, 98n
Hammond, Henry, 156
Hampden, Richard, 131n
Harley, Robert, 124, 140n
Harrington, James, 126–127, 151, 161, 170
Hercules, choice of, 20, 62n, 124n
Hervey, John, 130, 134
Hoadly, Benjamin, 32n, 130, 156
Hobbes, Thomas, 27, 31–32, 40, 53, 56, 63–69, 184
Homer, 203–204
Horace, 110, 176–177, 187, 205
Hughes, John, 6
humanism, 3, 28, 41–42
Hume, David, 53
Husserl, Edmund, 29n
Hutcheson, Francis, 2, 51, 53

identity, *see* self
individualism, *see* egoism
innate ideas, 66
intentionality, 55–56, 58
interiority, 55, 83–84, 91, 104–105, 184
irony, 96, 157

Index

Isocrates, 147

Jacob, Margaret, 17
Jesus, 158, 159
Junto, 132, 135
Juvenal, 184–185

Kramnick, Isaac, 129–130

La Bruyère, Jean de, 78n
La Rochefoucauld, Francois de, 63–64
Lang, Berel, 50
Lanham, Richard, 75
latitudinarianism, 31, 33n, 52n, 155–156, 162
Le Brun, Charles, 190
Le Clerc, Jean, 17, 176n, 199
L'Estrange, Roger, 15, 165
liberalism, 129–130
liberty: discursive, 4, 12, 97–99, 149–150, 150–151, 159–160, 195–198, 199, 201, 211; moral, 123; political, 123–125, 125–129, 133, 144–150, 175–177, 195, 198, 201, 211; *see also* autonomy; civic humanism; Whiggism
Locke, John, 15, 16, 27, 39–40, 49, 53, 61n, 64–69, 117, 126, 129, 130, 134, 138
Lucretius, 62, 64
Lukes, Steven, 63
luxury, 145–146, 181, 186, 188, 193

Machiavelli, Niccolò, 145–146, 148
Maecenas, 176, 187
Mandeville, Bernard, 2, 129–130
manners, 27, 131, 143–146, 177, 178, 183; *see also* politeness
Marcus Aurelius, 43, 60, 71, 74, 79, 83n, 89n
materialism, 61, 64
Menander, 199n, 205
middle class, 129–130
mixed or balanced constitution, 133, 149, 150, 178
Molesworth, Robert, 16, 126, 137, 138, 147n, 161
moral sense, 1, 56–58
More, Henry, 33, 162
Moyle, Walter, 16, 126, 137

Naples, 20, 124, 210
natural law, 33, 67–69, 126, 131, 134
Netherlands, 17, 133
Neville, Henry, 126–127, 146, 161
Newton, Isaac, 82
nominalism, 53, 55, 61–62, 64, 66
Nonconformity, 32, 52n, 156, 162, 164

Occasional Conformity bills, 156
opinion, 58–59, 65, 74, 94
oratory, 99–100, 107, 149, 201

painting, 188–190, 208n
Parker, Samuel, 164–165
parliamentary qualification bills, 135, 136
passion, *see* affection
pedantry, 5, 6, 108–109
Phillipson, Nicholas, 131
philosophy: aesthetics, 1, 35; analytic, 30n; ancient, 42–46, 60–63; empiricism, 29; epistemology, 29, 40, 54, 61, 65–67; ethical, 27–28, 31, 34–35, 39–41, 42, 60–69; historiography of, 28–30, 40, 50–51, 53–54; modern, 21, 27–28, 34, 37, 38–40, 46, 52, 53, 61, 63–69, 105; natural, 28, 38–39, 42; polite, 21–22, 34–36, 40–41, 43–47, 54, 69, 96, 97, 102–107, 108, 111–119; sites of, 36–41; style in, 43, 48–51; *see also* Epicureanism, humanism, scholasticism, stoicism
place bills, 135
plasticity, *see* theatricality
Plato, 43, 60–61, 108–111, 116, 166
pleasing and pleasure, 4, 58, 62, 97–99
Pliny, 188–189
Pocock, J. G. A., 126–128, 150
politeness: affinities with rhetoric, 46; in behavior, 3–5, 94; at Court, 175–176, 177, 180–183; in culture, 7–8, 9–10, 125, 131, 195–212; distinguished from sociability, 4; of Greeks, 199–206; history of, 3; language of, 2, 3–8, 34, 78, 102; in learning, 5–6, 13; paradigm of, 9–10, 11; in philosophy, 21–22, 34–36, 40–41, 43–47, 54, 69, 96, 97, 102–107, 108, 111–119; in writing, 6–7
post-structuralism, 30
Poussin, Nicolas, 190
pragmatism, 30
priestcraft, 22, 137, 160–161, 169–174
print culture, 11
Protestantism, 55, 161
providence, 60–61, 71, 158
public: the, 20, 41, 58, 68, 105, 184–185, 201, 212; discourse, 99, 167–168, 198; philosophy, 37, 45, 93–94; sphere, 2, 13–14, 98n
Pythagoras, 42

raillery, 50, 96, 98, 159, 168
Rand, Benjamin, 71
Raphael, 189
Raphael, D. D., 51

216   Index

reason, 55–57, 72n, 74, 96–100, 168: in religion, 155, 162–163
religion, 52, 53, 58–59, 155: revealed, 158
Restoration of 1660, 9, 38, 179–181
retirement, 60, 62, 79, 85, 108
Revolution of 1688, 1, 38, 125, 132–133, 135n, 140–141, 142, 207
rhetoric, 29, 33, 44–46, 69, 75, 89, 102–107, 147–150, 186–187, 201
Rochester, John Wilmot, earl of, 63–64
Rome, ancient, 146–149, 171: Court, 176–177, 185–186; literature, 186–188; painting, 188; compared to ancient Greece, 130, 200
Rorty, Richard, 29
Rotterdam, 17, 70
Russell, William, 136

Saint-Évremond, Charles de Marguetel de Saint-Denis, seigneur de, 5
scepticism, 53, 99, 159–160
schools, *see* universities
scholasticism, 28, 37–38, 39, 43, 69
science, *see* philosophy, natural
Scipio Africanus, 46
Scottish Enlightenment, 131
Selden, John, 67
self, 59, 73–74, 83, 85, 91–92, 96: and others, 4, 54–59, 72–80
self-command, *see* autonomy
self-fashioning, 81–90, 92–93, 106
self-knowledge, 27, 39, 42, 55, 71, 82, 83, 93, 103–105, 111, 116, 138
self-love, *see* egoism
Seneca, 186
sermons, 32–34, 100
Seymour, Edward, 140
Shaftesbury, Anthony Ashley Cooper, first earl of, 14
Shaftesbury, Anthony Ashley Cooper, second earl of, 14
Shaftesbury, Anthony Ashley Cooper, third earl of
  Life: family, 14–15; in Parliament, 15–16, 18, 135–141; personal crises and psychology, 17–18, 70–73, 78; personal relations with Locke, 15, 16, 27–28; political evolution, 131–132, 138–143; as political operator, 140, 142; retirement, periods of, 15–16, 17, 18, 20, 138, 141; sexuality, 76n
  Writings: "The Adept Ladys," 18; *Askēmata* notebooks, 17, 70–73, 82–83, 93, 138; *Characteristicks*, 1, 2, 16, 17, 19–20, 22, 34, 37–41, 48–49, 72, 78, 90, 96, 100–101, 111–119, 123–125,

132–133, 156, 158, 166, 210, 212; *An Inquiry Concerning Virtue*, 16, 17, 21–22, 48–60, 70–72, 80, 113, 117–118, 158, 166, 172, 196; *Judgement of Hercules*, 20; "A Letter Concerning Design," 20, 193–194, 210–212; "A Letter Concerning Enthusiasm," 18–19, 113, 150–151, 166–167, 196–197; "Miscellaneous Reflections," 19–20, 52n, 113; "The Moralists," 18, 19, 35–36, 37–38, 51–52n, 61n, 115–116, 118, 124; *Paradoxes of State*, 135n, 140–141; preface to Whichcote, 16, 31–34, 51–53; "Sensus Communis," 19, 51n, 64–65, 96, 113, 159–160, 196–197; "Socratick History," 18, 107–111; "Soliloquy," 19, 102–107, 113
Politeness and philosophy: critique of Epicureanism, 28, 42, 60–69; critique of modern philosophy, 21, 27–28, 34, 37, 38–40, 52, 53, 61, 63–69, 105; ethical ideas, 52–59; gentlemanly program, 20–22; moral discourse, 33–34, 34–41; natural sociability, 31, 33, 52, 53–59, 60, 62, 67, 68, 72–80, 89, 94, 112; philosophy, definitions of, 82, 90, 93; politeness, 2, 20–22, 80, 85, 94, 119, 125, 151, 160, 197, 207; politeness in philosophy, 21–22, 34–36, 40–41, 43–47, 54, 69, 96, 97, 102–107, 108, 111–119; relations with stoicism, 27, 55, 60–61, 62, 67, 71, 72n, 73, 74, 76, 79, 81–88, 93–94; sociability, models of, 8, 85–86, 93–96, 97–101, 151, 154; wisdom, 19, 21–22, 27, 34, 37, 41, 42, 44–45, 73, 77, 80, 82
Politeness and politics: on ancient constitution, 134; on British cultural history, 193–194, 207–210; as commonwealthman, 1, 16, 137–138; on commonwealthmen, 138–141; as Country politician, 16, 17, 131–132, 134–137, 139–140, 177; on Country ideals, 140–143, 207; on Court culture, 8–9, 151–153, 175–178, 183–194; cultural politics, 8, 16, 22, 124–125, 132, 143, 150–153, 198, 210–212; on ecclesiastical culture, 8–9, 21–22, 31–33, 37–38, 52, 54, 100, 106–107, 151–153, 154–160, 165–169, 173–174; on English language and literature, 209–210; on established Church, 32, 155–156; on France, 133, 139; on liberty, 123–125, 133, 195–198, 201–202, 207, 211–212; on natural law,

Index

67–69, 134; politics, 131–143; on 1688 Revolution, 1, 132–133, 135n, 140–141, 142, 207; on Tories, 133, 135, 139, 140–141, 142, 152–153, 177, 193; as Whig, 1, 125, 131–133, 142–143; on Whig cultural ideal, 8–9, 22, 195–198, 207, 210–212

Textual practices: allusiveness, 61; abstraction and deduction, 69; of *Characteristicks*, 72, 111–119; compared to Addison, 37; discursivity, 77, 88–90, 104–105, 112–119; dialectical method, 86–90; as ethical process, 82–83; formality, 159; genres, 32–34, 100, 112–118, 191–192; injunction, 83n, 93, 95n; of *Inquiry*, 59; irony, 96, 157; the magisterial, 110; of notebooks, 72, 80, 82–83; pedantry, 18–19; pleasure, 4–5, 108–109; simplicity, 110; of "Socratick history", 108–111; of "Soliloquy", 102; transvaluation, 87; variety, 112–113; voice, 112–117

Shapin, Steven, 6n
Sidney, Algernon, 136, 146, 147
sociability, 29, 34, 85, 202–203: distortions of, 94–96, 99–101; in religion, 154, 156, 158–160, 163, 165; as natural affection, 1, 4, 31, 33, 53–59, 60, 62, 67, 68; as stylistic idiom, 49, 96–101, 112–119, 177; as threat to autonomy, 72–80, 83–89; *see also* enthusiasm
society: nature of, 55; origins of, 62, 67–68, 200–201
Socrates, 27, 36, 42–44, 60, 76n, 107–111, 116, 176
solitude, *see* retirement
Somers, John, 16, 152, 210
Sparta, 146, 200
Spinoza, Benedict de, 61n
standing army, 137
Stanhope, James, 45–46
Steele, Richard, 2, 9, 12, 129
Stephens, William, 137–138
stoicism, 27, 55, 60–61, 62, 67, 71, 72n, 73, 74, 76, 79, 81–88, 89n, 93–94
Stuart monarchs, 133, 139, 178, 189
sublime, the, 203, 209

superstition, 58, 170, 172
Swift, Jonathan, 146–148, 157, 181–182

Tacitus, 147
theatricality, 4–5, 74–79, 85, 90–91, 92–96, 100, 105–106, 138, 202–203, 209; at Court, 186, 188, 190–192
Tillotson, John, 32n, 156
Tindal, Matthew, 65, 157
Toland, John, 16, 48, 126, 137–138, 157, 200n
toleration, 137, 156, 160; *see also* liberty, discursive
Tories: version of cultural history, 178–182, 207; Shaftesbury on, 133, 135, 139, 140–141, 152–153, 177, 193
Town, the, 11–13
Treason Trials Act, 135, 136
Trenchard, John, 16, 137
Triennial Act, 135

universal monarchy, 185, 187, 188–189, 202, 207
universities, 10, 36, 37–38, 100, 152
utilitarianism, 58

Virgil, 187
virtue, 52–59, 62, 64–66, 123
virtuosi, 37–38
Voitle, Robert, 98

Walpole, Robert, 129
Whichcote, Benjamin, 31, 33–34, 156, 163–164
Whigs, 16, 18, 125–131, 133, 176: legitimist, 129–131; oppositionalist, 1, 16, 126–128, 134–138, 152; and religion, 154–155, 157; *see also* Country tradition; civic humanism
will, the, 59, 81–82, 84
Williams, William, 136
wisdom, 19, 21–22, 27, 34, 37, 41, 42, 44–45, 73, 77, 80, 81, 82
Worden, A. B., 48, 137
Wren, Christopher, 193

Xenophon, 43–46, 76n, 107n, 108–111, 116, 205

Printed in Great Britain by
Amazon.co.uk, Ltd.,
Marston Gate.